Being

by

Roland Jaquarello

CONTENTS

ACKNOWLEDGEMENTS

I would like to thank the following for their help in getting this book published: Fulham fans Richard Codd and Alex Smith kindly looked over drafts for me. David Daly, Non-Executive Director, Fulham FC and Carmelo Mifsud, Media Relations Manager, Fulham FC, were most helpful in steering me towards useful contacts. David Lloyd, editor of There's only one F in Fulham, kindly corrected me on certain facts. Lastly and most importantly, I'd like to thank the supporters for sharing an exciting season.

Photographs and Design

The cover photograph of Neeskens Kebano, celebrating after scoring Fulham's third goal v Preston at Craven Cottage on March 4th 2017, was taken by Daniel Hambury for EMPICS Sport. The photographer of the author's picture on the back cover is Mira Faber.

The cover design is by Mateusz Bartczak.

Quotations

The author is grateful to be granted permission to quote from

Noel Coward's PRIVATE LIVES © NC Aventales AG,1930

Sources

This book has been extensively researched through archive and information in the public domain as well as by gathering the opinions of many fans. In addition, the author has met people connected with the club over many years.

TO

FULHAM SUPPORTERS

EVERYWHERE

Hope Springs Eternal

The season hasn't started so I'm free to dream. Fulham haven't played a match yet but there are the usual moans about how awful the team was last season, how we need new signings and how we haven't a hope of challenging for promotion. Supporters, who probably would berate governments for spending unwisely or bankers for handing out unacceptable bonuses, are only too happy for chairmen to splash the cash exorbitantly. Football is now more of a business than a sport and stakeholders want a return. Unfortunately, teams aren't built up gradually anymore, they're bought off the shelf. And talking about business, our star player Ross McCormack, who was bought for £11 million, seems to want out after two seasons during which he scored 42 goals. He has only played forty five minutes in the friendly games and when asked by supporters when he's going to next appear in the team, he seemed noncommittal. McCormack has been nicknamed by some as 'McContract' due to his canny running down of contracts at his previous clubs, Cardiff and Leeds. Despite his absence, Fulham have done well in the preseason friendlies, only losing one game narrowly, and giving a wide range of players game time. The 3-1 win against Crystal Palace was particularly impressive. What was most noticeable was the energy and commitment of the team, compared to the sluggish performances of last season. The new additions to the squad did well, bringing greater defensive solidity and more pace up front. However, as we know from our national team, good friendly results can be deceptive.

A View from The Sofa

I'm not a season ticket holder. Work commitments have forced me to be more flexible. Originally I sat next to Richard and Pete, mates that I met at Craven Cottage. They had seats in the Hammersmith End, the home of Fulham loyalists. This was during the glory days of Fulham being in The Premiership. I privately nicknamed Richard The Oracle as he seems to have a very wide ranging knowledge of the game and shows insight into the tactical manoeuvrings, or lack of them, by managers. Although I miss their banter during the game, we still meet after the final whistle, at The Wall, opposite the Hammersmith End exit. For years such walls were daubed by graffiti like 'Mullery is God,' 'Trinder Must Go,' and various CND signs supporting Pat Arrowsmith, the peace campaigner, who was sent to jail eleven times for her protests. These were our Banksy icons of yesteryear but eventually the council got round to erasing them, so memories of our erstwhile, volatile captain and celebrity comedian/chairman were consigned to history. Tommy Trinder always used to refer to the club in his act ('what time does the game start? What time can you roll up?') and in his final years as chairman when he was under a lot of pressure, I remember his stand-up abilities serving him well as he counteracted boos and jeers with 'I've been looking at my crystal ball, my crystal ball is never wrong and I see good times in the future for Fulham!' In fact, he departed not long after that and was given the ceremonial, non executive position of President.

As the first game is on Sky, I'm not going to Craven Cottage. I snuggle up with suitable food and drink, to watch it on my widescreen. The reason we're on tv is because we're playing Newcastle. Newcastle aren't expected to be in this division, they're a Premier League club with a huge following and a manager who was coaching Real Madrid only six months ago. Apparently, they're bringing seven thousand fans and they're expected to win. I worked in Newcastle in the 80s and I remember at the time Jack Charlton resigning because he was fed up with the intense local criticism-and he's a Geordie!. It's a one club city and there's a huge amount of pressure on the team to win something. Yet such a burden has yielded no silverware apart from the old Inter-Cities Fairs Cup in the 70s and an entertaining 'near miss', when they came second to Manchester United in the Premiership during Keegan's celebrated 'I will love it if we beat them' season. I found Newcastle a warm but inward looking place, riddled with politics with a small and big 'p'. It isn't an easy place to work for an outsider as many have discovered, notably Alan Pardew, a decent manager who did a good job but was never regarded as 'one of them'. Pardew's departure, which many fans encouraged, didn't improve matters but led to where they are now-in the Championship. It seems that fans can sometimes be a baying mob, hastening departures through public disquiet but not necessarily the best judgement.

The Newcastle fans love Benitez because he decided to stay despite having a pedigree that would command jobs at the highest level in Europe. I wonder why he didn't leave? It probably wasn't for the money. Of course, he has a family home in the Wirral, which isn't too far away, but maybe he just loves football. Apparently, on his first date with the woman who was later to become his wife, he was explaining 4-4-2, with the help of various restaurant cutlery. So maybe even in this cynical age, here's a man who loves his job above all else?

Maybe, our football cognoscenti are in for a surprise? Fulham are continuing where they left off in the friendly games. Keeping the ball well, defending stoutly and attacking on the counter with pace. Newcastle are certainly unlucky not to have a penalty but Fulham are sticking to their task and keeping in the game. Before the start, clappers were given out and it certainly is making a difference. Fulham have quite an older fan base and rely a lot on the younger supporters at the back of the Hammersmith End to make all the noise, so the ground can be a bit too quiet at home games. After all, the sound of clappers at Leicester helped propel City to last season's title.

As we approach half time, a superb header from Matt Smith into the right hand corner, puts the Whites in front. Arching his neck back to a pinpoint cross from Tom Cairney and attacking the ball with vigour, it's a goal worthy of those great headers of the ball like

Tommy Lawton and Tony Hateley. The goalkeeper has no chance as he forlornly dives to his left as the ball whizzes into the bottom right corner of the goal. The crowd erupts, Smith is embraced by all his team mates and our season is on its way. There's another more dubious penalty claim in the second half but Fulham survive and continue to conjure up chances of their own. They seem to gain control of the game as it progresses but given the slender lead, I'm relieved when the final whistle blows and promptly bounce off my sofa in joyous celebration. What a start!

As Fulham won, the three pundits are complimentary about our performance: our organisation, commitment and game management. More impressively, both Benitez and the Newcastle captain don't provide excuses and whinge about penalty decisions. What a contrast to Mourinho railing against the world like an Iberian gangster, who always expects to have his way. In fact, it's incredible how stupid managers can appear. I remember Alex Ferguson, during the 95-96 season, after Southampton had hammered United 3-1, absurdly putting the defeat down to the fact that his team had difficulty passing to colleagues because they were wearing grey away shirts! Even Wenger became an object of ridicule when he responded to clear bad tackles by repeating the evasive platitude, 'I didn't see it.' Spared of such insults to one's intelligence, I celebrate the first win of the season with a bottle of Pinot Grigio. Onward and upward!

On The Road to Leyton

I'm now going to my first game of the season, an EFL Cup game at Leyton Orient. I've never been to the Orient before. Probably because we've rarely been in the same division. It's a long trip for me from Ealing. After being squashed on the tube like a sardine in a tin, I arrive at Leyton. As I make my way towards the ground, I hear a snippet of some fans' conversation as I make my way-'he was too busy with the play station and she was too busy with the fuckin' washing up!' As I join the queue at the white portakabin ticket office, a Fulham supporter in pale baseball hat and shorts, observes 'it's more like a burger van!'

When I go through the turnstiles and enter the ground, I discover that we are behind one of the goals. It's full of groups of friends and families. A lot of them seem to know each other. One side of the ground to our left is completely empty. I don't think it's being used. Opposite us is the home supporters' Tommy Johnston Stand, named after the free scoring Scottish forward, who died in 2008. On the walls behind their supporters are homages to their legends of the past. Good to see the name of Laurie Cunningham being honoured. Cunningham was one of Britain's first black players. A highly talented, quick winger who went on to play for West Bromwich Albion as part of Ron Atkinson's 'Three Degrees,' which also included black team mates Cyrille Regis and Brendan Batson. Cunningham also played for Real Madrid but got killed in a road accident in Spain in 1983. He was 33. There's also an appreciation of those who played for Clapton Orient, the club's precursor. It states quite simply: 'The Footballer's Battalion The Somme 1916'. This is linked by an Orient rallying call, 'Journey To The Promised Land'. Opposite us on the right is a steep bank of home seats, towering over which, there is a wide grey balcony for the dignitaries to look down on the masses. It has all the appearance of something out of East Germany, before the wall came down, a rather abstract, ugly Stasi-like construction. On the pitch the Orient's mascot, Theo The Wyvern, a bizarre creature, with a blazing red dragonish head, prowls around to no discernible effect.

The Fulham end consists of middle aged men, some families and a fair sprinkling of youth. There's an overweight gentleman with a baseball cap proclaiming 'The Empire Strikes Back' and a shirt asserting 'The Best of British,' there's another balding man with a white t shirt covering a pregnant paunch, who has a khaki bag thrown over his shoulder. A couple are having a selfie taken against the background of the pitch. It's taking ages as a dark haired, bemused youngster, is having trouble working the device. Eventually he gets there and everybody's happy. Fulham are playing towards us in the first half and start at a cracking pace, moving the ball around really well. A few half chances are missed but we're playing some youngsters- Edun, Sessegnon, de la Torre and Adeniran-all of whom show considerable promise. In fact, it's Adeniran who scores with a great header from an in swinging corner. The stand erupts and he charges towards the Fulham fans. I discover later that apparently he was embracing his Dad. The celebration is punctuated by that traditional Fulham ditty: 'WE ARE FULHAM, WE ARE FULHAM, WE ARE FULHAM FFC. WE ARE FULHAM, SUPER FULHAM, WE ARE FULHAM, FUCK CHELSEA!'

I never really understand the obsession with Chelsea. Probably because I come from another era, when lovers of the game went to Stamford Bridge one week and Craven Cottage the next. Mind you, I did enjoy it when Fulham beat Chelsea 1-0 in March 2006 and Mourinho, the self proclaimed 'Special One,' had the indignity of having to endure the long walk across the Cottage pitch to the dressing room to the strains of 'YOU'RE NOT SPECIAL, YOU'RE NOT SPECIAL, YOU'RE NOT SPECIAL ANYMORE!' Nonetheless our rivalry with our close neighbours is hardly on a level with City and United, Everton and Liverpool and Arsenal and Tottenham. Nonetheless, the wittiest chant I've heard came from the Hammersmith End during a Chelsea game, after a local thief had stolen Frank Lampard's tv and admitted to the judge that he was a Fulham fan. As Lampard went to take a corner, the crowd chanted, 'WE'VE GOT YOUR PLASMA!'

Fulham start the second half really well. It isn't long before Cauley Woodrow, our young striker, scores two goals-one a 35 yard free kick, the other a well placed shot after cutting in from the left.

It's 3-0. I turn round to the young girl next to me and enthuse that 'it's a great score line'. She agrees but unfortunately the celebrations are premature. Through some canny substitutions, Orient get back in it through good crosses producing two well headed goals. There are now nine minutes to go plus injury time. Alarm bells begin to ring, given that Fulham had conceded over 160 goals in the last two seasons, but thankfully we hold out and emerge with a victory from an entertaining game.

Supporters then walk briskly to the tube, given that their journeys are probably long. Thankfully, there aren't big queues and I manage to get a seat quickly. I embed myself with a novel, whose heroine is entrapped by bad 'uns and happens, somewhat ironically, to be set in the East End. A good evening.

Politics or Sport?

The Championship is a relentless, industrial British league. Games come thick and fast. It's only four days later and the team are off to Preston. I'm having to do other things but I still keep an eye on the resurgent Whites. In fact, I'm going to hear Labour Party leadership contender, Owen Smith, speak at St Pancras Church but I've got my battered smartphone to keep in touch with football matters in Lancashire.

Just before getting the tube, I check developments-'Parker in for Tunni' otherwise no change. Walking down a sunny Euston Rd, ablaze with myriads of holidaymakers, I check again. Blimey, we've scored, 0-1, Sone Aluko, 33 minutes. I arrive at the large, cavernous church, which holds about 300. I'm asked by one of the organisers to go to the front. I reject this invitation. As I work in the theatre business, I hate seeing people perform up close on my days off. I slide into a pew at the back, passing a middle aged, fair haired man with a broad smile. I check the score-'I'm not going to let politics interrupt my football,' I exclaim. The man replies, 'who do you support? 'Fulham'. 'Oh right.' 'What about you? 'Sheffield United. My Dad took me to Bramall Lane first in '62.' I then extol the merits of Yorkshire, it's bold unabashed confidence and abrasive but warm humour. However, when I tell him that I look forward to seeing United at the Cottage, he reminds me that they are in League 1. Certainly, Hull being the only Premiership team in Yorkshire, is a serious omission. It's still 0-1. Good. 'I can't wait any longer,' says the Yorkshire man. 'I've got to meet my girl friend at Waterloo. Nice to meet you.' He departs down the church aisle to the exit. Still 0-1. Come on Fulham.

When a grey-haired woman with brown spectacles, who is now sitting next to me, hears of my reluctance to move to the front, she informs me that a lot of actors are in the local party. I remind her that RADA's down the road. 'Maybe that explains it,' she replies. Owen Smith is introduced by Keir Starmer, the local MP, who makes jokes about his tumultuous introduction into Labour politics, after being a highly respected lawyer. The squat, owlish Smith is eloquent without being inspiring. He has a difficult job on his hands as he probably knows he's not going to win. 'What do you think?' I ask The Brown Specs Lady. 'He's professional without that extra oomph to win people over,' she whispers back conspiratorially. Smith is now going on about his policies. He's making a pitch for a second EU referendum. The church is almost full. A variety of ages are present. 'A lot of old people have come back to the party,' insinuates The Brown Specs Lady. Does she mean Trots or Old Labour? 'Ssh' says a humourless, tall, dark-haired man in front of us. 'Sorry,' I retort meekly. Smith is now laying into Corbyn's inadequacies.

And then I transcend from one Smith to another, and discover that our Smith, the mighty Matt, has scored. 0-2 to Fulham! The other Smith, Owen, is now taking questions and a small microphone is thrust before many willing participants, who all rush to put their hands up like enthused infants in a primary school: 'I've been in the Labour Party since 1945...' 'This is the time to invest in housing when interest rates are low...' 'Are you fully prepared to explain the cost of such policies?..' 'I did vote for Jeremy last time but I'm not going to do so again...' I think I've had enough. I shuffle off past the desks with the badges and the earnest requests for support and hit the street. By the time I get home, Fulham have conceded. Can we never keep a clean sheet? Maybe I'm getting greedy? I'd better just enjoy the moment. Nobody's perfect! Least of all Fulham.

Leeds Past and Present

Leeds is next up for us. A team with fanatical and intense support. A difficult place to go even when their current history is full of strife. During the Revie years (1961-74), Leeds were a talented but dislikeable team. They could play some great football but made gamesmanship into a fine art. I have torrid memories of Jackie Charlton standing in front of the goalkeeper for no other reason but to impede him, and when winning, their players taking an age over a throw in. Then there were the 'dirty' players: Norman 'Bite Your Legs' Hunter and the two Scots: the short tempered, ginger haired Bremner and the diminutive, pugnacious Bobby Collins. Later John Giles, for all his creative play, could also 'put it about'.

In fairness, in the 60s and 70s, most teams had an 'Enforcer'. Just the memory of Arsenal's Peter Storey, later of this parish, makes me shudder. Bizarrely, Storey later went to jail for forgery and ran a brothel. Another 'hatchet' man, Liverpool's Tommy Smith ended up in a wheelchair. Ron 'Chopper' Harris also typified the era in which Chelsea had a particularly poisonous relationship with the Yorkshire side. When Chelsea's lanky forward Ian Hutchinson was asked about this tension, he replied. 'It was quite simple. We hated them and they hated us!'

Leeds were at the heart of 70s football and Don Revie, a genuine thinker about the game-as a player-he was behind the tactic of the deep lying centre forward-eventually became a controversial figure. A child of the 30s depression, he seemed obsessed with money and was nicknamed 'Don Readies'. By British standards, Revie was tactically astute with an eye for detail, and at Leeds managed to create a family atmosphere with his paternal regime. However, this approach didn't work in the more transient world of international football and he never successfully recreated his club culture. His celebrated dossiers became discredited and it was rumoured that some England players threw them into the wastepaper basket. He was hated by Brian Clough, who regarded him as a cheat. When Clough took over at Leeds, it was probably inevitable that his reign was going to be short. In fact was very short. Forty four days. The two men were both born in Middlesborough but were chalk and cheese. Revie morose and defensive, Clough opinionated and combative. Revie disliked the media, Clough embraced it.

I once saw Clough close up and personal when Notts Forest played us in an early season game. It was hot and Clough was in shorts. He came out of the Cottage and went up to a crowd of supporters and thanked them for coming. He kissed the women on the cheek and engaged with them as if he was talking to his own family. He then jumped into the front seat of the bus and got all the kids to stand in line while he autographed their books. Meanwhile, the players waited in the coach, immaculately dressed in suits and the club tie. In contrast, Clough was slim and tanned, a far cry from the detached, passive figure, who refused to engage with his team before extra time in the 1991 Cup Final. It was a sad end to a great career. Maybe it's not only a politicians whose careers are doomed to end in failure Revie ended up fleeing to to Saudi Arabia to negotiate a lucrative deal, while still England manager, although not in the exotic disguise reported by some tabloids. Maybe he saw the writing was on the wall. I'd seen Revie's England in those crudely designed Admiral shirts playing Holland in 1977. We had a good team out including Brooking, Keegan, Trevor Francis etc but Holland totally outplayed us. Neeskens and Cryuff completely destroyed our embryo team with total football. Slick, quick passing, interchanging of positions and in Cryuff's case, blistering pace from a standing start. Everybody was so comfortable on the ball. It was a style of football that seemed to pass us by in this country.

Nonetheless the thirteen year Revie era is seen as a golden benchmark at Leeds. It included 2 First Division Titles, 2 European Finals, the FA Cup and League Cup plus being second in the league five times. Despite winning the title under Howard Wilkinson in 1991-2, and David O'Leary later creating one of the most exciting young sides in recent times ('they're just babies,' he kept telling interviewers), no other manager has ever been able to maintain the consistency of the Don. After the initial success of getting to the UEFA Cup and Champions League semi finals, O'Leary's chairman Peter Risdale gambled by borrowing excessive amounts of money and spending exorbitantly, not only on players but also the office goldfish. When Lee Bowyer and Jonathan Woodgate were charged with grievous bodily harm charge, Leeds didn't qualify for Europe and were left in financial ruin. O'Leary then had an unsuccessful spell at Aston Villa and later like Revie went to the Middle East. Currently, the club is in the hands of the volatile Italian Massimo Cellino, who seems to have a revolving door policy regarding managers. He's gone through five in eighteen months at the last count. Gary Monk is the latest choice. Of the Swansea passing football school, where he did a good job, you wonder how long it will be before he too is guillotined. Especially as they haven't started too well.

It's Tuesday night and it's Elland Rd, 2016. I'm keeping an eye on the game through Sky Sports and BBC updates, while relishing a ham salad. We're dominating possession but there are no goals. On Sky, they're playing back key moments in the game. Leeds break away past our back line and should have scored. Then a bit later around the half hour mark, the sprite and nimble Sone Aluko, is tripped by their goalkeeper, doesn't go down and no penalty is given. There's no justice for not diving! We then hit the post twice: Aluko shortly after his trip, Matt Smith early in the second half. We're really playing well with good movement, passing and pace but can't finish. I continue my meal. Eventually, with thirteen minutes to go, Tom Cairney comes up with a great curling left foot shot on the edge of the box. 1-0. Sky play it back. Brilliant shot! Come on you Whites!

Now can we hold out and complete the job? Unlike the last few seasons, we seem reasonably comfortable. It's now injury time. See it through Fulham, for gawd's sake! Then the bell of fate tolls and Leeds score. My language deteriorates. The fatal moment comes up on the screen. We fail to clear our lines in the penalty area, the ball bounces and Wood scissor kicks into the net. 1-1. Game over. I rush to look at the league table. We could have gone top but we're still in a good position. Later the manager, the talented but somewhat doleful Serb, Slaviša Jokanović, says it was our best performance this season. From what I saw, we played some great stuff but we do need to see games out. Why is it that when teams get ahead, they often go deeper? Fulham have given away so many goals in the final minutes of games over recent seasons, so I'll just have to hope that such vulnerability wont reassert itself. Anyway, at least Gary Monk hasn't been sacked yet, and in Ryan Sessegnon, our sixteen year old, flying gazelle of a left full back, we have a real star of the future, as long as one of the top six big boys don't gobble him up. Fast, technically gifted and seemingly with a good temperament, this is a player with a great future. Let's just hope that a significant amount of it is with Fulham.

Back to The Cottage

I'm going to my first game at the Cottage. My partner, Mira, is away, so I do my duty and water the flowers in her flat. I once succeeded in drowning some, so I have to be careful. I enjoy a succulent steak and kidney pie. I listen to Any Questions? and get annoyed by politicians. Thankfully, it's now time to go so I make my way to the 220 bus stop. There's a middle aged woman sitting in the bus shelter. She's wearing a brown hat, a cream coat, dark cream trousers and brown sandals. Her hair is tied in a bun behind her neck. She's smoking assiduously. I don't think she's going to the Cottage. There are always traffic jams going to Shepherd's Bush Green. As we inch past Jamie's Kitchen, I see a kid with 'Austin 9' on his back. The shirt is out of date as Charlie A has now gone to Southampton. Mind you, my own Fulham away shirt is from the Tigana era in the 90s, such is the sentimentality towards mementoes.

Going up Shepherd's Bush Rd, we pass two landmarks. The fire station and the old Hammersmith Palais. The Old Fire Station with its elegant pillars is now a restaurant. The Palais has now been demolished and student flats have been built on the site. I remember the Palais as the home of Joe Loss's band in the 60s. To think that in those days they did four gigs a week. For a raw teenager a throbbing Friday night at the Palais dances was an exciting but daunting experience. The Loss band could play anything from standards to the latest hits. Supplemented by good singers-Rose Brennan, Larry Gretton and Ross McManus (Elvis Costello's Dad), they were a highly accomplished and successful popular outfit, even if somewhat in the shadow of their more sophisticated American counterparts, like Ellington and Basie. In fact, the Palais didn't just house Joe but in earlier days, great jazz artists and later The Beatles, The Rolling Stones, Bowie and The Clash. What a pity it couldn't remain a music venue.

In pursuit of exercise, I get off at the library round the shopping centre and walk across to Hammersmith Broadway. Once there, I notice Vince, a homeless guy who sells the Big Issue. I met him thirteen years ago, when I lived off the Fulham Palace Rd. From

Preston, he's an avid United fan, so we've always enjoyed footballing banter over the years. He now looks a lot older. Tall, thin but with a deeply lined face, he was again accompanied by his dog, a benign labrador, nestling sleepily on the pavement. When I ask him about his mate cockney Harry, he tells me that he's died. I'm taken aback. 'How?' I ask, 'he wasn't that old?' 'Collapsed,' Vince replies. Crowds are making their way to the game and he's selling his paper, so I wish him all the best and leave. As I cross the traffic lights under the flyover and its dramatically arched slab of concrete, I wonder how Harry had departed this life. In his case, I don't think it was drugs or drink. Maybe his way of life just caught up with him? Who knows?

As I made my way down Fulham Palace Rd, I now encounter 'the opposition'. A balding man has 'Bluebirds Forever' emblazoned on his shirt. His companion is having trouble with her shoes and is holding the railing of the Peabody Estate as she adjusts them. The Bluebirds Man waits for her with contained impatience. As I pass I hear somebody asking 'who was he?' 'Terry Lawless,' comes the reply.' Boxing talk about Frank Bruno's erstwhile manager. In fact, there used to be a sporting pub very near here, The Golden Gloves, run by Alf and Tony Mancini, part of the boxing fraternity, brothers of Terry, the QPR and Ireland centre half, who once served me a pint in that very hostelry. I remember the eccentric Terry becoming infamous for wearing a wig during a warm up and dropping his shorts and 'mooning' at the directors box, in protest at some criticism. Like Tony Cascarino, he was a 'cockney Irishman,' although the former striker recently confessed that he had no Irish relations at all! Certainly when you saw Mancini lined up during the Irish national anthem, his lips were glued. He looked like an intruder at the wrong party. He obviously didn't know a word of The Soldier's Song.

When I arrive in Stevenage Rd, I get a programme from the seller, who's standing behind a mobile stall, bedecked with today's tome. Fair, with a money pouch, straddled around her shoulder, I enquire about the whereabouts of the regular Scottish lady. 'Not at Tottenham, I enquire?' 'Yes,' she replies. 'She's gone over to the dark side!'. I then proceed to the ground. 'So if you had one Olympic ticket what would you want to see?' says a Fulham fan walking to his entrance. 'Any with Usain Bolt,' says his mate. Fair enough, I

15

thought, as I twist my way around the turnstiles Going to the Riverside Stand, you have to pass the away fans, which means more intense security. I surrender my small backpack, then meander past the boozing Cardiff supporters loudly chanting, 'BLUEBIRDS! BLUEBIRDS!' and clamber my way up into the higher echelons of the stand. Down below, the sprinklers are on and Billy The Badger is prancing about the perimeters of the pitch. Who is Billy The Badger underneath that costume? Is it the same person every home game? And I assume he's appropriated number 79 on the back of his shirt, in recognition of the club being founded in 1879? Whatever, he certainly adds to the gaiety of nations.

The players are now warming up. It's amazing how every team seems to do similar routines. Cardiff are at the Putney End and Fulham at the Hammersmith one, embedded with their own supporters. 'Come On You Whites!' flashes up on the surrounding hoardings. Nearby, an ample man in a khaki shirt, dark green shorts and brown shoes has a pair of huge headphones wrapped around his ears. After the players depart to a splattering of applause, one of the ground staff picks up all the balls and deposits them into a big string bag. After years of David Hamilton, the broadcaster and lifelong Fulham fan, being the match day announcer, it's now a younger man, Ivan Berry. 'Make some noise for Cardiff and (bigger stress) Fulham FC!' cries Ivan. Then comes the music, the triumphant Palladio, with its insistent violins, pounding drumbeat and orchestral brass. After the theatrics, the game starts. Fulham play well in the first half a lot of neat passing, without creating a lot. The game is drifting to half time, when suddenly in the last minute, after great work by Aluko on the right, there's a goalmouth scramble and who is it that scores? None other than Ryan Sessegnon, the 16 year old who has come on for the impressive but injured Ayité. The youngest player ever to do so in this league. Brilliant!

Unfortunately, the second half starts with Fulham struggling to find their rhythm. Cardiff increase the tempo and then suddenly score two 'wonder' goals in the space of five minutes. First, Ralls' powerful shot from outside the box goes into the top left corner and then Pilkington, cutting in from the right delivers a well executed curler past keeper Button. Fulham are then fortunate when five minutes later, Whittingham hits the bar and the ball rebounds kindly However, the way Fulham respond is impressive. They claw their way back into the game and in the final minutes their pressure is rewarded as Kevin McDonald shoots into the bottom left corner. Relief.

'We would have lost that game last year,' says Richard when we meet at The Wall after the game.

Richard aka The Oracle, is there with his genial, contemporary mate, Pete. They are long-standing, forbearing supporters and are both wearing the club's cap. Although they were born in London, they now live in East Sussex. Alex, a younger friend of theirs, is also there, fair, slim and resplendent, in the latest Fulham Visit Florida shirt. He lives locally and is about to go to a Greek island for his holiday.

'I thought we did ok first half,' I suggest.

'We had a lot of possession without penetration,' replies a frustrated Pete.

On reflection, he was right, I think I sometimes fall in love with the passing game too much.

Everybody thought the Cardiff goals were exceptional but were encouraged by Fulham's response.

'Great to see young Ryan get the goal but he found it hard in the second half,' I submit.

'You can't expect a sixteen year old to be consistent,' declares The Oracle.' Slav needs to get three or four extra players in. He knows that. Still, see you on Wednesday. He'll probably play the youngsters.'

We say our goodbyes and depart, ready to reconvene at in a few days time. Hopefully, 'You Can Win With Kids!

A Boro'Adventure

I'm at the Cottage. It's a warm, pleasant evening. I've had a calming walk by the Thames on a still night, straddling among some fans going to the game, who were debating the river's geography-'this is the Surrey Side. That's the Middlesex side. I went there with your Dad.' The Scottish lady is back from Spurs, selling the programmes. 'So you weren't kidnapped then?' I jocularly enquire. 'No I survived,' she replies with a twinkle in her eye. I then put a few pounds in the Bobby Moore Fund cancer collection bucket.

I have great Fulham memories of the celebrated England captain: Bobby being chased by kids down Stevenage Rd to get his autograph and organising them in an orderly queue as well as calming a besieged Fulham defence at Carlisle and Maine Rd, during our journey to the Cup Final in 1975. In fact, when John Mitchell scored what became the winning semi-final goal, Bobby didn't join in the ecstatic celebrations but like a teacher trying to marshal his recalcitrant pupils in the playground, he ordered them back into position, knowing the match wasn't over. He went on to be part of the George Best-Rodney Marsh era, during which, in an entertaining home victory against Hereford, the two celebrated forwards ended up showboating, tackling each other! During that colourful epoch, towards the end of his career, Bobby Moore could still read the game brilliantly. What he lacked in pace, he gained in brilliant anticipation. It was if his imaginative thinking gave him five yards on his opponent.

I'm watching in the Johnny Haynes Stand, named after the former Fulham and England captain. The stand, with its unique brick facade and wooden seating, is a listed building and is the oldest stand in the Football League, dating back to 1905. It was designed by architect Archibald Leitch, who also built stands at numerous other grounds, including Old Trafford and Anfield. Tonight is an EFL Cup game. I enjoy cup games because in the end one team survives. Sometimes league encounters can become sterile by teams playing the 'percentages'. Tonight our manager Slaviša Jokanović shuffles his pack. There aren't that many first choice player playing but again he gives chances to promising young 'uns-Adeniran, Edun and de la Torre all feature. Middlesborough score early when we fail to cut a cross out and things seem ominous. They're a Premiership team and they have fielded a strong eleven. They're moving the ball about well and Fulham are taking time to settle. Still at half time, we were still very much in the game. 'Get your tickets out' screams Ivan as he teases us with the winners of the lottery. When the names are read out like a roll call of honour, he proclaims the full glory of the prize. 'You have won two tickets to the Birmingham City game!' Then it's birthdays. 'Happy Birthday to Alan from Mum and Dad.' 'Happy Anniversary, Tracey, with love from Len.' However, Billy The Badger seems to be missing, maybe he doesn't do midweeks.

This doesn't stop Ivan from heralding the entry of the teams for the second half-'Now let's hear some noise!' Nine minutes into the second half, after the warm clouds burst and the heavens open, we equalise. Our tall athletic left full back, Scott Malone, is played into an attacking position and his shot rebounds off a defender's leg, past the keeper. 1-1. The goal raises the crowd of only 8,500, but it now sounds like more. It's certainly game on! Boro' have substantial support in The Putney End, especially for a midweek game, so that cranks up the atmosphere. If the game goes to extra time, those fans, like Cinderella at the ball, aren't going to get back home before midnight. And so it did. Despite the pitch getting a drenching, the game doesn't deteriorate in quality but becomes an intense contest that goes late into the night. It could have gone either way but with seven minutes to go Lasse Vigen Christensen drills in Malone's cross from short range and we hold out to win.

'How about that, Roly!' says Richard, walking towards The Wall, attired in summer flannelled shirt and white trousers.

'We played well,' I exclaim.

'Five or six did,' he replies.

'We got to catch a train,' says the accompanying Pete, arrayed in similar summer gear.

'Otherwise, we won't get back to Sussex until the early hours.'

'I'll ring you Roly. I'll be in contact, Alex,' says Richard, on the move, about to leave.

As the two Fulham foot soldiers depart into the thick of the night, Alex and I, make our way to the Fulham Palace Rd.

'It's great the way Slav is getting the whole squad involved,' I enthuse.

'Yes. They kept their shape really well. He must have worked hard on that on the training ground.'

'The way those kids played is really exciting. They didn't look out of place against Premiership opposition. Great to see de la Torre running at Boro's defence in extra time. When others tired. Some of the older players stepped up, like Ream.'

'I was disappointed with Ream for the goal but he was certainly good in extra time.'

'Thought Jozabed (our new Spanish signing from Rayo Vallecano) looked class, although he's obviously not match fit.'

'Yes, some great touches. Listen, I'd better go.'

'Ok mate. Have a great holiday.'

Shopping and Fulham

'Your card is inactive,' says the Morrisons attendant. I've got some stewing steak at last but I can't get my points. It's Saturday and I'm at Shepherd's Bush, while Fulham are at Blackburn. I need to keep in touch. It's the last game before the international break. We must get a good result before several players depart to their national sides. We're back to internationals already after a very average Euros. Having so many countries in the competition made for duller games as the 'minnows' often played with ten men behind the ball. I walk back to Mira's at Wood Lane. A young blonde girl with a pink jacket and scooter to match glides past me. An old, decrepit woman is pushing a trolley. Her head, with its bedraggled grey hair is bent down. I don't know how she knows where she's going. Later, at Mira's flat, after a tasty salmon and vegetables, I check the score surreptitiously, not to be too annoying, as I don't want to overplay my obsession. It's early days, 0-0. Time to go to the Shepherd's Bush market to get a cover for my mobile. Surprisingly. it isn't very crowded. A Sikh gentleman gives me a good fit and by the time I return I'm ready to take a short siesta. After my snooze, I realise that the game is moving towards full time. I must know what's happening at Ewood Park. Like a true addict I can't stop myself. I'm having trouble with the mobile so I rush to Mira's computer. Suddenly up pops the result on the BBC site. Cairney's scored. 0-1. Tom may be obsessed with his hair style but he's producing the goods. We're second!

It's Deadline Day!

It's transfer deadline day and Fulham supporters are looking to see money from the McCormack sale to Aston Villa used wisely. So far, the signings are good: Ayité, Odoi, Button, McDonald, Aluko, Kalas, Malone and Madl look more than comfortable in this league. So hopefully we'll get further good additions to the squad. However, Slaviša isn't satisfied and has publicly voiced his frustration. In fact, he's the Head Coach not the manager so I assume signings also have to go through the much derided Mike Rigg, the Chief Football Officer. However it seems as if they're also monitored by another department and, in a recent interview for Radio London, Slaviša voiced his frustration about the process, referring to himself as 'not an important person' in recruiting players, 'it generally depends on this guy (Craig Kline, data analyst) who is going to sign for us or not....the last decision is in the hands of this man. It is not my business....I'm a little disappointed as no one knows who this guy is....I've lost many players in this process....' Apparently, one of those he failed to contract was recommended by the 'best manager in world,' believed to be Mourinho. Kline is a friend of the owner's son and believes in the 'moneyball' model, which centres around statistical data and was successful in American baseball. For a player to be signed, he apparently has to pass the 'Both Boxes Checked' system, whereby he has a positive score regarding both traditional scouting methods and data analysis

On the face of it, Slaviša making such opinions public is alarming. However, a few days later, Shahid Khan, Fulham owner and chairman, issued a statement and didn't seem to be too upset. Rumours were rife about Kline's 'challenging personality,' especially when he apparently proclaimed that he had an 'ownership mandate'. However, Khan saw the comments as part of Slaviša's ambition, which he applauded. In these power struggles, the supporter tends to side with the manager. Probably because of our traditions. However, with such a rapid turnover of managers in the modern game and each one wanting their own players, you can understand chairmen wanting to keep control of such spending, especially when it has to be within the Financial Fair Play regulations. In fact, a lot of British clubs are now coming round to the continental Director of Football/Head Coach model. So let's put the Fulham fracas down to 'creative tension'.

Slaviša always looks like a man who wants to satisfy his own personal ambition but I'm sure that he has no illusions about the loyalty of club's boards. He's been reasonably successful as a manager but has never stayed long at a club. Let's hope this isn't the case with Fulham. The club have had too many changes over recent years. A period of stability would be welcome.

Battling with The Brum

It's Saturday I'm on my way to see us play Birmingham. After leaving Mira's, I catch the 72 bus from Wood Lane. At Shepherd's Bush Green, we pass the Empire, originally designed by theatre architect, Frank Matcham. It used to be a music hall venue. Fred Karno and Charlie Chaplin played there. Later it became the BBC Television theatre, when it hosted Juke Box Jury, Old Grey Whistle Test and Wogan, plus countless light entertainment extravaganzas. In fact, as a student in the 60s I visited nearby Lime Grove. Then the place was beginning to get run down and was nicknamed 'slime grove'. Not long afterwards it was sold and became a council estate, one area being named 'Gainsborough Court' in memory of the film company that made those costume melodramas there during the War.

Nearby, The Sundercombe Social on the Green is where The Bush Theatre started being a powerhouse of British fringe theatre. I once went there to see the mime artist Lindsay Kemp, a significant influence on David Bowie. His troupe performed 'Flowers', a drama in homage to Jean Genet, the gay French thief who became a major writer. It was brilliant with its daring visual imagination and challenging mime, but the small, claustrophobic space made me feel that I was locked into a gay party from which I couldn't escape. Then, suddenly, I'm jolted out of such artistic reveries by the powerful, grinding sound of a council lorry and a worker in an orange jacket and matching cap, blue jeans and large dark boots, noisily sweeping the pavements around the Green.

When I walk down to the ground from Hammersmith Broadway, I discover that Roman v Fousey is on at the Apollo. I've never heard of them. I thought it might be a boxing contest for one of those obscure world titles but in fact they're a comedy duo! What do I know? I have memories of seeing Louis Armstrong and Aretha Franklin there, in its previous incarnation as The Odeon Hammersmith. Memorable shows by two genuine, unmanufactured legends. Manoeuvring away from Fulham Palace Rd. I pass offices next to The Thames, where there's a warning against drunken yuppies 'please respect local residents when leaving the property'. In the distance, there's a supporter with a Dempsey 23 red away shirt. Distant memories of former times. Nearer The Crabtree pub, I hear Brummie supporters reminiscing-'Collymore played in that game,' 'turn left, you been here before, haven't you?' interrupts his commanding mate. Eventually, I enter the ground and pass the obligatory services at the Putney End: the Sausage House, Brewery Tap, Putney Pie Co. I'm in the Riverside Stand, derided as the 'posh' area by some in the Hammersmith End. And yes, the man with the huge headphones and the hairy legs is here again. Meanwhile, the away supporters, aided by various beverages, are congregating at the Putney End. 'Redditch BC FC Blues' and 'B45 Hoppy, Charly, Andy,' with a St George flag in the background, dominate the stand.

When the game starts, Birmingham appear a very well organised side. Gary Rowett is an able manager. He did a job on us last year and now he is repeating the same medicine. Birmingham are very well organised without the ball and quick on the counter attack. However, their Polish keeper Kuszczak makes a brilliant save from a curling shot from Cairney, to stop us taking the lead.

Then in the twenty fourth minute, Madl gives away a penalty but thanks to a great save from keeper Button, we don't concede. Johansen, who has just joined us from Celtic, is taken off after half an hour. A Mourinho-like decision. In this case, maybe tactical? Jozabed comes on ('WHO ARE YER?' chant the City fans mockingly), presumably to give greater creativity. Fulham still aren't fluent and just on the stroke of half time Madl, whose game is all about cleverly timed interception, commits a bad foul, gets a second yellow card and is sent off. We are now down to ten men but at least it's still 0-0 at half time.

In the break our previous announcer, David 'Diddy' Hamilton, is being celebrated. The former DJ is 78, so 'let's hear it for David Hamilton,' screeches his successor. Then after two minutes of the second half, we give away another penalty, Ayité making a reckless tackle in the box. This time Donaldson scores, to the accompaniment of Brummie cheers. In fact, we start playing better with ten men. We keep the ball well but when the openings come, they go to our left back Malone and twice he misses. While we press for an equaliser, Birmingham could have got another so unfortunately they end up worthy winners. This incites them to abuse their nearest rivals ('SHIT ON THE VILLA! SHIT ON THE VILLA TONIGHT!'). Certainly, Rowett and his team have taken us to the cleaners again. Given that City are currently going through turbulent times, with their former owner, Hong Kong hair stylist Carseun Yeung, going to jail for money laundering and new owners about to take over, Rowett is doing a great job. A Brummie himself, there's an infectious commitment in his team. An underrated manager, one of the best in the division, I think they could well end up in the play-offs.

At The Wall, the guys are low.

'Disappointing 'says Alex.

'I blame that goalkeeper fiddling with the ball when he's surrounded by the opposition,' proclaims Pete.

'That's the way he wants us to play, from the back,' Alex reminds us.

'They pressurised us from the back and played on the counter?' I suggest.

'We weren't good in the first half, gave away a silly penalty early after the break but played better in the second half. With ten men you've got to keep the ball and then be more direct in the last ten minutes,' Richard concludes.

'We still got caught at the back too many times,' says Pete, obsessively frustrated by our goalkeeper.

The East Sussex Fulham Brigade depart and Alex and I stroll up to Fulham Palace Rd

'Did Slaviša miss the war in the Balkans?' I ask.

Alex thought so.

'I think he was living in Spain after his playing career ended?' I surmise.

'He's managed back in Serbia though,' retorts Alex

'Must be strange. Those terrible things going on in your country, yet you aren't there.'

I then remember an Ulster international match.

'In fact, I saw the old Yugoslavia team play in Belfast. I think it was in the 80s They were terrific. They looked like they could win things.'

'Red Star won the European Cup didn't they?' remembers Alex.

'Yes. Pity teams like Ajax, Notts Forest and Red Star couldn't do that now,' I lament.

'We're now nearing Fulham Palace Rd with its streaming traffic.

'Did you have a good holiday on the Greek island?' I ask.

'Yes. We've only just got back. The weather was good. Most of the time.'

'Mostly Brits?' I enquire.

'No. cosmopolitan. Germans. French and would you believe it, Serbs! It was good. Better go. See you Saturday.'

Alex then disappears across the road with the departing crowd. It's our first loss and we're sixth

An Evening with Johnny

I'm going to the Burton game with Johnny. He's a writer and we've been working on a play together It's a sultry night and as we walk by the Thames, we're discussing jazz greats-Dizzy Gillespie, John Coltrane, Miles Davis and Bill Evans. We riff about Miles' politics.

'He was the son of a dentist,' I remind John.

'Yeah but he got involved with black politics of the 60s. Dizzy didn't really,' says ginger haired Johnny.

We then continue talking about Evans, the white pianist from New Jersey, who played with Miles.

'Less is more with Bill,' continues John.

'He never got the credit for his contribution to My Kind Of Blue,' I suggest.

'Least he does now,' John replies.

'He had a simplicity that resonated,' I propound.

'Great to hear people talking about great music,' says a tall, slim, older man stopping in front of us. 'Sorry, I overheard you talking.'

'No that's fine,' I reply.

'That was a great period. I was at school with Bill Wyman, then I heard David Bowie in a local pub. I come from Penge. Funny thing, my kids now love that music. Who would have thought it? Forty years later.' And then our music enthusiast turns and recedes into the distance, towards the ground.

At Stevenage Rd, the Scottish programme seller is back.

'Where were you last week? I quiz her. 'Arsenal,' she replies.

'Better than Tottenham?' I enquire. She nods silently.

John and I then snuggle into our seats in the Johnny Haynes Stand. We're a few rows from the back. Clappers are on our seat. It's a hot night but the marketing people have done their bit, offering three games at a reduced rate, which is a good idea for unfashionable sides like Burton. The teams come out and the clappers are banged rigorously and their sound echoes around the ground. Tonight Slaviša has made a few changes. Parker is back in midfield. Sigurdsson, another new signing, makes his debut in place of the banned Madl. Sessegnon, the 16 year old, returns at left back and our latest loan signing, Chris Martin, starts ahead of Matt Smith. There are only a sprinkling of Burton fans at the Putney End but the Fulham areas are almost full. Getting to evening kick offs is always difficult. You usually find that the ground is empty until about ten minutes to go, then suddenly a tide of humanity comes flooding in at the last minute. Predictably, two thickset supporters pass me, five minutes into the game. They don't bother to sit but stand somewhat menacingly above us in the next row. Fulham start really well. They're zipping the ball around, much more quickly than on Saturday. They're dominating Burton and pushing them back. There are a series of half chances but Fulham can't find a way through. 'They're playing well. It's just that last third,' observes Johnny. Unfortunately, Fulham miss that lethal goal scorer. After all, we sold two of them preseason (Dembélé to Celtic and now McCormack to Aston Villa). So far, the bulky Martin doesn't seem fully match fit and can't hold the ball up.

By half time, we haven't made the break through. While, kids are competing in a penalty shoot out, John and I remain in the stands. He's a West Ham supporter and he's still trying to get over Watford putting four past them last Saturday at The London Stadium, their new ground, which was especially built for The Olympics. Apparently, there were a few punch ups as well-early season frustration.

The game restarts. We lose our rhythm and Burton are looking more threatening. After quarter of an hour, a totally unmarked Irvine shoots from just outside the area into the bottom corner. 0-1. We seem to be loose in our play off the ball. Now Burton have got something to defend, they get ten men behind the ball and indulge in tiresome time wasting antics, much to the anger of the crowd. There are fouls and procrastination. One of their players is rolling about on the ground. 'Get up you fuckin' poof' says one of the gentleman behind me. I thought the 70s was over. 'Break his fuckin' leg' is his unsavoury advice to the Fulham defenders. The temperature is certainly rising. Fulham are now appearing anxious and aren't creating much. However, they do manage to end strongly and in the allotted six minutes of injury time, Sessegnon scores from an acute angle after the Burton keeper pushes out Aluko's shot. 1-1. A rescue act from the youngster.

At The Wall, I introduce Johnny to Alex.

'Martin was disappointing,' I comment.

'Yes, you can see why Derby were willing to get rid of him,' replies Alex.

'We didn't seem to recover when we lost the ball,' I venture

'That was really arrogant,' thought Alex.

We're yapping away when Richard and Pete join the post mortem.

'We created nothing in the second half. We didn't use the width of the pitch to break them down. Kept going inside,' says Richard.

'That bloody goalkeeper, fiddling away on his penalty area,' Pete booms frustratedly.

'I don't think he's your favourite player, Pete,' I suggest.

'Yes, only he got man of the match, last week,' says Richard, The Oracle, with a smile on his face.

We all laugh.

'Johnny's a West Ham fan.'

'So you weren't happy on Saturday then? '

'Lost it. In a quarter of an hour.'

As Richard and Pete amble off, I shout out, 'I hope Mr Button is on your Christmas card list!' Pete replies but it gets lost in the noise of the departing crowd and Johnny and I go to sink a few pints at The Crabtree.

Going Up North

We're away to Wigan. I've got an affection for this small northern town. Several years ago I went to a Jazz Festival there and stayed a week in a local hotel. Percy Heath of the Modern Jazz Quartet and Pete Rugolo from the Stan Kenton band plus a good local big band were among the attractions. I had some good evenings with the locals and encountered a lot of warmth and good humour. Mainly a rugby league town, Dave Whelan, a former Blackburn player and successful business man, invested in the club and they rose to The Premiership and won the FA Cup. At the time of their biggest triumph, they also got relegated, which is an unusual double. Like several clubs ejected from The Premiership, they've gone into irreversible decline and descended into League 1. Recently promoted back to the Championship, their current team includes Dan Burn, a Geordie, but a Fulham player for several seasons. Burn had some good games for Fulham but was unfortunate that his time at the club coincided with there being six different managers in five years. In 2014, before a game at Stoke, which we needed to win to stay in The Premier League, Burn was told to play right back by the manager, the Teutonic disciplinarian, Felix Magath. Burn had never played there and his gangly frame wobbled like Bambi on ice against the speedy Oussama Assaidi. It was no surprise that Burn was skinned. After that, he was in and out of the side and when his contract expired, he joined the Lancashire club.

Before having a late lunch, I'm checking that fountain of wisdom, the BBC website. Fulham make one change. Jozabed, is playing instead of the injured Sone Aluko. Apparently, we start well but both sides go on to miss chances. In our case, Chris Martin couldn't convert a Jozabed cross. I'm trying to find out if we've had a shot on target. The game seems to be becoming a stalemate. In the last twenty five minutes, Slaviša looks to freshen it up by making changes, including forwards Woodrow and Smith. Unfortunately, we still can't make a breakthrough and the game peters out for a draw. In fact, the match was so uneventful that after a lunch I took a nap and didn't rejoin the action until towards the end. That's what a nice piece of salmon and Fulham's impotent attack does to you.

After the match, fans aired their frustration at the lack of goals, while being pleased with our improved defence. In the league, we've only scored eight goals but we haven't let many in, six to be precise, the lowest in the division and after the game centre half Ragnar Sigurdsson, Icelandic hero of the Euros and scourge of England, was named Man of The Match. However, that's three games on the trot, where we've struggled to find a way through packed defences. There's a feeling that there's insufficient movement upfront, the build up is too slow, too many passes are played sideways and that our striker, Chris Martin, doesn't seem sharp enough. This may be true but Wigan, after some bad results, played 4-5-1 and defended deep, so they weren't exactly an attacking home team. As a part of this defensive fortress, the gangly Dan Burn played well.

One depressing postscript to the game was a fan who travelled to Wigan telling of his son being threatened by two Fulham fans, just because he was expressing his frustration at the team's play. Apparently, the father took the heat out of the situation, but that didn't stop the two guys dressed in trainers and dark jackets, reasserting physical threats at the final whistle. This is both surprising and sad as historically Fulham supporters have a pretty good record regarding behaviour but I suppose no football club can be totally immune from society's problems.

The Kids Are All Right!

I'm about to leave my flat in Ealing to see the EFL game v Bristol City when the bloody bathroom door handle falls off. Even somebody with my limited technical skills realises that the screws are too small. I'll deal with it later. A broken handle isn't going to stop me watching football. I make my way to South Ealing tube, over the small bridge which surveys the trains that shuttle past my kitchen window. Kids are often seen there, being lifted by a parent as a train passes. I suppose we all wanted to be a train driver in our early years.

I then walk through the nearby small park. There's a man with a grizzled white beard and floppy straw sun hat. As he lounges on a bench, an opened Super Skol lies forlornly on the path beneath him. I cross the road to the station amidst the hurly burly of National Grid roadworks. I'm confronted by an imposing, curly grey haired man in a yellow bib, pushing the Standard in front of me, which I gratefully accept. When I lived in Hammersmith, the newspaperman at the tube was an avid Fulham supporter, so was his brother. When the Standard went free he was made redundant. A short, genial man, I remember seeing him on my only trip to Anfield. He told me that Fecundo Sava used to buy a paper from him. Our former Argentinian striker was famous for bringing out a Lone Rangers style mask when he scored a goal. At one game, in our period as tenants at Loftus Rd., a large section of the crowd came with their own masks. It was a bizarre sight, worthy of a dramatic choral scene in an opera.

When I get off and pass the Hammersmith Apollo, Ricky Martin is appearing. Whatever happened to him? Oh yes, he said he was gay. Apart from that, I'm ignorant of his progress. As I cross through Frank Banfield Park, off the Fulham Palace Rd, (named after a former Mayor of Fulham), many locals are taking their dogs for their evening walks. 'Come here, Doris,' says a silver haired woman, shortening her long lead as the sausage-like animal rigidly obeys her stern calls. As I go towards the Thames Path, I see a young supporter with a FC Barcelona track suit top and a Fulham scarf. A contrasting mix of cultures and achievement, to say the least. The Thames is calm. Lighted oarsman drift into the distance, as a boathouse and placid woodland survey the scene. Cyclists drift by and birds float into the sky. 'Where are the girls?' I ask the programme seller.' I don't know,' says a young, fair-haired, twenty year old lad. 'You've got rid of them,' I suggest. He laughs nervously. I look to enter the ground but I can't do so via my membership card. 'But that's what they told me online,' I tell the pony tailed man with brown-rimmed, glasses. 'I'm afraid you're going to have to go to the ticket office,' he replies apologetically. As I leave, my backpack hits the next customer. 'Watch out mate!' he shrieks. At the portable office near the Cottage, I suggest to Luisa, a small, dark Italian woman in a black track suit top, that she tells the office about my difficulty. 'No you tell them. They won't listen to me.' 'Well tell them again!' I rather pompously insist.

I'm in the Riverside section T, nearer the Hammersmith End. The crowd is small. It later turns out to be just 6,000. I'm perched above a very respectable looking old couple. As the game progresses, my language deteriorates, so I look rather shamefacedly at the couple but I think they understand. We're in a football ground not a monastery. After a lively opening Fulham score. A good cross from Woodrow is well headed by our first Brazilian player, Lucas Piazon. 'He started it and he finished it,' I gleefully inform the jubilant oldies. In fact, many Brazilian players have played at the Cottage including the legendary Pele for Santos, when in 1973 they appeared to be doing a 'bum a week' tour to earn a few bob. Surprisingly, we beat them, 2-1 but it was more of a friendly game than a fiercely competitive one. The Brazilian national team, Ronaldinho et al, also played against Ghana on the hallowed ground in 2011. However, Lucas Piazon is the first to play for the club, even though he's on loan from our friends at Chelsea.

Initially, Fulham are lively but again miss several chances. Then, in the dying minutes of the first half, Bristol score. They break through the Fulham defence and Wilbraham cleverly chips Joronen, our young Finnish keeper. A few minutes after the break, Fulham are awarded a penalty but it's badly missed by Woodrow. Ugh! Bristol increase in confidence and strength. They miss several chances but at the death, on ninety minutes, substitute Tammy Abraham manages to scramble in, Irish international O'Dowda's cross. To make it worse

Abraham is on loan from Chelsea! When the game ends, boos ring out which seems unfair- why trash a team with a lot of kids who are still learning the game? Slaviša has successfully blooded several of them in these EFL games. Such a policy should be encouraged not booed.

Nobody's at The Wall. Maybe disappointment, train connections or perhaps the gang have given this game a miss. I walk back with the despondent, moaning evening crowd. Down Fulham Palace Rd, outside the pub, kids with outdated 32 Dempsey and 23 Burn shirts on their backs, look to persuade imperious bouncers that they're ordinary well behaved human beings, not violent hooligans. Nearby, helmeted pizza delivery men look like the food police, ready to establish a new eating order. I was going to visit my partner but I've left my mobile at home. I timidly go back to Ealing, ring Mira and watch the other EFL games. Unfortunately the Fulham game doesn't improve with a second viewing, sleep seeming a much better alternative.

Slaughter in The Sun

It's the following Saturday and its Bristol City Part Two. We're playing them again-this time in the league. It's a pleasant, sunny day. I'm in the Hammersmith End for the first time this season. Richard has given me his free seat. He tells me that his mate Pete is in Bruges. His wife is having a knee operation next week, so he's having a long weekend with her before she goes into hospital. Mikey, Alex's fair haired brother, is present. He's come over from Norway, where he lives. He's a goalkeeper in Norway's fourth division. His team, Fevang, played on Thursday and drew 3-3.

Fulham make ten changes from Wednesday and the first team regulars are back. In the first half, we're playing well but again don't take half chances. Even though, Martin is playing better, creating some decent layoffs, I'm concerned about Tammy Abraham, their number nine. Massively tall as well as nimble and skilful, he's a menace in the box. 'You need a step ladder to deal with him,' I suggest to the young fresh-faced fan next to me. And lo and behold in the tenth minute, we lose the ball in their half, get caught on the break, Patterson goes into the empty space, sends in a great cross and Tammy bangs it in. 0-1. The rest of the half is fairly even. Odoi heads off the line, keeper Button makes a good save, diving full length to his right, while Martin misses a headed chance and Parker goes close.

'Young Ryan got caught upfield, Rich,' I ventured at half time. 'Yes but we need to cover when we lose the ball,' replies The Oracle. 'Richard will be contacted by Abramovich soon,' says Mikey. 'Yes but could he afford him? These pensioners don't come cheap!' The start of the second half is a bit messy but Aluko hits the bar and then on the hour mark, Fulham give away a bad goal. Tomlin goes through tackles with ease, passes to Freeman-0-2. Three minutes later, Reid shoots across Button-0-3. It's beginning to be a carve up. Just when it couldn't get any worse, McDonald, who has been playing centre half as a part of Slaviša's substitute rejig, is sent off for a dangerous tackle. With seven minutes to go, it turns into a rout, the unmarked Patterson easily finding Flint-0-4. Massacre complete.

Sigurdsson is the only player who goes to applaud the crowd. He's a brave man.

'That's the worst performance, I've seen for 5 years,' says Alex having joined us in our part of the stand.

Mikey saw it more fatefully.

'I thought there were bad omens this morning. I was to come with my mother but her partner collapsed and she didn't make it.'

'Is he ok?' I enquire.

'Apparently, yes.'

Richard goes to the loo. The rest of the gang leave the ground and gather at The Wall.

'That makes Wednesday's result, not so bad,' I venture.

'We played with more freedom on Wednesday,' suggests Alex.

Richard now joins us.

'What's this, losers corner? Come on lads, let's go for a drink. See you Rols,' says a frustrated Richard.

They move off.

'Safe home, Mikey,' I cry, as they move towards Putney.

As I walk down Stevenage Rd., I see a tall man in a black jacket, walking with a mate in a check shirt and sunglasses wrapped on his forehead. They're with a young boy in a red shirt with 'Poplar Insulation,' printed on it. 'We're twelfth,' I hear the tall man say.

'No thirteenth,' I counter across the street.

'Lucky for some,' he replies.

Actually for me, it has been. Or should I say, it had to be, as it was my house number at school.

Other fans are already subverting the pain of Fulham's loss by talking about other subjects.

'I'll tell them if I've got it, otherwise they'll have to get it off the internet,' rails one supporter walking aggressively to Hammersmith tube.

I reach the station amongst the trail of disappointed fans. One of the dossers in the Hammersmith Broadway shopping centre is having a nap on a high metal stool hidden from general view but there's no sign of Vince selling The Big Issue. I make my way to the bus stop in the hope of a relaxing night. I need it after witnessing that nightmare.

Redemption at Forest

'I bet Bendtner scores his first goal for Forest on Tuesday night and Kasami (a former Fulham player) makes a mark. It's inevitable,' said Mikey on Saturday. We'll see. I'm watching a rerun of the Clinton-Trump Presidential debate, then listening to a Champions League game, while checking Fulham's progress. We again seem to be playing well but missing chances. Forest also don't take opportunities. Both keepers make good saves particularly Stojković of Forest, who brilliantly stops a point blank header from Matt Smith. Bendtner hits the bar and later scores from a Kasami cross in the sixtieth minute. 1-0. Unfortunately soothsayer Mikey's prediction has come true! Thankfully, twelve minutes later we equalise, after a clever header from Odoi plays in Cairney. 1-1. Later, we have two offside 'goals' narrowly disallowed, one a brilliant team move, and Smith and Martin also go close. Then it's Mr Ferguson's 'squeaky bum time' as Forest nearly score in the dying seconds, when a ball goes across the Fulham goalmouth but fortunately it isn't put into the net. From all accounts, Fulham recovered well from Saturdays debacle. They seemed to have reestablished their organisation and were more positive in attack. Although Martin was much livelier when he came on, I still think we're missing a quality goalscorer. Nonetheless, we're only three points from a play-off place, the season's target.

The Noisy Neighbours Make Life Hell!

Sam Allardyce has resigned as England manager after a grainy video reveals him agreeing to certain dubious practices. Meanwhile, we're playing QPR at lunchtime, 12.45 to be exact. I espy the first sign of the enemy at Westfield. Shaven headed, with white trainers blue jeans and 'Guinness' inscribed across those dreaded blue and white hoops, he looks up for the fight. However, he's a somewhat lone figure. There doesn't seem to be much of a derby atmosphere. Maybe both sets of fans are too depressed. After all neither team has won for six games. A couple of Fulham fans on the bus are talking about Newcastle University business courses and an ex-girl friend in Lena Gardens. 'She figures a lot in my book,' the older fan, teasingly reveals. Blimey, I hope he 's not writing a book on Fulham as well! 'It's a big decision if I'm offered a job in Leeds,' the fair haired younger lad exclaims. No doubt it will be, if you're exiled to Elland Rd for a few seasons! It's raining. fans are hooded and zipped up, which makes them look like anonymous pilgrims winding their way to hopeful salvation. 'It's an awful time for a football match,' I suggest to a man with thick rimmed brown glasses, as we make our way by the bank of The Thames.

'Isn't it just? I was hoping to watch it on Sky.'

'It's not on Sky, is it?'

'Naw, it's not.'

This swarthy elderly gentleman, ensconced in blue rain jacket, with matching hood, then goes on to berate the modern footballer

'I've been watching Fulham since the 50s. Johnny Haynes only played for one club. He could have played for any team in Europe. Nowadays, these players are only here for a short time, get their money and leave. There's no loyalty.'

Then he's off on the chairman.

'He's got somebody in to buy the players, who doesn't know anything about football. The manager should be doing that.'

'Oh the 'moneyball' guy,' I reply. 'I suppose some chairmen get fed up spending money on players who don't perform. So they're looking for evidence of consistency but it's not foolproof. There are other factors. It's just a guide.'

My friend didn't reply but I don't think he was convinced.

Instead, he moves on to our former striker. 'Ross McCormack scores goals. Yes, we're missing him and young Dembélé, but everywhere Ross goes, the team doesn't do well. Cardiff, Leeds, Fulham, now Villa.' As I then join the queue at the corner of Stevenage Rd to get my programme, I say good bye to my querulous friend.

When I get into my seat in the Johnny Haynes Stand, I'm next to a dark haired man in his thirties, who's with a female companion of similar age, attired in a Fulham shirt with Marathon Bet, embroidered on its front. We talk about football programmes. He tells me he's keeping the Fulham v Juventus one. 'Yes do,' I advise, 'I have a friend who sells programmes and that one's apparently worth a few bob.' The sun's out, the pitch looks good. and again Fulham start well. Then the drama starts, when after just five minutes, Fulham are awarded a penalty. And what happens? Tom Cairney misses it. He goes to the keeper's right but it isn't hit hard enough and Smithies is well positioned. Now Fulham aren't in a great place. They've missed lot of chances and penalties in recent games and needed to break that hoodoo to play with freedom and confidence. Then, predictably QPR score. There's a wicked deflection as Washington's shot fatefully spins past keeper Button and nestles into the net. Midway through the half, we miss a sitter. The slight but skilful Lucas Piazon is sent through on goal by Parker. He draws the keeper, passes to Martin, who then shoots wide. Fulham certainly aren't helping themselves. They have further half chances before the interval but can't capitalise. The alarming thought is that they should be at least 2-1 up.

At half time, the cheerleaders from the Jacksonville Jaguars, the Fulham chairman's American Football team are strutting their stuff. In fact, it's a little subdued by American standards and they're athletically cavorting in modest tops and black leggings, while frenetically waving their pom poms in the air. During the break, the bloke next to me has gone to get some Fulham cuisine. In fact, he misses the equaliser immediately after the interval, when a Parker cross leaves the QPR defence clearing half heartedly and American Tim Ream, whacks the loose ball and scores. 'You must go and get more food mate, you brought us good luck,' I joke, as my neighbour tucks into his unappetising pie. The game now gets more intense. It's not long before big Matt Smith, who's replaced the beleaguered Martin, heads the ball down to Parker, who has a shot cleared off the line. Kebano then comes on for Cairney and immediately misses another sitter, left back Malone floating in a perfect cross which the Congolese international can't nod home.

I get a bit anxious when the injured Scott Parker departs and is replaced by Jozabed, as it leaves us defensively frail. Predictably, QPR now have more of the ball as we can't win it back. When Jozabed gives the ball away in their final third, Rangers work the ball out to the right, Cherry puts in a great cross and the unmarked Sylla's diving header plants it in the goal. 1-2. There's now only three minutes left, and, somewhat desperately, Fulham play it long, looking to use Smith's height. When Jozabed's powerful free kick, resounds off the bar, you think that might be it. But no, just when you think it's over, the unexpected happens-this is Fulham after all! In the final minute of injury time, when abrasive QPR defender Onuoha kicks Jozabed in the face, a penalty is awarded.

Now who's going to take it given Cairney is off the pitch? Oh no, it's Sone Aluko. Although his approach play has been good, he doesn't look as if he could hit the proverbial barn door at the moment. I'd have gone for somebody else, who hasn't already missed chances. Still you've got to admire his bravado. But then-oh no, Sone. He tries to fool the keeper by shooting in the right hand corner, only for his effort to hit the post and go out of play. Immediately, the referee blows his whistle. Aluko lies prostrate in the penalty area. Other Fulham players look equally distraught and are standing rooted to the spot as if time has stood still. This was definitely defeat snatched from the jaws of victory.

'I don't know what to say after that,' says a bewildered Alex at The Wall.

'Richard said to me- how did we lose that game?' explains a frustrated Pete, resplendent in a white baseball cap.

'If you miss two penalties, you don't deserve to win,' responds bespectacled Shane, a friend of Richard and Pete's. It's the first time I've seen him this season.

'Carney signalled that penalty. And I don't think Sone should have taken the second,' I remonstrate.

'Should have been Malone taking it and putting the ball straight down the middle,' asserts The Oracle.

Pete still worries about our keeper. 'Should be Bettinelli.'

'Slaviša looked to attack with his subs but it was difficult,' suggests the author.

'When Parker went off we couldn't get the ball,' Richard explains.

'Let's hope the next time we meet up, Fulham have won and scored lots of goals!' proclaims an ever optimistic, Richard as the East Sussex Wall members depart gloomily towards the Putney Bridge tube.

Meanwhile, Alex and I make our way towards the Fulham Palace Rd.

'I don't think I've seen a Fulham side miss two penalties before. Although I saw Juan Pablo Angel miss two for Villa at the Cottage.

'No,' says Alex 'but I remember a Huddersfield player missing two penalties, away at their place. Bettinelli saved both.'

'Maybe the international break will be good for us. It's like starting all over again.'

'Won't be easy with Norwich and Huddersfield coming up,' warns Alex.

'Barnsley away also won't be easy.'

'I'm not sure what more Slaviša can do apart from rebuild confidence. I think, he's found his best team. Bar McDonald and Ayité, there's nobody else pulling up trees, staking a claim to be included,' asserts Alex.

'After watching that I need a break for psychological recovery!' I declare.

'Take care. See you in a couple of weeks,' says a departing Alex, as he merges with the departing crowds into the late evening glow.

George, Johnny and Yesteryear

The QPR game saw the unveiling of a statue in honour of George Cohen. George played 459 times for Fulham, won 37 England caps and was right back when we won the World Cup on that glorious July day in 1966. Plagued by injury in his latter career, he had to retire at twenty nine. In later life, he has worked in property management and courageously fought bowel cancer. Certainly a great Fulham servant and deserving of such recognition. The statue was unveiled behind the Hammersmith End, where it replaces Mohamed Al-Fayed's previous installation not of a footballer but pop icon, Michael Jackson, who only visited the Cottage once. Later, when Shahid Khan bought the club, he took this edifice down and 'Michael' was transported to the National Football Museum in Manchester. Al-Fayed wasn't happy and implied that Fulham's relegation from The Premiership was due to the bad karma emanating from the statue's removal.

George's statue was designed by the same sculptor who created the Johnny Haynes effigy outside the Cottage. That was much admired but some are more critical of the latest conception: 'I thought we were commemorating George Cohen not Bobby Moore', 'looks bugger all like him,' were some of the comments. Others objected to it being tucked away in the corner of the Hammersmith End-'you can't build a tribute to a club legend and have it installed in the back garden.' Still who says it isn't the thought that counts. Certainly, the homage to Johnny is magnificent. It catches his posture perfectly.

In fact, it was Johnny who made me a Fulham fan. He was captain of England at the time and I had come as an eleven year old with my mate, the brainy, bespectacled Danny Wiseman, to do some autograph hunting. We'd already been to Stamford Bridge and Highbury where we got the signatures of goal scoring wonder boy Jimmy Greaves and the Brazilian international Didi, who was training with the Gunners. In those days, the team trained at the Cottage. After getting Johnny to sign, we cheekily asked him if we could watch. 'Ok. If you don't make a lot of noise,' he replied. Two schoolboys then felt as if they had just been given the keys to the kingdom of heaven-or the Putney End terraces, to be more precise. By modern standards, training seemed pretty basic but my abiding memory was a scene that took place between 'Tosh' Chamberlain, Johnny's mate from school football and reserve goalkeeper, Ken Hewkins. 'Tosh,' loud and rumbustious, was practising his shooting and every time he scored he jokingly baited Hewkins. 'Pick that one out of the net, haggis,' he yelled. In fact, Hewkins is South African but such distinctions seemed minor to 'Tosh', he'd played for Clyde after all. 'Tosh' had a hard shot, which would either zoom into the floodlight pylons or hit the back of net. As he continued to score and humiliate Hewkins, playful tension arose and they ended up having a mock fight in the penalty area. As this altercation progressed, Jimmy Hill, the bearded wonder and inside forward, was showing a rather glamorous tall, slim woman around the ground. Witnessing the comic fracas, he came over and berated 'Tosh', telling him, 'cut it out Trevor'. At this moment 'Tosh' was entangled with Hewkins in a rather eccentric embrace on the hallowed Cottage turf. Extricating himself from Hewkins' forceful entreaties, he peered up at the imposing Hill and screeched suitably foul invective! The stylish looking lady, appeared somewhat bewildered, marooned on the touchline.

After their pugilistic efforts, the two Fulham truants departed to get changed. In fact, as Danny and I descended from the terraces, I'm sure I could hear 'Tosh' singing in the shower. Later, we talked to Ken Hewkins at the top of the stairs of the Cottage. It transpired that he was waiting for his mate. After getting his autograph, I asked him what was the best save he's ever made. 'Probably for Clyde in the Scottish Cup Final,' he replied. Big, genial and relaxed, Hewkins went on to talk generously about his colleagues, not least a really good young goalkeeper. This proved to be the brilliant but erratic Tony Macedo, who would later supersede not only the then first team keeper, Ian Black, but also Ken himself. As we were talking, the effervescent 'Tosh' appeared and both players went off together to lunch or was it a betting shop? On the following Saturday, I went to my first Fulham game against Rotherham United. Roy Bentley had just joined us from Chelsea and there was a big crowd of over 30,000 thousand. When 'Tosh' scored in the same way he had been practising with Hewkins, he went into ecstatic orbit, while some of his team mates just stood and laughed. There seemed to be something eccentric about Fulham, later described by some fans as 'Fulhamish'.

This was borne out when later I went with my sister to see a charity game and at half time, the club allowed hundreds of kids to go on the pitch and play, chasing a very small football. It was like a throwback to another century as parents laughed at such crazy antics. I'd also met a lifelong Fulham fan working for a small car hire firm my father was managing. Joe, immaculately suited with a wide-brimmed felt hat covering his expansive bald head, was then working part time, after having been with car hire supremo Godfrey Davis for many years. He used to always watch the game from the old Putney End. In those days, there was a tree at the side of that terrace. 'I'm always by the tree. If I'm not at the tree, you know I'm not there,' he had proclaimed. Fulham seemed to be full of such characters, both off and on the pitch, led by the comic interaction between the brilliant perfectionist Haynes and 'Tosh,' his frustratingly inconsistent mate.

In those days, although you certainly wanted Fulham to win, it wasn't the end of life as we knew it, if they didn't. Maybe, because the club embodied a human and community spirit that went beyond that. Am I being sentimental? I don't think so. After all, even reserves like Ken Hewkins were at the club for seven years. In fact, Hewkins took penalties for that team and on one bizarre occasion, he missed, hitting the crossbar so hard that the ball rebounded such a long way, that the opposition were immediately able to launch an attack and score, while Ken was desperately trying to get back into his goal! The club certainly has always had an eccentric and unique allure. Previously, I'd gone to Chelsea, as it was nearer to where I lived, but now the Whites were the club for me. I'd got the Fulham bug.

Tykes and Canaries

It's Saturday October 18th. We've had the international break. Several players were away playing for their countries, so it must have been difficult working with the squad. However, the team needed to recuperate and go again. Hopefully they've been on the sports psychiatric couch trying to heal the pain of missing open goals and penalties. Whatever remedies have been administered hopefully they'll do the trick and we'll get a result at Barnsley. After a little shut eye, I start reading my book about what happened after World War 2 in Eastern Europe-a litany of misguided idealism and oppression.

Then suddenly, I couldn't checking the score. Oh no! We're 1-0 down after four minutes-ugh! That defensive frailty has manifested itself again. I take refuge in my book and get so absorbed that I don't check the score until an hour or so later. Blimey, it's 2-3. We've scored three away from home. They walked through us for a couple of goals but our left back, Scott Malone is playing a blinder. He was part of the build up which saw Lucas Piazon's deflected shot go into the net for the first goal and his intended cross went past the keeper for the third. Norwegian international Johansen, is another player who is also having a good game, playing a great through ball for Sone Aluko to score the second. And would you believe it? That man Malone has now done it again and crossed for Martin to score his first goal in over twenty games, for the fourth. Brilliant. 2-4. Yes, we've scored four away goals. After missing too many chances in our previous games, that's a real fillip for confidence. What's more we did this after conceding the first and going behind twice in the match. That's a good sign of the spirit in the group.

The following Tuesday it's Canary time at the Cottage, our battle with Norwich City, the current leaders in the Championship. My sister has lived in Norfolk for many years and her husband is an ardent Canaries supporter, but I'll deal with family loyalties later. It's dark and chilly and I've left the flat inappropriately attired. My light blue jacket is flimsy and more suitable for spring. Still it's too late and winter is on its way. I enter the Johnny Haynes Stand and pass the Fulham Food Company where several young people are earning a few bob. I can't say the cuisine looks very tempting. The teams are warming up. The Fulham players are passing impressively to each other. 'They look good when there's no opposition,' I jest to the security man. He laughs nervously. I find my seat, near the Hammersmith End and discover that I'm amidst a lot of older men like myself. One of them, fat, suited and booted, wearing a blue jacket, is twisting and turning, doing some exercises. When I look at him, he stares somewhat accusingly. I swiftly avert my eyes elsewhere. Meanwhile, Ivan, our announcer, informs us that there are free drinks if Fulham win but at an Islington pub. Obviously the more local hostelries, The Crabtree, and The Golden Lion were fearful of going dry! Billy The Badger gets a predictably big build up accompanied by loud music. Next to me is a talkative middle aged gentleman, with brown glasses and a faded red jacket. All the people in this section know each other and are probably season ticket holders.

'You're the wrong side of him,' screams my neighbour, when Jerome skins Ream. Jerome then puts a header over the bar. 'There was no one near him,' the fan yells scoffingly. Then he turns to me and knowingly asserts 'the defence is still a problem.' When Fulham attack and lose the ball, Norwich are turning over very quickly on the counter and that's how they score. Sigurdsson's pass goes astray, Norwich attack, Jerome entices Malone into a rash tackle, and a penalty is given. 0-1. The Canaries are singing. Then later, things get worse, Malone's hands are apparently all over Jerome as a corner is taken. Penalty. It seems harsh. 0-2. The crowd are incensed. 'YOU DON'T KNOW WHAT YOU'RE DOING!' rings round the stadium. As the ref blows for half time, he's booed aggressively and the ground is rocking with anger. While the ref waits for the players to go off the pitch, Scott Parker, the Fulham captain, approaches him and looks for an explanation. He's already been yellow carded, so he needs to be careful. A member of the Fulham staff comes over and diplomatically ushers him away.

'London Calling', The Clash's post-punk Armageddon anthem, is playing as the players come out for the second half, probably because of its rousing rhythm rather than its gloomy lyrics. Clappers are also being banged vigorously on seats. Fulham respond by upping the ante and playing with greater intensity. They're dominating the game with quick decisive passing and greater energy. When Fredericks replaces Odoi, it gives us greater space and width as their defence tires. Fulham look as if they're determined to fight back and it's not long when they score. Great work by Martin, leads to the tirelessly marauding Johansen shooting powerfully into the net. 1-2. The crowd are certainly up for it and get behind the team. The players are responding and are rewarded with a second goal, this time by Chris Martin, who has been purposeful and aggressive all night, and after being played in by Johansen, he scores against his former club, with a perfectly placed shot into the left hand corner Fulham have used up a lot of energy to get back into the game and Norwich come back into it in the last twenty minutes. Both teams have chances but in the end, 2-2 is a fair result for what was an excellent game.

At The Wall, nobody's there and I'm about to leave. Then I suddenly hear Alex:

'Roly. Richard's in the loo.'

'Oh I thought he'd gone to catch his train.'

'No. He's on his own. Pete's been working in Birmingham.'

'Ah Roly,' says Richard as he strides towards us, wisely encased in a heavy jacket. 'Fredericks made the difference. Pushed them back, gave us width.'

'I think there's great team spirit and character in this squad. You get the feeling that they think that they've been unlucky recently and can beat anyone. They've come back well twice now.'

'You're on to something there, Roly. Other teams would have lost that game.'

'They played with such intensity in the second half.'

'Yes, that was the best since we were in The Premiership,' purrs The Oracle. 'Mind you Norwich were good. They'll be there or thereabouts. Better go to catch my train lads. Have a great time in Bari, Alex. See you at the Huddersfield game.'

Alex and I then wander off to Fulham Palace Road.

'You're going to Bari,' I enquire.

'Yes for a long weekend. Thursday to Sunday.'

'Have you been there before?'

'Yes, when I lived in Italy.'

We then talked about Huddersfield being our next opponents.

'My Dad supported Huddersfield.'

'Did he come from Yorkshire?'

'No. But in the thirties Huddersfield were a big club. Their manager Herbert Chapman went on to manage Arsenal. Pity Hull's the only Yorkshire club in The Premier League.'

'Not quite the same as Leeds or the Sheffield clubs.'

'No. Those big city clubs have got such huge support.'

'In fact, my Dad took me to Charlton. My parents were divorced so that was a way of having a day out with him as he lived in south east London at the time.'

'The crowds were big then. 40,000.'

'That's right. In fact, once aged about eight or nine, I got parted from my father due to the force of the crowd moving round the terraces. Then suddenly a man behind a stanchion saw that I was in trouble and shouted to my Dad, who was now thirty odd yards away. 'Don't worry guvnor, I'll see he's ok and wait for you at the end of the game.' Not much health and safety in the days of Sam Bartram.'

'Charlton have plummeted recently haven't they?

'To think their fans were criticising Curbishley!'

'Yes ten years in The Premier League wasn't failure.'

'No wonder he seems to have had enough.'

'Yes, he doesn't seem to be pursuing management jobs anymore.'

'Johnny who came to the Burton game knows him. I must ask him.'

'I then tell Alex that I might go to Villa Park next Saturday.'

'I went once,' he replied.' I remember Simon Morgan and Steve Hayward scored there in an FA Cup tie. We were in League 1, they were top of the Premier League. It was early in the Al- Fayed reign. We won and it was the start of me thinking that something was going to happen at Fulham.'

'I also remember as a kid, us losing a Villa Park semi final there in '62, when the Burnley goalkeeper Blacklaw controversially brought down Maurice Cook and we didn't get a penalty. Did you see the semi there with the Tigana side?.'

'Yes, I came over from Italy for that one. Pity.'

'It was an awful goal to concede as well.'

'I remember it was being played late on Sunday afternoon.'

'A stupid time.'

'Afterwards, I had a rush to get back to Stanstead in order to return to Italy.'

'Well while you're holidaying in Bari, hopefully I'm cheering on the Whites to victory!'

'See you.'

Away We Go!

I'm going away for the first time in the season to see the Aston Villa game. Mira is driving me there so I'm not late. I've been playing butler this morning getting the breakfast prepared-'a very good butler' apparently. We get in the car and I'm worrying about a missing plug for the bath. 'You don't need it, so why worry about it. We always shower,' says Mira. That's logical but unfortunately I'm getting a bit obsessional, not least about being late, especially when I haven't yet got a ticket. My fears are irrational, it's early Saturday morning and the traffic is light. Eventually, I see a fellow traveller, a woman with a slight limp wearing a Fulham scarf. Mira seems quite keen to unload me quickly, as she's going to her yoga class, and after arriving outside the Cottage, she wishes 'good luck to your team' in her warm Polish accent and disappears down Stevenage Rd, in her newly acquired Ford.

'Are you Barbara?' I ask the lady with the limp, who's now next to the departing coach. 'No, she's up there.' I then ascend the coach's steps to confront a woman with auburn hair and dark make up, wearing a black cardigan. She's in the front seat, next to a genial driver, who welcomes me on board and is wearing a black waistcoat, a white shirt and sunglasses. 'What's your name?' Barbara asks. I tell her and she gives me my match ticket. I'm about to depart up the gangway, when she calls me back to look at the coach ticket. 'Just to make sure, there aren't any problems. I'm sure there aren't.'

After it's found that everything's in order, I find a seat in the middle of the coach. I put my thick coat in one of the shelves and place my bag on the floor. Opposite me is a middle aged man with horn rimmed glasses and greying temples. He's with a young woman, maybe his daughter? 'Is this the only coach?' I enquire. 'Oh no, there are four leaving Motspur Park (Fulham's training ground).' That makes sense as not so many Fulham fans actually live in the area anymore. A lot live in Surrey and Sussex. We then start talking about our beloved club.

'No I never went to the Cup Final in '75, I was fourteen,' he tells me.

'Did you go to Hamburg? he asks.

'No unfortunately, I didn't'.

'Glad I went. I doubt that I'll see Fulham in a European final again in my lifetime.'

It's approaching ten o'clock. The coach is filling up. A smart, young lad in his teens with dark black hair comes to sit in the window seat next to me. I ask him if he's been to away games before. He says that he went to Orient for the cup game and the Barnsley game with his Dad. They stayed the night in the Yorkshire town overnight and drove back the next day. 'We haven't lost away this season,' he reminds me.

The coach is dark and grey. Most of the supporters in this coach are older like me. There are several women, mostly middle aged. There's a digital clock looking down on us like a technological god. A blank tv stares back at us out of the murky light. After a brief discussion about Fulham's inability to put away penalties-three missed so far this season, the young lad gets his headphones on and plays with his mobile. I know when to shut up. It's all dark and quiet as we drive down the M1. We stop off at that homage to modern architecture-the motorway cafe. Inside this monstrosity, it's teeming with people. They're eating, chatting and controlling kids. It's like a café in a tube station.

When I get back in to the coach, wiggling my way past Barbara and our driver, who's looking more and more like a musician in a fifties rock group, I chat to the young supporter, who follows me into his seat. I bang on about diet and the bad food in the café. The conversation then veers off onto the EU referendum. I'm telling myself to shut up but I can't help myself. Then I manage to stop, just in time-before I go on too long. One should never get too heavily into politics with supporters, unless you know them very well. Especially, something as controversial and divisive as the recent referendum. However, from a football perspective, you do wonder how it will all impinge on foreign players, especially those who aren't top internationals. Although we probably have too many overseas players in our game, the better ones have helped to considerably raise the standard. However, you need more of a balance like in Germany, where there are foreign players but indigenous ones are given more opportunity and the national team is protected.

After our repast, it's not long before we're approaching the ground. We're in the Doug Ellis Stand. He of 'Deadly Doug' notoriety-the chairman who sacked eleven of his thirteen managers. And what's more he's still around at ninety three. 'AVFC Prepared' is strewn across the stadium exterior. I go and get a programme. The seller is stationed against a wall and protected by a small canopy. 'How much is it?' I enquire. 'Three fifty,' she replies in a light Brummie voice. We're early, which is good and the coach is in a car park near the assigned stand. Opposite the ground, is a concrete multi-purpose pitch, surrounded by green wire fencing. There are old netball hoops and a cracked playing surface. Young children of around ten years old, are happily playing football. Semi-detached red bricked houses and a small church spire hover over their innocent game.

When I enter the ground, I go through the wrong entrance and am nearly frisked twice. A security man tries a second time but I tell him that 'I've already been done,' which thankfully he accepts. When I get into the stadium, I enter an area which is more like a detention centre: dark, eerie, impersonal. There's only one refreshment bar, a match day betting counter and a gents, which is impressively big compared to Fulham's rundown equivalents in the Johnny Haynes Stand. Spurs v Bournemouth is on the tv. There seem to be very few supporters, especially as I was told by the gent on the coach that 1,500 travelling. Maybe they're on their way.

Villa Park is impressive. It's towering and overbearing with stands, arching to the heavens. It holds over forty two thousand and has its finest moment, which led to the club winning the European Cup, inscribed on the side of the North Stand-'Down the left. A good ball played by Tony Morley. Oh it must be! It's Peter Withe!' That was in 1982 but today in the humbling environs of the Championship, will they ever fill all those claret and blue seats? I'm in the lower section of the Stand but another security man says I can sit anywhere, which is strange. Where are the other Fulham fans? Then I discover, they're all upstairs in the higher section.

The players are warming up. It looks like there are a couple of changes from the Norwich game, Madl for Ream and Sessegnon for Malone. Not dramatic ones but hopefully enough to refresh a squad, who are playing a lot of games. Madl and Sigurdsson are passing to each other. They chat like members of the defenders club, away from such trivial beings as forwards. The selected team are near us. The substitutes with their coloured bibs have been banished to the other side of the pitch. For some unknown reason, we seem to have three goalkeepers here as Jesse Joronen is delivering crosses for Bettinelli, the reserve keeper. The mascots come out. Fiona Laban is Fulham's. Billy The Badger doesn't seem to do away games. The Villa mascots, who are dressed like something out of Planet of The Apes, but are apparently lions, disappear. Four young men come out with flags raised high, followed by the teams. They go to the centre of the pitch, stand in a line with flags aloft, Trooping of the Colour style. The announcer screams the predictable 'let's hear some noise for Fulham' and then-with inevitable greater emphasis-'Aston Villa!' The players enter and go through the ritual of rather meaningless handshakes.

We're off. We're having a lot of possession without looking dangerous. Villa are playing on the counter. Button makes a few routine saves. The game's a bit of a stalemate but the Fulham fans are in good voice. The Villa supporters are quiet. After all, they've suffered a lot in recent times. 'IS THIS A LIBRARY? chant the Fulham faithful. This is followed by 'CAN'T TAKE MY EYES OFF YOU,' our version of the Frankie Valli song. Aluko responds by having a shot but nothing much is happening. Fulham aren't playing with the intensity that they showed in the second half against Norwich. Our build up is slow. We manage to make inroads on the left with the pace of Sessegnon but overall our game is too predictable and narrow. Parker and McDonald, two defensive midfielders, seem to be duplicating each other, the passing is laboured and we're not getting behind their defence. Half time arrives. We're sort of managing an away game but it's a pallid performance so far.

After the break, Villa play with more aggression. Their new manager, the much travelled Steve Bruce-Roberto Matteo having already departed after poor results-has obviously geed them up.

However, Villa are just a workmanlike, 'percentage' team. We aren't playing very well but the game is under our control. Tom Cairney, our midfield playmaker, who didn't play in the Norwich game, comes off the bench, and for Villa, so does former Fulham striker, a seemingly overweight Ross McCormack. I have a feeling that this tepid match will either peter out to a bore draw or will be decided by a mistake. Unfortunately, it transpires to be a Fulham error. Button gets his kicking out all wrong, the ball goes to substitute Adomah, who centres and Kodjia acrobatically volleys the ball into the back of the net. Time to respond is running out. Smith comes on and we play it long, to not much effect. Ayité, our other substitute, certainly brings us pace and greater threat, but it's all to no avail. It's too late and Villa end up winners. Another game, we shouldn't have lost.

There's anger from the supporters about Button's kicking, playing from the back, the manager etc. Personally I have no problem with playing from the back. I know what Slaviša is trying to do but it'll take time to get a new squad time to implement it successfully. However, there's not much patience in the modern game, so while we lose, he's vulnerable. When Jean Tigana was with Fulham, he said to the players. 'pass it from the back and if you make a mistake, I'll take the blame.' Unfortunately, some English supporters don't take naturally to the possession game. Probably because many have been brought up with second ball football, athleticism, 'getting stuck in' and 'work rate'. Of course these things are important parts of the game but so is imagination and technique. Look at how many English footballers can't kick with both feet. Saha came to Fulham and took penalties with his left and right. No wonder we can't make consistent progress at international level.

Back on the coach, the mood is quiet and sombre. I make way for the young lad who passes returns to the seat next to me. We share commiserations and frustration. 'Still we're still only a few points off the play-offs,' he reminds me.' 'It hasn't made much of a difference then.' 'Not much, no.' On that relatively optimistic note, he gets stuck in to his mobile. We're now in a traffic jam. It takes ages to get out of Birmingham. I hear the coach driver talking to Barbara. 'It's like being in central London again!' On the journey back, conversation is muted. Disappointment and travellers buried in their various technological devices, contribute to a subdued atmosphere. The man on the other side of the gangway, has huge headphones wrapped around his head like an elderly, grey haired DJ. Barbara interrupts his ruminations. 'Money for the driver.' There's no reply, so she repeats her request more emphatically. 'Money for the driver.' Eventually, the man finally emerges from his headphones. 'You don't have to if you don't want to,' says Barbara, slightly disapprovingly. The man finally contributes, dropping coins into a big white envelope. I give a couple of quid. Eventually we reach inner London. 'Does the coach stop at Hammersmith?' I ask the young lad. 'Yes. it does,' replies my companion reassuringly. I get off opposite the tube with a few others. I'm feeling a bit drowsy and stupidly start to cross the road at a red light. An approaching car brings me to my senses and I withdraw to the curb. 'Not worth it mate,' says a squat, baseball-hatted fan, 'not even Usain Bolt would have made that!

Taming The Terriers

It's a beautiful autumn day. I'm on the 220 bus to the Huddersfield game. The visitors are now managed by the German David Wagner, former manager of Borussia Dortmund II, close friend and colleague of Liverpool's boss, Jürgen Klopp, who was best man at his wedding. They have started very well and are currently third, although recently they've begun to falter. They have a small squad and seemingly limited resource but nonetheless they're expected to give us a hard game.

As I make my way down the Fulham Palace Rd, I hear the wise sages giving their advice, 'with all that possession, they've got to use it better,' 'they've got to have that desire to win,' 'they need to show that intensity from the start, not just in one half.' As I wind my way down the back streets to the ground, a man with a fluffy beard encased in a grey helmet, passes on a motor bike, seemingly disinterested in football fanatics. Two foreign gentleman are proceeding apace to the game. They are speaking animatedly in what I think is Turkish. One is wearing light track suit bottoms, a white sweater and steel rim glasses, the other a black jacket and dark trainers. As I reach Colwith Rd, where the leaves on the trees are a beautiful autumnal brown, the Turks' discussion becomes more animated and intense as their pace quickens. At The Crabtree pub, a Halloween Party and Comedy Night are advertised. As I ascend the incline to the Thames Path, a jogger attired in blue velcro descends upon me. When I move aside, the courteous traveller, removes his white i pod and says, 'thank you.' However turning the corner to behold the Thames, I nearly crash into a hefty gentleman on a bike, who brakes just in time, but then moves on regardless, his headphones blaring loud rock music into the ether.

As I proceed towards the ground, I hear, the Yorkshire tones of the opposition. 'No I'm ok now, I've had eight hours sleep. I'm quite fresh. Going down there, it's a six hour drive, with a four and a half hours break. I were there last week. We've lost the contract on that one. Mind you, boss isn't bothered as we have a lot more work.' By the time, I get to the Johnny Haynes Stand, I'm met at the turnstile by a young, extrovert lad wearing an official orange bib. 'Sing loud and proud,' he proclaims. 'Loud and proud,' I reply 'that sounds like a gay anthem.' He laughs and I go up the ancient wooden stairs to the stand. I'm in the upper area and without thinking I make a mess of sitting down and stupidly fall flat on my arse. 'You forgot to unfold your seat,' says a large, benign gentleman with a wide grey moustache. 'Thanks. It's a bit primitive,' I reply, absurdly blaming the old seat for my lack of judgement. 'It's not that bad,' he wisely responds. His attention is then distracted by his companion, a young hyperactive boy, who transpires to be his grandchild. 'Grandad!' squawks the kid, not wishing the elderly man's attention to be engaged elsewhere.

Fulham have made several changes from the Villa game. The most important is the impressive Kalas is back at centre half and McDonald is the only defensive midfielder. The game starts and just as I'm settling down, a trio of young fair haired, well groomed ladies appear. 'Sorry. Excuse me,' the first one says. 'Oh, certainly,' I reply. Normally such an interruption would be annoying but the sight of the three tight-jeaned women, with their elegant scarves and jackets, trim figures and wafting scents, is a pleasant diversion. This prompts me to think that Fulham seem to have quite a lot of female fans.

I refocus on the game. Fulham are off to a flyer, they're moving the ball quickly and playing with the intensity they showed against Norwich. It's no surprise when they get the all important first goal, Chris Martin scoring when Stefan Johansen's free kick is nodded into his path. The Terriers then respond well and could have scored from both a well directed cross and corner but no one gets on the end of the deliveries. After Wells has a thirty five yard volley saved by Button, Fulham reassert themselves and Kalas of all people volleys in Scott Malone's well weighted cross. The Whites press on and when Sone Aluko's surging run ends with another good cross being nodded home by Piazon, we're 3-0 up at half time. Brilliant! 'Grandad,' cries the kid behind me. He's getting so excited that I think he needs to go to the loo. During the interval, that well known celebrity, Billy The Badger is being interviewed by Fulham FC TV. Meanwhile, our announcer, Ivan Berry, is commentating on a game, whereby if you manage to kick the ball into a certain hole, you receive a prescribed amount of money. He also tells us that 'Dead Zombie' and 'The Devil' have won the Halloween competition.

The second half starts where it left off. Ryan Fredericks, who's making a difference down the right with his pace, crosses but Martin can't get on the end of it. Then Tom Cairney goes close with a shot over the bar. When Aluko is fouled in the box after one of his mazy runs, Martin expertly converts the penalty. Thank goodness for that as we've already missed three this season!. Later, Aluko figures again when he finds the unmarked McDonald in the six yard box and the big man from Carnoustie rifles the ball into the back of the net. 5-0. Tim Ream comes on as a sub and is booed by a section of the crowd after an erratic start to the season. In fact, Ream should have made it six as his unchallenged header goes wide. Still, we mustn't get greedy. It was a fine performance. The movement in the team was terrific, the balance in the midfield with Johansen doing the ball carrying made us less static and with Fredericks in full harness at right back, we had more width and pace.

'Where did that come from?' asks Richard coming to The Wall.

'I didn't see that coming,' admits Alex

'He did what we were talking about Roly,' says Richard, 'we can't have both McDonald and Parker in midfield.'

'Yes. I think he's found his team now. There's a better balance in the system (4-2-3-1).'

'We certainly managed to make the pitch wide and play narrow when we needed,' declares Alex

'First half maybe we were flattered but second half we had so much movement, I think all the teams in the league will struggle against us, if we play like that.' Richard then changed tack:

'Gentleman. I'm now going to have to go as I have the journey from hell. The trains are not running as usual and I am going to be transferred to a bus.'

'Don't worry when Corbyn comes in and nationalises the railways, all will change.'

'Not in my lifetime, Roly,' declares The Oracle, cheerfully departing to negotiate his transportation minefield.

Meanwhile, Alex and I leave together:

'It's good Slav has back up in every position. There are some decent players not getting a game'

'Yes,' says Alex.' He's also got a good way of playing now. He needs to get the whole squad familiar with it.'

'There are so many fixtures, so he'll need to change personnel at some stage.'

'Good that he has alternatives.'

I then change the subject:

'Did you enjoy Bari?'

'Yes it was seventy degrees'

'Blimey.'

'Are you going to Brentford?'

'I'm watching it on tv, Alex. Got to save the money.'

'Richard and I are booked.'

'Ok. See you at the next game at the Cottage.

'Right. Safe home.'

Beating the Bees

I'm going for my evening run. As I puff through the South Ealing streets and reach the tube, I'm confronted by the enemy. A swarm of Bees supporters pour out of the station wrapped in their red and white scarves and thick coats to counter the cold night air. I zig zag my way past the enemy lines and beat a hasty retreat, like a soldier in battle retrenching to a safe position. There may be 'Make America Great Again' Trump v 'Deplorables' Clinton, Remainers v Leavers, but I've got Fulham v Brentford.

I return exhausted and after showering prepare a delectable salmon and rice before settling before my plasma. Sky have got Scott Minto (ex-Chelsea, Benfica), David Prutton (ex-Southampton, Leeds etc) and Peter Beagrie (ex-everywhere) sharing the pundit duties. Beagrie is talking about our poor away form and refers to our need to 'crack the code at the Cottage'. I didn't know Fulham were featuring in a Le Carre novel. It's been raining heavily all day but the surface looks good as three soldiers lead the players out. It's the Friday before Remembrance Sunday so it's time for an appropriate tribute. The soldiers lay three wreaths on the pitch. The players congregate in the centre circle. The names of players from both clubs who died in conflicts are read out. A Brentford supporter wearing the club shirt, raises the Club's flag with an inscription saying, 'Brentford FC Lest We Forget'. There's a minute's silence. Fulham unsurprisingly after the hammering of Huddersfield are keeping the same side. Daniel Mann, our commentator, informs us that David Button, our goalkeeper, formerly at Brentford, has been 'receiving banterous texts' . One apparently had his head in the middle of a dart board. He also explains that his number is 27 because that's the day he met his wife and it's also his age. Not a lot of people know that!

Fulham start well. Their movement and pace is good. Cairney shoots just wide and Aluko's drive misses. Our full backs are getting up the pitch and having a field day. We create a lot of chances but can't put them away. Let's hope we don't regret taking our opportunities. Then just before half time, Johansen plays in Aluko, his initial drive is beaten out by keeper Bentley but he follows up and scuppers the ball over the line. At last-1-0 to Fulham. In the second half it's different. Brentford tighten up and winger Clarke forces a magnificent save from Button, who pushes his powerful shot over the bar. Later, the creatively persistent Aluko shoots over, then wide. Floyd Ayité comes on for Piazon, and as Brentford push forward, he's set up by Martin on the break but also misses the target. Come on, Fulham, score another and settle it! Cairney first produces a good save from keeper Bentley and then, in injury time, in another counter attack, he sells his opposing defender a dummy and cleverly places the ball into the far corner. 2-0. The Fulham supporters go wild. Game over.

Scott Malone is made Sky Man of the Match. After the obligatory interview, he raises his statuette and claps the Fulham fans. Ex-Bee Button gets booed but I detect that he has a wry, smile on his face. Sone Aluko from Hounslow is interviewed. He speaks well and admits that he should have scored more goals. Back with the pundits, Beagrie thinks Fulham were 'sensational' especially in the first half. 'Brentford came back into it, especially with the introduction of the substitutes, so it was a very entertaining game.' Prutton believes that the Huddersfield game could be a 'sea change'. 'Out of possession Fulham worked so hard.' There was talk about how players who can run at the opposition are so dangerous as they can take players out of the game. Aluko is praised for this as are the two full backs, Fredericks and Malone.

However, Beagrie thinks that they can get better support for Martin and that the midfield can push up more. He believes that they need to do better at Craven Cottage and that the club's expectations to return to The Premiership quickly might have daunted some of them. Prutton thinks Fulham need more penetration in the final third of the pitch. He was impressed with the way Johansen carried the ball, which 'attracts players' and makes space. Beagrie admired Sone Aluko for continuing to be positive even after many misses. 'He still got on the ball.' And as for Man of The Match, Scott Malone, he was 'phenomenal' with his non-stop running 'off the shoulder', giving width and putting the opposition on the back foot. Regarding Brentford, it was remarked that they are a young side, one of the youngest in the league, and they'll learn from this. For Fulham it's a great win and they earned their bragging rights over their neighbours. The Bees were well and truly stung.

Facing Down The Owls

Donald Trump is the President Elect of the United States of America. This reminds me of a Question Time, many years ago during Robin Day's tenure, when the whole panel were in hysterics. Denis Healey, who loved to name drop, mentioned that he heard about JFK's philandering before his inauguration when an American colleague said they'd introduce him to the 'President Erect'. The panel found it difficult answering the next question.

I'm now having a meal before leaving for the Sheffield Wednesday game. After the spinach soup, I get down to the chicken and potatoes. I'm at Wood Lane and Mira is offering to give me a lift as she's going to North End market. While in the car, Classic FM is playing Haydn's Trumpet Voluntary and we discuss the relative merits of Alison Balsam and Wynton Marsalis. We're getting round the Green slowly. When we finally emerge in Shepherd's Bush Rd, I suggest to Mira that she drops me off near Hammersmith Library. 'No!' she cries as I move towards the car door, 'I want a companion, when I'm driving!' The trouble is that the time is ticking to kick off and I'm not sure she knows exactly how long it takes, given the traffic. Eventually we get to Fulham Palace Rd, where inevitably there's a jam. I tell Mira I'm going, open the door quickly, saying goodbye as I hurriedly depart.

I'm now walking down the road with other supporters. In Frank Banfield Park, a kid comes hurtling down a grassy mound. 'Harry tripped me!' he screams. His mother, a middle aged woman wrapped in a Fulham scarf and black coat, is suddenly joined by other members of this Whites supporting family. They're convening with the kids and no doubt Harry is getting sorted out. Further down, as I enter the Thames Path, a sturdy, bearded man wearing sunglasses and a red jacket, descends on his bike but brakes just in time. As I progress, I can see the floodlights hovering on the horizon, searchlights in the distance. It's low tide and I pass a pigeon, who's standing on the river bank's ledge, indignantly unperturbed by the football hordes passing him so dismissively. Meanwhile, his fellow pigeons are nestling in an oasis of land in the middle of surrounding shallow water, pecking away indiscriminately for food.

I get my programme and ask a young, dark haired woman in a thick, dark coat if she's got the Scottish lady sacked. 'She's not here today,' she giggles. 'Maybe she's at Tottenham?' I reply mischievously. I enter the ground at the Johnny Haynes Stand near the Cottage. I've now got a half season ticket which is a good deal, although I have to perch a bit like a bird on a ledge to see the furthest areas of the pitch at the Hammersmith End. I make my way to my seat. I'm there with a few minutes to spare. It's Fulham's first home game since Remembrance Sunday. The Fulham programme has a picture of a poppy on its front cover and a quote from the Robert Laurence Binyon poem, 'Age shall not weary them, nor the years condemn, /At the going down of the sun and in the morning /We will remember them.' Like the Brentford game, four soldiers with wreaths lead the team on to the pitch. The same ritual takes place. This time though the players are in lines opposite each other. Also during the minutes silence, the Last Post is played by a solitary trumpeter. As a respectful stillness hovers over the ground, a tall, lanky man in a long black coat clumsily clambers across in front of me, up to his seat above.

The game starts and Sheffield Wednesday make a strong start. They're passing the ball well. They've lost the last two games and seem determined not to lose another. In the tenth minute they score. After an incisive pass from the diminutive Bannan, Forestieri shoots and although Button gets a hand to the ball, it goes in off the post. The vociferously supported Wednesday are ahead. In response, McDonald leaps high and heads powerfully over the bar. Then Johansen is denied a possible penalty as referee Geoff Eltringham waves appeals away. In fact, Eltringham's not stamping his authority on the game and letting a lot of fouls go unpunished. However, it's Wednesday who are dominating the game. They're well drilled, decent passers and physical. They're doubling up on our speedy full backs, so they can't get forward and on the few occasions in the half that our quick players like Aluko pass them, they immediately retaliate with a foul. Later, they miss a few chances and the first half ends with the visitors in the driving seat.

During the interval, in the row above me, a gentleman with a white beard, receding greyish hair and light rimmed glasses says 'it's got to get better. That was awful.' He's wearing a blue jacket and has what seems like a country Irish accent. He's accompanied by a young red haired man with a check 'cheese cutter' cap. 'They've got to do something different in the second half,' the older man proclaims. 'What do you suggest, pray?' I reply. He laughs at my call for spiritual help and we resettle for the second half. Fulham are trying to get forward but Wednesday are a really hard, difficult side to play against. Chances emerge for both sides and the game's in the balance.

The turning point is the arrival of Scott Parker as a substitute for McDonald. An experienced, well seasoned pro, he'd obviously noted Wednesday's fouling and as Fulham start to press forward more strongly, one of his first actions is to put in a very hard 50-50 tackle. He's booked for it but he's made his point and as Wednesday tire, the gaps open up. Parker himself goes wide but in injury time, the unmarked Malone, arriving late in the box at the back post, scores with a powerful left footed shot. 1-1. Even the Irishmen are delighted. Shortly afterwards, they make a quick early exit to beat the traffic. The game ends as a draw. We're eighth. We'll take it.

At The Wall, I meet a darkly clad Alex

'That was a hard, niggly game'.

Shane, Richard's stocky mate, wearing a dark woolly hat, joins us and berates the man in black;

'The ref didn't give us anything.'

'I thought he was in danger of losing control of the game,' I concur.

'Was that a penalty in the first half?' asks Shane.

'I thought so but I couldn't see it clearly,' I reply.

Richard comes to join us.

'We would have lost that game last season.'

'Their goal was a good one,' I suggest 'and Forestieri is a Premiership player.'

'It was a hard game,' pondered The Oracle. 'They stopped us getting forward and squeezed the middle of the park. If we broke free, they clattered us.'

I then launch into a rallying cry.

'I've got faith in this squad. They've got a good spirit. They've shown commitment and resolve coming from behind!'

After everybody seems to agree with the author's intense declamation, Richard and Shane depart to get their train to East Sussex.

Alex and I wander away.

'Is Pete ok? 'I enquire.

'Yes. he's at a family do. He's missed more than he's seen this season, what with his wife's knee op, and the recuperation as well.'

'Right. I wondered as I haven't seen him much.'

I then veer back to the football.' .

'Pity about the international break.'

'Yes. We would have liked to continue. Playing after the break isn't easy.'

'Especially given the opposition, they were a 'nasty' side who can play.'

'Still I think we can still do well.'

'Yes. I agree. I think there could be exciting times ahead.'

'On that positive note I'll leave you. have a good weekend.'

I walk up the Fulham Palace Rd past the long line of Yorkshire coaches and the Owls fans perched on ledges by the roadside as they wait for all of their supporters to assemble.

Frustration at The Seaside

Fidel Castro has died and Fulham are playing away to second placed Brighton. After having a bizarre conversation with Mira about cosmic energy, I arrive at Stevenage Rd and discover the departing coach. Next to the vehicle is an older man with greying sideboards, a red jacket, a Fulham FC scarf and a multitude of Fulham badges on his cap. He tells me that the coach is full and that there's another one along in six minutes. Meanwhile, inside the existing coach, the driver is giving instructions on a microphone like a Butlins Redcoat. When the second coach eventually arrives, I clamber up the steps to be greeted by Barbara, the lady, who's in charge of travelling supporters. When I hand her my ticket, she responds critically by telling me, 'that's the wrong one'. Inadvertently, I'd given her my match ticket. 'Sorry,' I reply. 'That's ok. These things happen,' she responds sympathetically. 'In any case, I've got your name and address.' Having passed this hurdle, I make my way to the middle of the coach, dump my rucksack on a seat and settle down for the journey.

As I do so, I discover that across the aisle, I'm next to a fair haired man in his late twenties-early thirties, who's permanently looking at his smartphone. He's next to a blonde lady around the same age, who's wearing a Fulham FC shirt. When I manage to distract this man from technology, he tells me that Fulham are taking 2,400 supporters to the game but he thinks that most of them are travelling by train or car. That explains why the coach isn't full. He has a friend, who's in the seat in front of him and has come with his son. 'Brighton are second,' screeches the child. 'Don't worry about that,' says my smartphone friend in a firm, paternal tone. 'My first game was against Middlesborough. McCormack scored. Number 79. Da Da Dee Da Dee,' chants the kid. Then he adds, 'I've not seen Fulham in the Premier League yet, 'cause I've just started.'

Later, while this group discuss the cost of games online and Black Friday bargains, my smartphone friend distributes crisps to the young boy. What has Gary Lineker done for healthy eating? Then suddenly Barbara makes an announcement. The driver is over his time, so we'll have to wait seven minutes. She then counts the number of people on the coach, announces that there'll be no stops on the journey and that we'll go straight to the ground. This will be repeated when we come back, apart from a stop at Putney. This is her destination, so she's glad that she'll be getting home early for once. The driver seems unsure of the journey but a grey haired gentleman in the front seat sketches out the directions and tells him 'we'll keep an eye on you.' Eventually we get going. We pass Fulham Park Gardens, where I used to live in the 80s amidst lots of young, smartly suited yuppies going to Putney Bridge tube, on the way to making their fortunes. Nearby, Suzy Lamplugh worked for an estate agent. She mysteriously disappeared after showing a property to a 'Mr Kipper', not far from Craven Cottage. She's never been seen since.

As we make our way over Putney Bridge, I discuss the season with the two lads opposite me. The father of the young boy, a young man with short fair hair, dressed in a grey t shirt, bemoans losing to our nearest neighbours.

'QPR was a bummer,' he laments.

'Yes, those missed penalties didn't help us,' I reply. 'Who's missed the penalties this season? I ask Smartphone Man. We then go through the names of the 'criminals', like a roll of execution: Cauley Woodrow, Sone Aluko and Thomas Cairney

'Still we bought a lot of players this season. They do need time to bed down,' says the young Dad, optimistically. 'We've also got a good manager but you have doubts,' he says looking accusingly at Smartphone Man.

'No. I like him,' remonstrates his mate.

The lads get diverted and I get disturbed by all the notices coming up on the tv in the coach: 'This vehicle is equipped by CCTV'. 'Do not obstruct spare seats by placing belongings on them.' 'Telephone conversations should be conducted quietly.' 'Smoking and Vaping aren't allowed in this vehicle.' Certainly the modern football journey is quieter and more security and health conscious but it lacks the boisterous character of days of yore. Everybody is much more in their own bubble. Still those in the back, the traditional home of the 'rebels,' are doing their best. 'She was with his Dad's mate for ten years', one of them cries.

Then we're interrupted by a young blonde woman wearing brown rimmed glasses and casually dressed in a white sweater, grey trousers and matching trainers. She wants us to fill in a questionnaire to improve the 'customer experience' and get more fans to travel to away games. I suggest that there should be more social activities. The supporters don't even have an amenable, widely accessible bar at the Cottage these days. Al-Fayed wanted to use all available space for corporate activities. While I understand the need to raise more revenue in a small ground, I think many hard core supporters have lost a place to fraternise. Even while we were located at QPR, there was a bar in a portakabin, and I used to meet many more fans. There were also end of season get-togethers. Now there's nothing. Barcelona style, Fulham should have more activities beyond football, to induce a greater sense of community and loyalty. You could work on away support from there. At the moment, there aren't many connections between supporters, beyond message boards and the short contact at matches.

I fill in the form and a young man in his twenties in a brown sweater, comes down the aisle and asks 'anyone have one of these?' dramatically waving the questionnaire. I give him mine. He thanks me and departs. Meanwhile, the lads at the back start hurling names around: Hardy, Justin, Cleo. They describe characters that go with the names and start laughing. I'm not sure the meaning of all this but it invites suitable backseat hilarity. Then as we approach the ground, the child opposite me asks, 'what colour is Brighton, Daddy?' I can't hear the Dad's reply but I hope he gets him up for the coming battle by saying 'blue, like Chelsea!' After evacuating the coach, I buy a programme from a balding man in a yellow florescent jacket, with hair only at the sides of his head. He owes me ten pence but says 'I've got no tens yet.' I forget it and depart, only to be insistently called back to receive my newly found paltry change.

Making my way to the entrance of the South Stand, I'm greeted by a young man in a khaki jacket who coolly exudes bonhomie- 'Welcome to The Amex, man. May the best team win.' Then suddenly a coach with black tinted glass crawls past us to the main entrance. I think it's the Fulham team. I walk behind the coach to where various supporters are congregated, behind a cordoned off area. The team come out but there's only a small gap between the coach door and the entrance, so I only get a slight glimpse of the players. Slaviša Jokanović, the manager, exits the opposite side. I give him a shout but he remains impassive, no doubt, concentrating on the task ahead. I go back to the South Stand, where the away supporters are starting to enter. There's still one and a half hours before kick off but there's not much to do outside, so I join the queue, get frisked like a convict and enter into the area under the stand, where food and drink are being served. Four pints are being offered for sixteen quid and the food hatch is offering four items for ten quid. BT and Sky games are being relayed at various strategic positions. I chat with a young, short, unkempt Fulham fan with fair hair and a stubbly beard, who's sipping his beer. Apparently, he hasn't been to many away games but he went to Brentford and enjoyed getting those local bragging rights. On the tv, Aguero equalises for City. 'He's something else,' Stubble exudes. He thinks we have a good chance of being near the play-offs. Robbie Savage is summarising for BT. 'I hate him' says Stubble. Aguero gets another goal. 2-1 City. 'Better go.' 'Ok mate, see you,' replies a cheery Stubble, relishing the last remnants of his booze.

After going to the expansive toilet with vast troughs ready for marauding football hordes, I go up into the stadium, which is another modern concrete bowl. Impressive but impersonal. It seems to be dropped into the community rather than coming out of it. It has none of the character or intimacy of Brighton's old but grubby Goldstone Rd ground. A St George flag inscribed with Brighton FC is behind the goal facing us. Enshrined on the edge of that stand is 'Stand Or Fall For Sussex On The Sea.' I go to my seat and discover, I'm next to a dark haired youngster in a long black coat. He doesn't think we'll make the play-offs. I disagree.

'You'd like a play-off game at the Cottage wouldn't you?'

'That'd be great,' says Black Coat.

He then says he prefers Bettinelli to Button in goal.

'It's good to see a Fulham Academy player in the first team.'

I agree but suggest that Bettinelli might be omitted for a perceived lack of discipline. In one game I saw him walking a hundred yards out of his goal to confront a referee.

'But he is young,' counters Black Coat.

'You're right, but I suppose Slav's gone for experience.'

Black Coat doesn't like the ground either. We then get into a discussion about the way various people have wanted to flog Craven Cottage and end up in a ground like this somewhere else. In the late 70s owner, Ernie Clay, a tough northern businessman, bought Craven Cottage's freehold from the Church Commissioners for £900,000 and then sold it for £9 million to Marler Estates, developers, whose director David Bulstrode became chairman and wanted to amalgamate the club with QPR as Fulham Park Rangers. Later, Al-Fayed with his dream of Fulham being the 'Man Utd of the South', flirted with moving the club to a bigger stadium. Black Coat and I agree that these were unrealistic and unwelcome propositions. Thank goodness for the efforts of Jimmy Hill, Fulham 2000 and the supporters, who insured that the club maintained its unique ground.

Getting back to the game, Black Coat also feels sorry that Madl isn't in the team.

'I'm not that impressed with Sigurdsson but I suppose he's got more height and maybe Slav wants one big guy.'

He's now questioning the subs.

'Why's Ream a sub before Madl?'

'Because he can double up as a full back. Also he gives a left sided option?'

'Oh maybe you're right,' replies the smoothly coiffeured Black Coat. 'I'll take a draw today,' he continues.

'Yes. it's going to be a difficult game but I genuinely think we can beat anyone,' I optimistically enthuse.

The players are now out doing their predictable warm ups.

'What animal is the Brighton mascot?' I enquire.

'Some kind of bird,' suggests Black Coat. In fact, unsurprisingly it's a seagull called 'Gully'.

The fans are now warming up. They're singing their Al Fayed song inspired by their desire not to leave The Cottage, 'TAKE ME HOME AL FAYED, TO THE PLACE THAT I LOVE. CRAVEN COTTAGE BY THE RIVER, TAKE ME HOME, AL FAYED!'

The game starts. Fulham are attacking away from us. Initially Brighton have a couple of shots saved but in the eighteenth minute

Johansen's corner is headed by Kevin McDonald to the far side of the goal. Our old mucker, Steve Sidwell, tries to clear it but all to no avail-it's over the line. 0-1, to the Whites. Now we boss the game. Our passing and movement are superb. Ayité, who appears lively and quick has a deflected shot well saved by another of our old boys, David Stockdale, who seems to have lost a lot of weight since his Fulham days. The Fulham fans are moving from the abuse of 'YOU'RE FUCKIN' SHIT!' to the celebratory 'IF YOU LOVE FULHAM STAND UP! 'When they do, a few old'uns behind us, sitting on their seats, respond humorously with 'SIT DOWN!' Despite our impressive play, we just can't take our opportunities and score again. In the second half, Brighton, up the tempo. Seven minutes into the half, a poor header leads to us not clearing our lines and Baldock volleys home superbly. 1-1. The home crowd spring to life with chants of 'WHO ARE YER?' . The Fulham faithful respond with 'WE FORGOT, WE FORGOT THAT YOU WERE 'ERE!'

After Sidwell appears to strike Kalas and only gets a yellow card, the game becomes more intense and we seem to lose our rhythm, Although, we're still causing them occasional problems and Stockdale saves well from Ayité, with ten minutes to go a cross from Baldock finds Murray unmarked, and he calmly volleys home. 2-1. Fulham respond aggressively and create chances, the best in the last minute when Martin in a good position to shoot passes to Cairney, who, ten yards out, scuffs his shot and gives Stockdale an easy save. Game over. We've played well and should never have lost this game.

As I'm about to ascend the concrete stairs to the car park, I hear a familiar cry in the distance.

'R-ol-y!'

It's The Oracle, fully gloved and coated to combat the increasing cold.

I'm freezing and frustrated.' How did we lose that? I mourn.

'They had two chances and scored from both,' responds Richard.

'Where's the coach?' I ask

'The Fulham one's over there on the right. I'm over here, I took one from Brighton.'

Maybe The Oracle was a solitary Fulham supporter surrounded by Seagulls?

'We played the better football. They knew how to win,' concludes Richard.

You're right. See you next Saturday. Better catch the coach.'

'Ok. Bye, Rols.'

There's a funereal, eerie silence on the way back. There are the isolated sounds of music on headphones, supporters bent over smartphones looking at results and weary loyalists lying prostrate on unoccupied seats. Chatter is sporadic as if it's an intrusion on a cortege's grief. Still, I ask Smartphone Man where we are in the table. Eighth-only three points off the play-offs. We've got to hang in there up to the final games. The child opposite me is asking about Chelsea, who have kicked off at 5.30 pm-that's all I need. I sneeze. There's a chorus of 'bless you!' from the back seats. When we get near Putney, I decide to get off. As I descend, a small man with horn rimmed glasses peers out of the dark. I ask him, 'where's the station? 'You turn left at the main road and it's over on the right.' replies my guide. I then walk past the Putney Bridge tube to get the 220 bus. On the journey home, two young women are talking animatedly-'Claire told me he's leaving his wife or partner and their kid'. Life goes on all right but Fulham have lost at Brighton.

Cottage Carve Up!

Gareth Southgate has been appointed full time England manager, the police are looking into eighteen cases of sex abuse in football and seventy one people have died, when a plane carrying the Chapecocnse football team crashed in Columbia. I'm leaving Mira's flat, to go to the Cottage to see us play third placed Reading

At Hammersmith Library, I alight. I pass St Paul's Church, where Johnny Haynes' memorial service was held. I remember that there was a big attendance and the vicar spoke knowledgeably about both Johnny and the club. I think at one time he was attached to Fulham. I'm not sure that such a post exists now during these secular times. That Johnny died in such a violent car crash was particularly upsetting. Still, apart from his wonderful passing skills with a heavyweight leather ball, one affectionately remembers his frustration with his team mates missing the chances he created and his mate 'Tosh' rushing up to the ref, when JH was being admonished for a verbal indiscretion, apparently pleading that 'he was only talking to me!'

Down the Fulham Palace Road, a steady stream of supporters are making their way to the game. A young man is earnestly discussing the merits of higher education with an older friend. He seems more interested in going to a university in the States than Oxbridge. Apparently, he loves New York. You get all types at Fulham. Some bring The Guardian to read at half time, others have a different perspective and, in the eighties, I once overheard a discussion about whether a supporter should vote for the National Front.

While continuing on my way, I get a phone call from Mira to tell me that the trouble with her car has been sorted. She wishes 'good luck to your wankers!' Well that's one way to wish a team well, I suppose. Meanwhile, a group of Polish men throng around a bench in Frank Banfield Park, demolishing lagers. The sun burns down on The Thames. It's a beautiful, brisk afternoon. 'I can smell dinner,' says a white haired lady in a fur coat, stretching her head in the direction of the adjoining Thames Path houses. On Stevenage Rd, the Scottish lady is still not back selling the programmes. Maybe Spurs have kidnapped her! 'Get your latest Fanzine!' cries a man in sunglasses, black coat and jeans, looking like a macabre character out of The Sopranos. I buy one. 'Thanks' he says. 'Enjoy.' Getting into the Johnny Haynes Stand, an old'un is having trouble with getting his card to be recognised. 'Bring back tickets! I cry. 'Nah, I'm all right,' he pleads, struggling away as the nearby attendant in an orange bib grins in amusement.

Next to my seat, there's a young man seated with an older man in a dark coat, possibly his father. The young bloke, with a light brown, tweed cap, tells me he's really a rugby fan. 'Oh, so you're coming to see us plebs play with a round ball.' 'Exactly,' he replies, with a beaming smile. 'Who do you support then?' I enquire. 'Leicester Tigers'. Yes, at Fulham, you do indeed get all sorts. Not surprising as diehard Fulham fans probably amount to no more than 10,000. The players now come out wearing black armbands in memory of the Chapecoesne players who died. They were flying to play Athlético Nacional in the final of the Copa Sudamericana in Medellin. Their rise to such dizzy heights is regarded as similar to our own Leicester City's trajectory in winning The Premier League.

The game starts and Fulham play flowing attacking football, continuing the positive play of the first half versus Brighton. They finally get their reward when Fredericks thundering down the right, puts in a tantalising cross in the 'corridor of uncertainty' and Gunter instinctively reacts by putting the ball into his own net. 1-0. Fulham continue the good work but again can't capitalise on their chances, Aluko and Martin, with a header, being the main culprits. Such is Fulham's dominance that Reading don't have a shot on target until the end of the second half. However, after Brighton, doubts linger about whether we have that killer instinct to finish a game off. At half time, white discs are placed on the turf in selected areas. A group of very young kids, who go to the academy a few days a week, are playing five a side football. Watching the skills of these boys is quite alarming. They look really good. What's more they seem to be enjoying it, which helps.

Shortly after the game resumes and not long after the interval, Martin powers forward towards goal and scores from a low, strong shot going into the left hand corner. Thank goodness for that. 2-0.

We have that cushion. Martin then misses two chances-one a weak header from a Johansen cross, the other a shot which goes over the bar, after Ayité played him in. In the fifty fourth minute there's a dramatic change in the game when Williams is sent off for lashing out at Johansen. Although more space opens up for Fulham, Reading are still looking to go forward resolutely and Fredericks makes a great tackle to stop a dangerous counter attack. Nonetheless, Fulham add to their tally when our swivelling and swerving man, Sone Aluko, beats two players out wide, cuts in and sends a delightful shot into the far corner. A wonderful goal. Ah but hold on, the assistant ref thinks it's off side. There's a dramatic pause until thankfully the ref points to the centre circle. 3-0. What a great individual effort.

This is the cue for Fulham to get expansive. Johansen evades three defenders, goes into the box and fires a brilliant shot via the outside of his left boot into the net. 4-0. The Cottage is rocking. The clappers are being whacked, the decibels are increasing. 'CRAVEN COTTAGE BY THE RIVER' is resounding around the ground. To cap it all, Martin powers into the box, wins a free kick and then dispatches it way beyond keeper Al Habsi. 5-0. Now we're getting greedy and the fans are shouting, 'WE WANT SIX!'. A great performance and a terrific win.

On my way to The Wall, a man is waiting outside the Hammersmith End puffing a cigar. After that result, we can all bring them out.

Pete is back in the Fulham fold. He tells me he can't get rid of his chest cold but his wife's ok after her operation but 'she's lazy, she won't do any exercise!'

'Well that was better than Brighton. That was ninety minutes,' says an approaching Richard.

'They certainly are playing the best football since the Tigana days,' I suggest.

'I think that's better than the Tigana days,' counters Pete

'There aren't the consistent goals of that time,' says The Oracle.

'Yes I get worried when they don't take their chances,' I admit.

'It takes time to weld a team together but it's happening,' offers Alex.

Suddenly we are interrupted by a young boy of around eight years of age.

He's wearing a dark blue woolly hat and is carrying a tray, full of cakes and fudge.

'Taste and buy,' he cries.

'Did you make them?' says Richard

'With the help of my sister,' the boy replies

'How old is she?' asks Richard

'Eight.' The boy hesitates. 'Well my Mum did help.'

'I'll give you a pound,' says Pete

The boy gratefully accepts the deal.

'A good entrepreneur. That's what I like to see,' declares Richard

Then we all contribute a few bob.

Suddenly his South African Dad appears and takes a photo with us all.

'That's before we mugged him!' Richard declares jauntily after the picture has been completed.

Eventually we all depart our separate ways.

As Alex and I are walking towards Fulham Palace Rd, he tells me that next week he's going to meet his partner's aunt in Zagreb.

'I'm meeting her at the airport and coming straight back to London with her. She doesn't speak a word of English.'

Into The Black Country

I'm at the Cottage waiting for the bus to Wolverhampton to see the Wolves match. I've had a small contretemps with my partner, Mira, who said she'll give me a lift but who seemed to take an age to get ready. 'A lot of traffic isn't there?' says a cynical Mira, revelling in a vacant Shepherd's Bush Rd. We arrive in reasonable time only for the coach not to appear. I haven't had online confirmation of my ticket, so I'm little concerned. My doubts are allayed when Barbara, dressed in a decorative pale coat, asks me 'are you Mr Jaquarell? 'Yes,' I reply not bothering to correct her pronunciation of my name. I've been called all sorts of name- Jaquaretto, Jaquarelli- and worse, so I go with the flow.

I pass the time talking to a very committed Fulham fan, with long grey hair and a light blue jacket. He managed to avoid the latest delays on the Piccadilly line and tells me that he had a few beers the previous night and is going to get some kip on the coach. He's seen many Fulham teams come and go but he's happy enough with this one 'Johansen has particularly impressed me. Wasn't so sure at the beginning but he's won me over.' I tell him that I like Ayité and the way he shoots on sight. 'Yes, but it'd be good if it wasn't straight at the keeper,' he replies acidly. I've a feeling that this is the bloke who used to live in Hammersmith but is now in the East End. From a previous brief conversation, I think he and his family lived in my old flat in Parfrey St.

At last, the bus arrives and we get into the coach. I settle behind East End Man and don't say much as I know he wants to kip. Barbara tells us that we can't leave until 10.20 because of the driver's rota. 'Oh that's a pity, I could have gone for a drink,' says the bald, beefy man opposite me. He's wearing grey trainers, a black shirt and has a tattoo on his left arm. Meanwhile, the woman behind me is talking to the man behind her. Apparently, she's been in therapy after dislocating her shoulder. She's also has had a run in with somebody about 'their bloody dog':

'I said to her. You see that thing-it's a lead. You're not supposed to let him run by the river.'

'This is not the river,' replied the lady with the dog and told The Woman Behind, in no uncertain terms 'to piss off!'

When we get to the top of Fulham Palace Rd, the bus, for some strange reason, stops. A young man in an elegant brown hat and dark coat embarks-'sorry, I had terrible problem with traffic,' he explains, mustering all available charm. 'Wish I'd known, as I live near here' cynically comments The Woman Behind, after the young man passes down the aisle. I jerk round and see that she's a fair haired, middle aged lady wearing light rimmed glasses. There's a general air of critical surprise that one fan is getting special favours. This is dispelled by a diversion from The Bald Man. 'Hope they're going to win today,' he surmises. Then he adds somewhat fatefully, 'they played great last week but there's no guarantee, they'll repeat it this week.'

The coach is fairly quiet. It's near Christmas so maybe some regulars couldn't make it. As we pass the home of our rivals, those bees from Brentford, an ominous sign menacingly rears up amidst the drizzling rain-'When It Rains It Kills. Slow Down'. Suddenly an isolated cry of 'Come On You Whites' breaks the purgatorial silence. As we reach Heathrow, the traffic is temporarily heavy. The coach isn't full. Probably, more supporters will be coming from Motspur Park. Opposite in a row just behind me, an Irishman with a mop of grey hair is on his mobile talking to a mate-'I'm away going to a match. I'll give you a buzz during the week. Ok Andrew?' he says diplomatically, not wishing to indulge in a public conversation

After a stopover at another overpriced motorway cafe, we continue up the M40. The Bald Man opposite me asks me if I've travelled away much. I tell him that I've seen some away games. Apparently, he's going to Newcastle-he's already booked a plane for £60.

'That game's in April isn't it?' I enquire

'I suppose that's why it's cheap,' says The Bald Man.

'It's a long way to get beat,' he adds

'Blackburn got a result there. I think they're beatable,' I optimistically assert.

'Yeah. Maybe,' he hesitantly replies.

We then discuss the merits of the 1966 and 1970 England World Cup sides. I always thought that the 70s side was better, after all they were playing away and nearly beat Brazil,-one of the greatest sides to ever play the game. The '66 side was good but it's sometimes forgotten that they did play all their games at Wembley and most England sides do well in competitive games on their home patch. The Bald Man isn't totally convinced and the conversation veers to that old chestnut, the England manager. The newly appointed Southgate hasn't a great record as a club manager but he's done well with the England Under 21s.

'He could be our Joachim Löw,' I declare.

'A civil service type,' the Irishman counters

'You need a ruthless type like Ramsey,' insists The Bald Man

We then discuss Leicester City's indifferent form after surprisingly winning the Premier League.

'Maybe Leicester gave us all false hope. Mind you, if Fulham were to win the Premiership and go down the following season, I'd take it,' says The Bald Man.

He then goes on to paint a vivid picture of Fulham in the final of the Europa League.

'Never experienced anything like it. No trouble, yet everyone was drunk!'

'The Athletico fans were good,' suggests the Irishman

'Yeah, but they won so they could afford to be,' replies The Bald Man.

'Then I went to the Euros,' he continued

'To see England?'

'Naw. I'm Welsh,' he asserts in a ripe estuary accent. 'Saw all the games. Chris Coleman did well. He did ok at Fulham but it came a bit early in his managerial career. It was great over at the Euros. Mind you, my credit card is still suffering.'

He then gets back to Fulham FC. Despite, Mohammed Al-Fayed's considerable commitment and success with Fulham, he never warmed to him

'They all chant his name but I don't.'

Mohamed Al-Fayed laid the foundations for the rebirth of Fulham. He then oversaw us becoming both an established Premier

League club and UEFA Europa League finalists. However, some supporters remain sceptical of his dealings elsewhere.

'He conned Shahid Khan into buying the club,' says The Bald Man.

'How much did he get? 'I enquire

'Between £150-200 million,' suggests the Irishman in the dark red sweater

And then in a short time, we went down, immediately decreasing the club's value. The Bald Man then continues by telling me that both of his sons are in New York.

'It was New York or Wolverhampton. I got the short straw. On the trip over there, they were showing 'Sully', that film about a plane crash! That's a bit odd. Still, apparently it's a good film. They're staying with a cousin in a flat overlooking the Hudson, so they're all right.'

He then applauds Roy Hodgson's management and the team that reached the Europa League Final, Fulham's greatest achievement.

'Mind you, I don't know why he bought Konchesky to Liverpool. They obviously didn't do research on his Mum. Apparently, she'd already swung her handbag at somebody during a Fulham game with Reading. So when she told the Liverpool Echo that she didn't like Scousers, that was it!'

'Ok' says the Bald Man, changing the subject, 'who's the dirtiest players who've played for Fulham?'

'Terry Hurlock?' I cautiously submit

'How do you remember him. He was a monster.'

'Peter Storey?,' I add

'Michael Brown?' proffers The Woman Behind.

'He didn't look hard. Still, he could be nasty,' adjudicates The Bald Man.

The Woman Behind then tells us about 'sledging.'

'You know-like in cricket-bad mouthing. At the Cottage, some of the Sheffield Wednesday bench were doing it as the Fulham players warmed up.'

The Bald Man then regales us with his experience at Liverpool.

'They'd just beaten us 10-1 and after leaving the ground, I'm met by a bloke, who proceeds to pull at my Fulham scarf. Wait a minute,

I tell him. you've just thrashed us, why do you want my scarf? Here, I said, calm down, you can have it!'

We're deep in the Midlands, now.

'Sutton Coldfield's near here. When I was in the army I was based there. Worst place I've been to. When you go out on the town, you can meet some real hard nuts,' continues The Bald Man.

Eventually, we get into Wolverhampton. Molineux is in the centre of the town. We approach The Stan Cullis Stand. Cullis was the Wolves manager from 1948 to 1964, when Wolves were one of the best teams in the country. Cullis, a bit of a Sergeant major type, was hard but effective. He played a strong, very English, athletic game. Later we pass the Billy Wright Stand. Wright was a major footballer in my childhood. He played 105 times for England, 90 of those as captain. With Wolves, he won the old First Division three times and later played for and managed Arsenal. I remember him as one of the first major footballers to marry a person in show business. His wife was Joy Beverley, one of the Beverley Sisters, a popular singing group in the 1950s. They were the Posh and Becks of their day. After mentioning this to The Woman Behind, she reveals that she dealt with the Beverley Sisters' accounts. 'Most of the sisters were ok,' she tells me.

While I'm remembering a bit of Wolves history, it becomes quite clear that our Asian driver, formally dressed in a white shirt, multicoloured tie, black pullover and grey trousers, seems to be getting lost, as we go right round the ground without parking. 'That's why I don't like coming by coach,' expostulates The Bald Man. 'It's too much like hard work. At the front of the coach, they've spent too much time cracking jokes, rather than concentrating on the way.' Eventually, the driver succeeds in finding the car park, which heralds an outburst of ironic clapping.

The coach is parked some way from the ground. We then have to cross a busy motorway by walking four hundred yards to our right and going down a series of steep steps. When we emerge on the other side, we have a short meander to the stadium. Here we are greeted in the pouring rain by a programme seller, protecting himself from the elements with a huge black gabardine mac. 'I'm not hiding!' he says from under his camouflage. He then emerges and extracts a programme from under a waterproof cover. Inside the ground, there's no tv, so we can't watch a game. However, I encounter The Bald Man in the bar and tell him to 'have a good one.' I then bump into a Fulham fan with a red and white Santa Claus hat. 'You're in festive mood,' I declare. 'Why not, it's an away game?' replies Santa.

Inside the stadium is coloured by a dramatic bank of gold and black seats. 'Love Knows No Division.' is displayed across the Steve Bull Stand, named after their long serving striker. Two big screens hug the diagonals of the pitch. A long glass panelling is behind us, probably for guests and VIPs. Above this is a digital screen updating the score. Maybe, the fifteen yard gap between the fans and the pitch makes the players more remote but the stadium certainly has a sense of ambition We have a great view around the half way line, which is unusual for away fans. Two young, heavily muscular lads are near my seat. When I show them my ticket, they depart. I'm not clear where they intend to sit.

The announcer then mentions the death of two Wolves players, Ian Cartwright and David McLaren. We are invited to applaud. Clapping rings around the ground. This is followed by six men in golden jackets appearing with 'We Are Wolves' signs. They take up strategic positions, at various sides of the ground, gently swinging their flags in the breeze. They are followed by two Wolves mascots in golden shirts, black skirts and fluffy brown shoes. Are they both 'Wolfie,' Wanderers' official representative, or is there a subversive double in our midst? It remains a mystery as the Fulham supporters strike up 'Come On You Whites' and the mascots have their pictures taken with some children. Meanwhile, Wolves fans lustily sing their version of Jeff Beck's 60s hit, 'Hi Ho Silver Lining!' which blares over the loudspeakers to deafening effect. Apparently some Wolves supporters would prefer to sing the reggae song 'The Liquidator' but it was banned by the previous regime because it incited a mass swearing accompaniment!

The players come out and the game starts. As the two teams tentatively suss each other out, it's clear that this section of our fans are going to stay standing. Not everybody is happy about this. Behind us, I hear an aggressive voice shouting.

'There aren't real fans here but the fuckin' Riverside lot. I've been Fulham all my life, you're not real fuckin' fans,' he cries menacingly at his protagonists.

One of the men next to me wearing a dark blue jacket, decides to challenge this renegade.

'Stop the swearing. They're kids here.'

'It's a football match, if you don't like swearing, then don't come. I've been Fulham all my life,' retorts the youthful rebel.

'You like listening to yourself, don't you?' replies the man who's now facing towards the angry youth.

I'm not turning round to look at him in case it increases aggravation. To me, he remains a turbulent voice in the crowd. For a moment, I fear it might kick off but 'the voice' gradually moves away and gets lost in another part of the stand. Although The Man In The Blue Jacket saw him off without resorting to anger, the majority of fans are still standing and you can see that some people, especially those with children, remain frustrated.

Fulham start well with the fast passing and quick movement they've shown in recent games. Then Wolves score. Our old aerial failing manifests itself again. A corner is whipped in and Hause heads past Button, who seems to get down late and can't stop the ball crossing the line. 'WE'RE WINNIN' AT HOME! WE'RE WINNIN' AT HOME! YOU MUST BE SHIT WE'RE WINNING AT HOME!' chant the Wolves faithful. 'Button's a disgrace. Bettinelli's a much better keeper,' says an irate man next to me, his face contorted with frustration. A young Dad says his kid can't see and loudly pleads for fans to sit down. Some do but when others don't, they're forced to get up again. Thankfully, after thirty minutes Fredericks' low cross is hammered into the net by Johansen and dilutes the tension. 'YOU'RE NOT SINGING! YOU'RE NOT SINGING! YOU'RE NOT SINGING ANYMORE!. YOU'RE NOT SINGING ANYMORE! shout the Fulham fans derisively. They're now in fine voice. and 'CRAVEN COTTAGE BY THE RIVER!' is followed by 'CAN'T TAKE MY EYES OFF YOU'.

Wolves then miss a great chance as Cavaleiro in a good position slips and his shot flies well over the bar. Thank goodness for that. Fulham take advantage and just after the half hour Johansen's superb cross is headed in by the advancing Ayité. 1-2. Now we're ahead, some of the fans are compelled to hurl abuse. 'YOU'RE FUCKIN' SHIT! YOU'RE FUCKIN' SHIT!,' is followed by 'I WANNA GO HOME! THIS IS A SHITHOLE, I WANNA GO HOME!' Then three minutes before half time from Johansen's free kick, Tom Cairney scores a great goal-a tremendous volley. 1-3. Cue for ex-Wolves stalwart, Kevin McDonald to get jeered. To which, a corpulent fan responds, 'he left you 'cause you're shit. The same reason Stearman (now on loan with Wolves) went back!' A few minutes later, the ref blows for half time and the Fulham team get an ovation as they leave the pitch. I turn round to a young blonde mother, who's with her husband and two very young children. 'Can the kids see?' I enquire. 'It's ok. I've managed to balance them on the top of the seats.'

After a rather subdued interval, the game restarts. Wolves are upping the tempo. They're playing more intensely and directly, getting at Fulham's back line. We're not responding well, missing tackles and looking flustered. The warning signs are there as McDonald heads a Doherty header off the line. The Fulham supporters are more subdued. However, Cairney raises cheers by forcing keeper Burgoyne into making a great save, when he sweetly hits a well timed shot from a Fredericks cross. Shortly afterwards, the Sir Jack Hayward Stand over to our left really erupts, when Codey's cross is hit home by Doherty. The noise is deafening. It's now 2-3 and it's game on! Fulham don't seem to be able to reassert their passing game.

Wolves are playing on their terms and Fulham aren't coping. McDonald is trying to push us the up the pitch but we've lost the rhythm of our game and when Cavaleiro powers forward into the penalty area and unleashes a powerful shot, it leaves Button with no chance and it's 3-3. Unfortunately, the momentum is with them. We've been bullied in this half and haven't managed to withstand their intensity and when Edwards scores from an acute angle, it's 4-3 to Wolves. Talk about throwing a game away. Hey, but wait a minute, we're pushing forward, there's a cross, a knock down and would you believe it, Floyd Ayité, gets on the end of it, heading in to give us a draw in the dying seconds. The Fulham fans then cheer ecstatically, enjoying Wolves' last minute humiliation. There's nothing like a late goal to give supporters a lift on the way home.

I grope through the dark back to the car park behind the Kweik store. In the coach, The Bald Man is giving out about the substitutions 'why didn't he bring on a striker and Parker earlier, and why give Kebano only a minute? Mind you, I suppose it's easy to be critical. Do you feel relieved or disappointed?'

'Disappointed. It's a game we should have won. They've only won one game at home.'

'Trouble is we don't have a leader,' asserts The Bald Man.

'What about Parker?'

'But he's at the end of his career and can only play for twenty minutes.'

'McDonald was powering us on.'

'I know but he's not a leader. He's not going to talk to people. Like a Tony Adams or a Bryan Robson.'

'Bobby Moore didn't talk that much. He led by example.'

'Yeah but England is different.'

He then turned to 'turncoats':

After that bloody David Mellor, Lily Allen is the worst. She said she was in tears after we lost the Europa Final, then she started to go to watch Chelsea just because her husband supports 'the filth'. Then they split up. I never liked her stuff. Did you? he says looking at a nearby supporter with a neat, grey, military-looking moustache.

'No. Terrible stuff. Never liked it,' Military Man concurs.

As we eventually get out of Wolverhampton, there's a discussion about managers. The Bald Man and Military Man agree about Roy Hodgson's powers of organisation.

'We could have been relegated in 2007-8 under Roy,' I remind them.

'That wasn't his fault, that was Sanchez.'

That's probably right but if Danny Murphy hadn't scored in the seventy sixth minute against Portsmouth to complete The Great Escape 2, who knows how Fulham would have developed? Such are the twists of sporting fate. In fact, I had some dealings with Roy when he was at Blackburn and he seemed a really decent person but I never fully warmed to his style of football, which always seemed just efficient and functional. During our Europa Cup run, Shakhtar Donetsk were a much better footballing side and Juventus underestimated us, but nonetheless nobody can deny that Roy got the best out of that particular squad. Certainly the game at the Cottage versus the Italians provided the biggest turn around in the club's history. I remember when Juventus scored first, I turned round to a bloke behind me and said. 'Well I suppose that's it then?' How wrong I was. Clint Dempsey's final glorious chip crowning a brilliant night,

The conversation with The Bald Man then moves on to Martin Jol. 'Never seemed to get on with the players. Zamora never liked him and left. Somebody said his brother (his assistant) would have done a better job. Magath? I liked him at first because he came to youth and reserve games but he destroyed the club. Look who he bought. He also got rid of too many experienced players. Hangeland and Sidwell wanted to stay.'

When I tried to say there were some extenuating circumstances and that money needed to be saved, Military Man pipes up 'what was the parachute payment for?' The Bald Man was also certainly not having it. 'Naw. I can't excuse Magath. In fact, if I saw him, I'd give him a belt!'

My efforts to marginally defend the controversial German then lead to The Bald Man directing most of his conversation to Military Man, as if I'd breached some article of faith. They then get into talking about the attitudes of the modern player.

'Sometimes, I can't relate to them. For instance I was with my kid and I asked Steve Sidwell to sign a programme and he just put a squiggle on it, no thought behind it. I told him, have a bit of respect. I've paid for the programme, don't squiggle on it. I mean, where does that come from? Mind you, he did come over later with a new programme and a proper autograph. Now George Best, he always did a nice one. Same with Andy Murray-it's not his fault he's Scottish and his mum can't dance!'

Eventually we arrive back in London. I get off at Hammersmith, East End Man, the fan with long flowing grey hair, with whom I chatted while waiting for the coach. When we get to the tube, he corrects me about his family living in my old flat in Parfrey St.

'It wasn't me that lived there. We lived In Hammersmith Grove, my cousins lived in Parfrey St. That must have been from '43-54. Later we moved to Wembley. I hated doing that but a family member was in bad health, so we had to be on hand.' Then, in the 70s, he went to live to Hackney where he has been ever since. He departs east, hoping that the tube is now functioning properly as I go west for a meal. It's been a long, Fulhamish day

The Millers' Tale

Rotherham are one of those teams we're expected to beat. They have one of the smallest squads in the league and tend to struggle to avoid relegation. Last season, they had an amazing late run under that much-travelled manager, the cantankerous Neil Warnock. This season they've already gone through two managers (Alan Stubbs and Kenny Jackett) and Paul Warne is currently the interim incumbent.

Fulham have some connections with Rotherham-that fine Scottish player, Graham Leggat, who scored 134 goals in 280 Fulham appearances, played for the Millers at the end of his career. I saw Leggat score the fastest hat trick in English league football: three goals in three minutes against Ipswich Town at the Cottage on Boxing Day 1963. I was standing next to the river with my friend and schoolmate the genial, chubby Duncan, who had minimal interest in football and just came out of mere curiosity. When the game ended 10-1 to Fulham, I told him that 'it wasn't like this every week!' Ironically, Fulham lost the return seasonal fixture two days later 4-2. For today's game, another Fulham stalwart, Stephen Kelly, the Irish international, who was part of our squad which reached the Europa League Final, is among the Rotherham substitutes.

On the tube to Hammersmith, I'm reading the Standard. There's an article by former Fulham midfielder, Lee Clark. He's optimistic about the club's future. He thinks things are now going in the right direction. Apparently, he still has a strong affinity with the club. 'I still keep in touch with people at the club. I love the place.' I feel like singing that old Fulham refrain 'THERE'S ONLY ONE LEE CLARK!' but I restrain myself from interrupting mirthless commuter rituals.

At Stevenage Rd, I ask the Scottish programme seller where she was for the last home game. 'Arsenal. The dark side. It's great to be back'. I don't think she likes north London much. In the gents toilet, that bastion of sporting revelation, an old Fulham fan, while urinating, shouts across to his mate: 'Hello Dominic. I thought I'd come down tonight as they seem to be scoring goals'.

There's a couple of changes this evening. Sessegnon comes in for Malone and Madl for Ream. In the seat directly above me, the son of the grey haired Irishman is there with his ginger hair and rusty complexion, although in fact, he speaks with a standard English accent. He tells me his father, who came to the Sheffield Wednesday game, was in London for years but recently returned to Ireland. Apparently he now lives in Limerick, prefers rugby and goes to see Munster play.

When the game starts, Rotherham look the sharper side. Fulham are having most of the ball but the Millers are looking dangerous on the break, prompted by Chelsea loanee, Isaiah Brown. They carve out a few half chances and then in the nineteenth minute, they score a really good goal, Newell hitting a powerful shot from twenty five yards into the right hand corner. 0-1. Thankfully Fulham up their game and after a series of half chances, we score. Fredericks' fine run down the right, leads to a Martin shot being blocked and when the ball runs to Sessegnon, he lays it off for Johansen, who hits it low and powerfully into the net. 1-1. The lively Brown then goes of injured for Rotherham and Fulham end the half strongly.

After seeing a none other than Billy The Badger score in the half time shoot out, the game restarts. Fulham pressure eventually tells and when substitute Lucas Piazon puts in a brilliant low cross, Ayité moves like lightning to ram the ball into the net. 2-1. Later, after Johansen's free kick grazes the post, Madl is hauled down at a corner and Martin misses the ensuing penalty. Blimey, that's four penalty misses this season. I don't believe it! Now there's no daylight between the sides. Fulham put themselves under unnecessary pressure, for even though we continue to dominate, you know Rotherham will have one chance and that's exactly what happens. Substitute Frecklington finds space and has a shot from ten yards out but thankfully he doesn't connect well and his effort is easily saved by Button. On another day, that could have been a goal. Nervously, the Whites see out the game and get the three points. We were lack lustre but just did enough to win the game.

At The Wall, Mikey is back from Norway for his first game since the Bristol City debacle

Earlier he was playing golf with Alex in Wandsworth, while Richard and Pete were also swinging their clubs in Sussex.

'That Chris Martin miss has let me down. I had 10 to 1 for 3-1,' says Pete

Mikey tells me he's driving down to Stanstead, having a kip in the car and then catching the 9 am plane in the morning.

'How did the golf go?' I enquire.

'It was better for some than others,' says a tactful Mikey.

'Some played crap,' responds Pete, masochistically admonishing himself

Richard, The Oracle, brings us back to the game.

'It was a bit flat tonight.'

'Still we got the three points,' I remind everybody.

As its Mikey's last trip over before Christmas, he and Alex are going off to have a drink with the other golfers. I wander in the opposite direction into the dank night.

As I make my way towards Hammersmith, Mes Amis restaurant is buzzing behind shadowy curtains. Down the road, the wealthy come out of The River Café to drive away in their expensive cars. By the time, I pass The Apollo and cross the road to the tube, I see Vince selling his Big Issue. His face is wizened and he looks older. He's wearing a long floppy woollen hat with flapping extensions that hang over his ears. He's with his labrador, who loyally accompanies him. As his dog is being admired by some female Fulham fans, I wait until the ladies buy the Christmas Big Issue and depart. Vince is a big United fan but I didn't get into the faltering start to Mourinho's reign. Instead, I wanted to know more about his street mate, Harry and how he died.

'Riddled with cancer,' Vince tells me.' He had no relations alive. I became his next of kin. I had to deal with the Social Services. It took four months to have him cremated. They treated him as if he hadn't existed. It made me physically ill. It was a shock. You know how lively he was.'

Vince tells me he's living at Shepherd's Bush. I leave him with a few bob, take the Issue and make my way home. Vince goes back to selling his wares, his dog and a tarpaulin splattered with coins, lie by his side.

Derby in Town

I'm on the way to the game against our play-off rivals. The traffic is slow and it's foggy. The Bubbly Bath are at the Apollo, the pizzeria opposite The Crabtree is doing a roaring trade and the Thames looks like something out of a ghostly Victorian painting. I walk towards the river to the sounds of squawking seagulls, past Save Charing Cross Hospital signs and the green grass of Rawberry Mead. While doing so, I hear a father and son behind me discussing the workings of quanto mechanics, a conversation that floats airily above my head. I then pass two older white haired female supporters wrapped in thick coats, ensconced on a bench, having a snack before making their final stroll to the ground. The quanto mechanics duo are now talking about possible exam grades-'if I get below a 'b'...' At Stevenage Rd, I greet the programme seller-'they haven't moved you north then? 'Not yet,' she laughingly replies.

When I'm in the ground, Fulham are practising shooting. They're all missing, so I hope it isn't an omen of things to come. Billy The Badger in his Santa hat is walking around the ground, waving to the crowd, followed by security men. As he approaches the disabled bay he has selfies taken by curious fans, while men and woman in their wheelchairs look on, somewhat bemused. When the teams come out and the game starts, the Derby fans are in typical voice-'WE HATE NOTTINGHAM. OOHAH DERBY!

This is turning out to be a hard tough game between two evenly matched sides. Fulham are playing fluent football but they're up against a well organised resolute side, managed by former England manager, Steve McLaren, who has never really recovered from being dubbed 'The Wally With The Brolly', after the 2008 Euro defeat by Croatia at Wembley, in the pouring rain. Like Louis Van Gaal, he's always armed with a computer and has the air of a modern technocrat. Both sides are having their moments without a clear cut opening. Then after half an hour, centre back, Sigurdsson, badly mistimes a clearance, lets Ince break free and the Derby winger beats Button inside his near post. A bad goal to give away from an individual error-0-1. However, again Fulham show resolution and defiance and in injury time, Ryan Fredericks produces a searing run down the right and Floyd Ayité meets his perfect low cross to make it 1-1. The Irishman isn't present this week. so I talk to a man in his seat, who's wearing, a dark green coat and an ostentatious, multi coloured scarf. He's not very vocal but his son, a man of dark complexion, who's sporting a green woolly hat, is more animated. 'Tight game,' I suggest. 'Yes, probably a fair score, so far.'

After the break and the ritual entertainment with kids attempting penalties, Parker appears for Sigurdsson, which is an attacking move of sorts. Is Sigurdsson injured or has he been removed from the fray after his error? Whatever the reason, McDonald and Madl are now our makeshift centre back pairing. Fulham pressurise and on the hour, Johansen scores after creative persistence from Sone Aluko. There was a helpful deflection on the shot, but such are the quirks of sporting fate. 2-1. Johansen and his team mates then go to the touchline for a very personal celebration. They hold up a shirt giving a message of support to Noelia Foeyo, Fulham's sports therapist, who has recently been in an accident. This display seems genuine and sincere rather than posturing, which makes a change. Now it's a question of whether Fulham can hang on. Derby up the tempo and make substitutions, one of whom, Darren Bent, is greeted by jeers. The fans never warmed to the much travelled striker's time at Fulham, even though he was at the club during some dark times.

Ten minutes after our former errant striker's introduction, we are punished for missing a few half chances and give away an awful goal. From a corner, Pearce is left totally unmarked and scores with a powerful header. 2-2. It looks like our temporary centre back pairing has been exposed. Or did they expect Button to come off his line and collect the cross? In the modern game, it seem that teams can't see games out and Fulham are no exception. With three minutes left, young 17 year old Stephen Humphrys from our academy makes his debut. Shirt hanging over his shorts, like an unruly schoolboy, he shows some nice touches and a physical presence. The game is in the balance. Piazon hits the bar from a free kick and in the dying embers of the match, Michael Madl gets his legs in a muddle, loses control of the ball, fouls Johnson as he is about to break free towards goal and is lucky not to be sent off. Finally, the game ends, probably fairly, in a draw. 'Pity to give away two bad goals.' I say to the young man next to me, sporting an elegant, brown felt hat. 'Still it was a good game,' he replies in an unengaged manner. Maybe, but I just wish Fulham could be more ruthless. We continue to play some fine football but it's still undermined by poor finishing and individual defensive errors.

At The Wall. I wait in vain for Richard and co.

A couple of fans pass by and one of them gives his own derogatory street ode to Darren Bent:

'Thank God Bent didn't score. Useless cunt!'

Just as I'm about to depart, Alex comes bounding towards me.

'Richard and Pete left dead on ninety minutes. Got a dinner date this evening.'

'Sporting one?'

'I think so.'

'I'll ring Dr Richard, The Oracle, when I need my football therapy. My friends have no interest and when they attempt to proclaim on the game, they talk a lot of nonsense.'

'When we win, they can't share your elation. When we lose they can't share your frustration,' suggests Alex.

'Yes. Something like that.'

'Pity we gave away those goals.'

'We threw them away rather than they created them. Still I'll take a point against Derby. They've just won seven on the bounce.'

'I wonder why Slav took Sigurdsson off. Was it because he didn't want to expose him after his mistake?'

'Maybe but he has been injured recently and out of the side, so I'm not sure.'

I then tell him about the tension among supporters at Wolverhampton.

'I was worried that it might all kick off. If it had, we might all have been rounded up. Then I'd have been classed as a seventy one year old hooligan!'

'That would really have been a case of the wrong place at the wrong time!'

We wish each other a happy Christmas and look forward to meeting up in the new year

No Tractors For The Invalid!

I've had an awful cold over Christmas and I can't make The Ipswich game. So I won't be seeing the Whites take on The Tractor Boys. I'm staying at home listening to continual George Michael records. The singer has passed away at fifty three and the radio stations are all playing their tributes- 'Careless Love,' 'End of Christmas' etc. What a year, Prince, David Bowie, Leonard Cohen, now the former Wham front man.

I'm not going to Suffolk but look online for the teams. Ah, here we are. Slav has made a few changes. Odoi for Fredericks, Ream for Sigurdsson, who's on the bench. Madl also starts, so there's a new look back line. Apparently, we're playing well, and after thirty six minutes, we make the break through. A free kick for a foul on the influential Johansen is taken by Chris Martin and his twenty five yard shot powers into the net. We boss it until half time, but after the break, Mick McCarthy, changes his formation and goes to two up front. Best and McGoldrick come on, which signals a strong aerial threat.

I've always liked McCarthy, even though his pragmatic football can be an eyesore. Still, when he had some decent players in the Irish team, he did well, whatever Roy Keane said about him during their World Cup 2002 dustup at Saipan. In fact, it's somewhat ironic that McCarthy should be a rather better manager at Ipswich than the combustible Man U legend, who now sits on a sofa with Lee Dixon doing punditry for ITV. Keane often appears bearded and bespectacled, looking more like a like a left bank intellectual than a midfield hard man.

After I discover that Odoi is adjudged offside when Martin scores, I fall asleep. The effect of those Lemsips. However, it isn't a deep slumber and when I awaken, I discover that Floyd Ayité has missed a good chance and Ragnar Sigurdsson has come on for Aluko, presumably to counter Mick's aerial bombardment. Apparently, we continue on top but can't get the crucial second goal. Then, after Ayité is denied by their keeper, from the ensuing corner,

Sigurdsson rises above everybody and heads a fine goal. 0-2. Game over.

I'm feeling better already. We did the business, got the points and are now seventh. A good thing too as those near us in the table also won. Big games coming up- Reading and Brighton. Hopefully, we can push on nearer that coveted sixth position. If we do so, it'll be without Mike Rigg, Fulham's Chief Football Officer, who's leaving the club after two years. Maybe this is a battle Slaviša has won before the forthcoming transfer window?

A Foggy Night at Reading

When I get to the Cottage, I'm told that there are two coaches. I go for the second as there seems to be more room. When I ascend its steps, I'm met by an elderly gent, whose jacket is emblazoned with Fulham badges.

'Ticket young man'.

'Young man? I'm over seventy,' I reply.

'You've got some way to go,' he chuckles.

'Oh, it's all to come is it? Let's hope so!'

Brian a man in his fifties in a red sweater is getting the passengers organised.

'Tell them,' he yells to The Man With Many Badges, 'that there's a couple of two by twos at the back.'

Our decorated steward assembles the fans accordingly and then precedes to count the occupants-'eighteen, nineteen, twenty...'-after which he gives the driver the ok.

The driver is dressed in a white shirt with a navy blue pullover and matching trousers. He now delivers a speech.

'First a few rules. Or should I say polite notes. You're advised to use seat belts. It's foggy and even though I have decent visibility I can't account for what other drivers do. There's a toilet in the middle of the coach. It's small, so gentleman please sit down. There's a white bag for the rubbish, so it'd help me clearing up if you'd put your stuff there. At the end of the game, remember we're coach number two. And one last thing please tell the steward if you're not returning by coach. Ok. Thanks.'

The man in front of me, a bushy eyebrowed gent called Dukey, has been talking about Fulham of yesteryear with his mate, a shaven headed sturdy man, who moves into the seat in front of him.

'Is your back all right, mate? 'Dukey enquiries

The sturdy man wearing a light green sweater and navy jacket, seems to affirm that he's more comfortable with greater space.

'I am the walrus, I am the egg man,' sings somebody from the rear of the coach for no particular reason.

At the Hammersmith Apollo, Club de Fromage are playing on New Years Eve. Who the hell are they?

A green overhead light makes the coach an eerie grotto. A battery of car lights flash past us down the M4 on the way to London.

Behind me there's a young woman in a crimson sweater sitting with her strapping boy friend. She's wired for sound but then removes her headphones. Apparently, she hasn't checked her mail to find out her results- maybe she's at uni? She then describes watching James Corden on You Tube training with the Arsenal team. That'd be something to behold.

Her boyfriend then goes on to berate a friend of hers:

'She's no good for you. She's doing you down, just cause she hasn't gone to uni. She aims low cause that's what she knows.'

'I'll never be friends with her,' protests The Lady In Crimson.

'You are friends that's why we're talking about her. I don't like the way she's treated you. She's bad news.'

'I can never like her now,' explains the young woman

'I'd hate anybody who was rude to my Mum.'

We get to Reading in an hour and a quarter. The roads were pretty clear. Many people seem to be still away on holiday. Most supporters get off the coach, but as there's two hours before the game starts, I prefer to stay in the warm.

'At the least we beat the other lot,' says the driver, proudly, referring to the other coaches.

When asked if he's going for a meal, he replies:

'I had myself a hot lunch. I'll have chips later.'

Dukey and his bald mate, a family in the front of the coach and myself, remain on board.

'Are we holding you up?' The Dad of the family asks the driver

'No. That's ok. Just tell me when you want to leave.'

Meanwhile, Dukey and his mate are reminiscing

'Do you remember the 66-67 season? We had crowds of 40,000. I remember going to Barrow-it was 3-3...Clyde Best. Have you seen him lately? He's awesome. He's got a book coming out. He was on Talk Sport. He's huge now...Goalkeepers were much smaller then-Hodgkinson, Banks...You go to Newcastle, it's like watching ants, you're so high up there. Mind you, the night life is good there...Do you remember when we beat Sunderland up north in the 60s? That Irish guy scored on his debut What's his name? Mullan. Yes. Brendan Mullan. I remember there was a picture in the paper of Johnny Haynes playing the drums after that!'

Then I hear from the Dad of the family that Martin isn't playing. Allegedly, he's refused to play for Fulham and Slaviša has apparently made a strong stand. Good. He has a contract with us and shouldn't suddenly return to one of our nearest rivals at a whim. That reminds me when some years ago, I fortuitously met Ken Bates, the then Chelsea Chairman, in a Paris café. When I enquired about player loyalty, his wife started laughing and said 'they're only loyal to the value of the Euro or pound'. Certainly, Mr Martin's behaviour wouldn't persuade Mrs Bates to review her opinion of the modern footballer. Ok, for them it's a job and they want to get out in their mid-thirties with enough money for life but there are limits.

The mother of the family puts it another way:

'If there's a smell in the room you need to fumigate it.'

Jokanović seems to have done exactly that.

I'm starving, so at 7pm I get out of the coach and get some chips. While eating them next to the catering van, where young people are serving food, I chat to a tall bloke in a grey woolly hat.

'Enjoying your chips for three quid,' enquires the lofty Fulham fan.

'A bit expensive,' I complain

'My mate is having sausage and chips for £3.99. Suppose it's not bad, when you think that they have to pay everybody. Just been to the Hobgoblin. Now that's a real pub. There's real ale, an outside loo and no bloody mobiles allowed. My mate said it was terrible, but to me it was great.'

'Least it's not the same, like shopping centres.'

'Yeah. Shopping centres. Look all the same. Terrible. I like places with character. That's what I like about Burnley Football Club. Working class with character. See I'm a Brexiteer. My son disagrees. He thinks leaving will make things worse.'

We then chat about how automation and robots are going to probably mean less jobs in the future.

'I don't think we'll solve the problems of the world tonight but I'm Fulham born and bred so let's hope the team will cheer us up!' concludes The Bloke In The Woolly Hat.

'Have a good one, mate!'

Inside the ground, I'm welcomed by another concrete bowl. The Royals mascot, Kingsley Royal, is bouncing around. He's a seven foot bipedal lion and apparently is the only mascot to have been sent off, for 'confusing the linesman and assistants' during a match with Newcastle in 2007. Neil Diamond's 'Sweet Caroline 'is blaring across the ground. The crowd shout at the end of each verse. 'BOOM! BOOM! BOOM! SWEET CAROLINE!' The announcer tries to get the local fans to be more vocal. 'You did a great job last game so let's hear it tonight,' he pleads. The team's then come out. Fulham get a great reception. They have good support tonight.

The game starts. Fulham are playing towards the North End. We're in the South Stand behind the goal. When Ryan Fredericks, our right back, gets booked, the referee is immediately abused by the away support. 'WANKER!' they cry. The game is pretty even but when McLeary gets one on one with our keeper, Button makes a good save and pushes the ball round the post. As the game proceeds, a fog envelops the ground. I can see Fulham attacking at the far end but I'm not sure exactly what's happening. However, I'm certainly able to view Reading's forays and Kermorgant's header being saved by Button. The game drifts on. Now our supporters are chiding the locals. 'YOUR SUPPORT IS, YOU'RE SUPPORT IS, YOU'RE SUPPORT IS FUCKIN' SHIT! YOUR SUPPORT IS FUCKIN' SHIT!' Meanwhile, the fog is getting worse.

After 35 minutes, there's a delay. The referee is having a talk with the managers, Slaviša and Jaap Stam of Reading, the former Man U centre half. Play continues, the fog seems to clear only to reappear like some controlled theatrical projection. Fulham deride the lack of home vocal support-with a big 'SSSH!' followed by that celebrated refrain, 'THIS IS A LIBRARY!' Williams is booked for a bad foul on Fredericks, much to the delight of the away fans. There's a further delay and discussion. Maybe the officials are struggling to see across the pitch? The game restarts. A fine bit of play by Harriott leads to a powerful rising shot and a great save by Button, diving to his right. Soon afterwards, Harriott gets injured and is replaced by that doughty evergreen Paul McShane, as the game fizzles out to half time.

During the break, I go and get a bottle of water. After the chips, my throat feels dry. I queue at the bar amidst a caterwauling of drunken songs and shouts. I manage to get away quickly, although the drink cost me £2.50. Amazing how you can get ripped off on a football trip. When I return, I talk to a young dainty blonde with a pale green woolly hat, who's been sitting next to me. She has been accompanied by a young, small fair haired Fulham supporter, who's gone to get some drinks. I think they're at uni together.

'Have you been to Craven Cottage?' I enquire

'No this is my first time to a game. But Bob goes. He comes from Putney.'

I then comment about the fog and how it might stop the game.

'At least we are staying with my parents tonight. They live in Reading.'

'So you're all right then!'

She laughs with a delightfully warm, open smile.

The Tiger Marching Band from Alexis I. Du Pont High School Delaware, USA are playing but according to the announcer, they've been relegated to the touchline, because of 'pitch issues'. They sound good and were part of London's recent New Day's Parade. After they earn a deserved smattering of applause, the Fulham team come out but aren't followed by Reading. A voice of doom then bellows out an official announcement on the loudspeakers, in a manner, worthy of some authoritarian state. We are told that the match has been abandoned because of adverse weather conditions. The announcer then intones about a rearranged date being announced later etc. As the fog has lifted and the conditions are now actually much better than they were for much of the first half, both supporters chant together in anger and disbelief: 'YOU DON'T KNOW WHAT YOU'RE DOING! YOU DON'T KNOW WHAT YOU'RE DOING!'

Back in the coach, I move across the aisle and sit next to the Irishman who travelled to Wolves. I've lived and worked in Ireland for thirteen years of my life, so I'm interested in his story. Apparently, he came over to England when he was fourteen to attend a college seminary. He was a great Fulham supporter in the 60s but got disillusioned when the talented but wayward Rodney Marsh was sold. Those were the days of Vic Buckingham, the Felix Magath of that era. Both Buckingham and the controversial German managed at a high level. Buckingham was manager at Barcelona and Ajax, while Magath won three Bundesliga titles, two with Bayern Munich and one with Wolfsburg. However at Fulham, despite making radical changes, they were both unsuccessful. Admittedly, the debonair Buckingham did buy one of our great goal scorers, Allan 'Sniffer' Clarke, who went on to have a fine career with Leeds. However, like Magath, he also got rid of some players too quickly.

During 'The Great Escape' of 1965-66, I bumped into none other than our rugged blonde centre half Bobby Keetch on a bus-yes times were different. When I enquired about the team's recent great run, Bobby waxed lyrical. 'Fucking Buckingham. Nothing to do with him. It's Dave Sexton, the coach. He's the one that's made the difference.' Bobby then leapt off the number 11, probably to attend to his 'Swinging London' business, when he got mini-skirted girls to drive tourists around town. Bob was also an art connoisseur and on Sundays he was sometimes pictured looking at the latest exhibition on the continent. I remember him partaking in more mundane matters, like kicking lumps out of Spurs centre forward, Bobby Smith. That was in a game at White Hart Lane, during which we were leading the great Spurs sixties side 1-0, only for Tony Macedo to throw the ball to Greaves on the edge of our penalty area, thinking that he was a Fulham player (Fulham were in an away strip, Spurs in white-Fulham's usual colours). Jimmy duly scored, the game ended in a draw and a moment of triumph was lost. As he left the pitch, Greaves put his arm around Macedo, as if to say, 'sorry mate, had to do it!'

But back to the Irishman, who tells me he's from Tipperary. He lived here for many years but went back to Ireland in 1993 only to return in 2011 for personal reasons.

'I know Ireland pretty well but I've never been to Tipperary,' I tell him.

'Probably because there's not much going on there. Still it's known for the title of a famous song.'

We then talk about Irish nationalism and the corrosive insularity of the De Valera years.

'I knew a friend's family who wouldn't open a letter with an English stamp on it. They just burnt it. Mind you a couple of brothers were murdered by the Black and Tans in the Anglo-Irish War.'

We are then diverted by Brian doing steward duties, collecting money in an envelope:

'For the driver lads and lassies'

I give him a quid.

Suddenly, a drunken supporter, young, dark and lean, stumbles out of the lavatory below us and hurls himself into my seat. I extricate my bag and ask him if he's ok. He mumbles incoherently.

The Irishman continues:

'The Celtic tiger made people go crazy.'

'Like kids with new toys? 'I suggest.

'Exactly'

'Too many high profile gamblers selling the people short.'

'Still we're chastened and recovering.'

The drunken supporter then asks me. 'What happened?'

'It was abandoned after half time at nil-nil.'

'Oh,' replies the inveterate.

'You'll have to come back again, mate.'

The Irishman and I continue to weave our way around the labyrinth of his nation's history. It's not long before we're in Hammersmith. The Irishman, now wearing a splendidly imposing NY baseball cap, walks with me to the tube. I tell him that in the 80s, there was a Dublin woman who came over every week from Ireland, to see games both home and away, but he didn't know her. In fact, strong hard core support was developed during those years in the lower leagues, under the likes of Micky Adams, when we witnessed such wonders as Mike Conroy scoring against Wycombe from the half way line. As we approach the ticket barrier, I ask the Irishman his name.

'Jim.'

'Nice to meet you Jim. I'm Roland'

'Where do you watch the games?'

'Johnny Haynes J'

'I'm in Johnny Haynes D. I was in the Riverside but at a very high seat and the climb was a bit too much. I might return there if I'm up to it.'

'See you around Jim'

I go upstairs to the bus station. As I'm waiting for a 220 bus, I see two young female Fulham fans. One of them, a rotund figure with brown hair and black glasses, is explaining the abandonment to someone on her mobile. Her friend, shorter and slimmer, wearing a dark brown jacket is standing next to her. We share our frustrations about the evening. On the bus, we discuss Slaviša's comments about Chris Martin and that 'Fulham isn't a train station. You can't come in and out when you want.' We all approve. I voice my apprehension that we might not hold on to our talented manager:

'We need to keep hold of Slaviša. His contract runs out in the summer.'

'Yeah,' says The Rotund Girl, 'Malaga are after him.'

'We need a few additions,' I propose 'but we want to start next season with the core of this group, whatever happens.'

Then we move on to their favourites.

'I like Marcus. He's a lovely bloke. We've met him,' says The Rotund Girl proudly.

'Tom Cairney's nice,' says her friend, changing the subject.

'When he's not too busy combing his hair!' I suggest.' Mind you he's a good player. He's having a great season.'

'I like Tom. We've met him as well,' says The Rotund Girl. 'He could be in The Premiership. He's had offers.'

'Well you girls better stop him going,' I cry, as they depart near White City. Oh gawd, maybe they live close to Loftus Road!

The Seagulls Return

It's a fine, crisp day but I'm not in a good mood. A fraudster has hacked into my account and taken the best part of three grand. They say football can make you forget. I hope so.

When I arrive at Hammersmith Broadway, I see that The Yardbird (named after the 60s group?), a nondescript pub in the shopping centre, is looking for staff. Down the Fulham Palace Rd, a guy in a navy woolly hat is complaining that 'the rates are too bloody high'. Near Parfrey St, various young men return 'Boris Bikes' to their stands. Each bike is embroidered by a Santander advert, which doesn't make me feel good. They're my bloody bank! Later, at Stevenage Rd, I see the Scottish programme seller being given a lot of notes, so I try to help:

'I've got some change'

'I've got plenty o'that,' she replies

'I should never underestimate you.'

'Happy New Year.'

'Same to you.'

As I make my way to the Johnny Haynes Stand, I hear a woman say, 'did you get my text about the fire?' The mind boggles. In the ground, I'm next to a middle aged man in a light brown jacket. I tell him that I saw us play brilliantly against Brighton and lose, 'I know. I was there,' he dismissively asserts. There are some changes for this game. Sigurdsson is in for Madl, who's ill and Matt Smith replaces Ayité, who's gone to join the Togo national team for the African Nations Cup.

Fulham start well again but lack penetration in the final third. Johansen shoots wide, Aluko has a shot blocked. Then an American woman, an attractive, slim, middle aged blonde wearing tight jeans is looking to find her seat. 'I think we're first in the row. Amelia, honey,' she says to her young kid, 'this way honey. Sorry,' she apologises as she brushes past me. Eventually, Fulham's pressure is rewarded. Bruno, Brighton's bearded Spanish right back and captain, flicks the ball on to his hand and a penalty is awarded. In the absence of the controversial Martin, Johansen takes it. It's a poor shot. Our former keeper, 'Stocko,' David Stockdale, guesses correctly and makes a comfortable save to his right. This really frustrates me. That's the fifth penalty we've missed this season! This has given a strong psychological advantage to the bloomin' Seagulls. However, Fulham do respond as if they're determined to purge such sinful waste. However, unfortunately, Malone miscues and McDonald goes wide. Brighton are under the cosh but when their striker Baldock gets away from Ream, Knockaert nearly puts Murray through but luckily his pass is over hit.

It's half time. Billy The Badger is struttin' his stuff and the usual penalty competition is going on.

I turn round to Charlie, a ten year old, who's sitting behind me with his father.

'I think you like Stockdale,' I suggest. His Dad smiles.

'Didn't you say 'good save' when 'Stocko' stopped the penalty?'

The khaki jacketed Charlie then confesses;

'I met him. We should have never let him go.'

'But he appeared to be overweight. Look at him now. He seems way below 'the timber' he was carrying at Fulham'

He then quizzes me about other departures.

'What about Sidwell?'

'A decent, solid pro.'

He was our best player in our last season in The Premiership.'

'Yes. Of a bad lot.'

'What about Berbatov?'

'Good player but not in a struggling team. He's not going to track back and tackle. That's never been his game.'

I'm not sure Charlie is convinced. Oh dear, I hope I haven't torn apart his heroes and punctured his dreams.

Back to reality. The second half starts. Fulham continue to press and after ten minutes they're rewarded. Tom Cairney finds Piazon in a crowded area in the last third and the Brazilian curls a wonderfully executed shot inside the far post. Brilliant! 'WE ARE! WE ARE ! WE ARE THE FULHAM BOYS!' rings out. Fulham look for a second but Piazon lobs a looping Malone cross into the arms of beloved Stockdale. Then after seventy four minutes, calamity strikes. Sigurdsson's legs get tangled with Hemed and a penalty is awarded.

Whatever happened to the Bobby Moore principle of standing off attackers and not jumping in? Unlike most of our penalty takers, Hemed is calm, cool and calculating. Button dives the wrong way and he rolls the ball into the left hand corner. 1-1. This better not be a rerun of the away game at The Amex. Immediately Brighton go for the juggler. The 19 year old substitute Humphrys can't hold the ball up, Aluko misses a tackle as centre half Dunk runs from deep at the heart of our defence. Why is he being allowed to get that far? Dunk passes the ball to Knockaert, whose shot is parried by Button back into his path and he scores from close range. 1-2. The Brighton players rush to their fans at The Putney End and fall into a predictable celebratory heap.

They've been outplayed for most of the game but they have a strong defence and when their chances have come, they've taken them. We seem lightweight off the ball with too many players who can't really tackle. Fulham look to respond. A good move involving Humphrys and Cairney sees Fredericks narrowly miss the post. Fredericks is now moved further forward and although he makes inroads, we can't eke out a chance. Brighton are managing the game well, even though it isn't pretty to watch: they initiate niggling fouls, bring on substitutes and waste time-all to break up the game. In the end, they get over the line. I can't believe it. We've dominated them for most of both games and have come away with nothing. We're a better footballing side but we lack a cutting edge and seem soft centred. I turn to the man next to me in the brown jacket, looking for an explanation, instead I get a fateful reply, 'you could see it coming, couldn't you?' And to think that not so long ago, we tried to sign that bloody Dunk!

At The Wall Pete wishes me 'A Happy New Year'.

Richard looks a bit morose, even though we're tenth, still only six points off the play-offs.

'We haven't got a striker and Ream and Sigurdsson are a disaster waiting to happen. And the missed penalty? Stockdale could have sat on it. Smith missed a couple of chances. We just can't take advantage.'

'Important game. Not sure we'll make the play-offs now. Mind you, now you'll get good odds for us getting there,' says Pete.

107

'Was Smith shot?' I ask

'Yes. He'd gone,' says The Oracle 'but it made it easier for their centre backs without him.'

Richard and Pete reiterate New Year wishes and go to catch their train. Alex and I move off.

'I don't agree with Pete,' says Alex 'I don't think it was a defining game.' There's still a lot of points to play for. We're only half way through the season.'

'How many games are there?'

'46'

'That's 22 to go. 66 points!'

'We've played most of the top teams. Yes we've got to play Leeds and Derby again and we travel away to Newcastle but we have still to play many teams from whom we should get points. Better to have a good run at the end than be burdened with expectation, having been in pole position for most of the season. Are you going to Cardiff?'

'No. The start is too early and it's on tv.'

'Well I'll see you at the Barnsley game then,' says Alex departing into the thick of a winter night.

The Cup on the Telly

We're playing an FA Cup game at Cardiff at 11.30am. The coach departed at 6.30am. Too early, when it's on tv. Some supporters thought the commentary was in the Welsh language-'a waste of taxpayers money' insisted one of the Fulham faithful. In fact, this wasn't correct and, yes, the commentary is in English. A few minutes before the game, I start panicking. Where the hell is BBC 1 Wales? I then go through nearly all the Sky channels until I eventually find Channel 952, just before kick off.

The ground looks very empty. Not surprising. Cardiff aren't doing well and it's on tv at an unsociable time. Fulham field a strong team. The sixteen year old wunderkind Ryan Sessegnon replaces Malone at left back. Odoi is at right back and Fredericks is pushed forward into a more attacking wing back position, with Smith relegated to the bench. Marcus Bettinelli, the favourite of those girls, is in goal for his first game this season. We start well, passing with pace and accuracy but, against the run of play, they score from a wicked deflection from a Pilkington free kick, given away on the edge of the box by Denis Odoi. Standing in the wall, Piazon fatally turns his back and Bettinelli has no chance as the ball suddenly diverts to the other side of the goal. Piazon needed to show more courage there and take the ball on the head.

Commentator Rob Phillips and pundit, former Welsh international Iwan Roberts, are waxing lyrical about our style of play and domination of the game. When the pacy Fredericks, gets behind his opposing full back, reaches the byline and delivers a perfect low cross, Stefan Johansen smashes the ball home. 1-1 and deservedly so. What's interesting about our line up is that we seem to be playing without an acknowledged striker, so there's a sense of a false no 9, as the rotation and movement mean that different players appear in that central position. It therefore seems that Matt Smith, a rather static target man, despite his wholehearted perseverance, doesn't really fit in with the way we're playing. We continue to control the game and it's no surprise when Fredericks' speed again plays a significant part. Another cross from the right is met by Tom Cairney's left foot. The ball hits the bar, bounces tantalisingly down on the goal line but is bundled over by the advancing Sessegnon. The commentators are discussing whether young Ryan might have been off side but eventually they agree that it was the correct decision.

At half time, both pundits: ex-Fulham manager Kit Symons and ex-Cardiff defender Danny Gabbidon are critical of Cardiff for not tracking runners for both goals. Kit thinks that they're 'neither pressing nor dropping off and playing deeper.' Certainly, Cardiff seem lack lustre for a Neil Warnock side, which always tend to be highly competitive. Warnock only replaced Paul Trollope, the former Fulham player (1997-2002) as manager in October, so he's probably not found his own team yet.

Before the second half, begins I notice East End Man in the crowd. His long flowing grey hair and severe black sunglasses, make him stand out like a voodoo doctor. As long as he doesn't put a spell on the Whites! We start the second half well, but the high line we play does make our centre backs vulnerable to balls over the top. Surprisingly, an under strength Cardiff side, don't pursue such possibilities. Even allowing for the changes, you would think that the selected players would be more galvanised to show what they can do. That said, Fulham aren't killing the game off and Cardiff are still in it, when they shouldn't be. The wide pitch suits Fulham's passing game and we continue to control the match without really threatening their goal. As the game gets into the final ten minutes, Fulham start retreating and get a bit edgy, which is absurd given this is such a one-sided match. We're not going to self-destruct are we? Cardiff's powerful centre half Bamba goes up front in an effort to heroically rescue the tie but it's all to no avail. and Fulham nervously see the game out.

Kit, Danny and Rob Phillips are now on the pitch.

'That was a footballing master class from Fulham,' gushes Phillips

Kit thinks they did very well but they should have been more productive.

'They didn't have an out and out striker but they should have scored more goals. Cardiff were under pressure the whole game and didn't seem to have a game plan.'

'Fulham were very well drilled. They worked hard defensively off the ball as well,' says Danny.

Slaviša comes on the pitch to be interviewed. He's at the other end of the line to Kit, who was sacked as Fulham manager to make way for the Serb, which must be uneasy for both of them. He talks about how it was a contest between our passing game and their directness and ability to win second balls. He's happy with the result and the team.

Ryan Fredericks is made Man of The Match. He tells us how the team are encouraged to pass the ball well and that's their strength. Cairney is also interviewed and expresses his frustration at not finding a third goal and how it became nervy at the end. He also mentions how the team are coached to keep to their passing game and that 'mistakes don't matter'. Kit thinks Cairney is a pivotal player for the team. The programme finishes. It's a good result. Let's hope we get a good home draw in the next round. Now, where's that chicken for lunch?

The Tykes at Home

It's Saturday January 14th. It's cold, wet and foggy. Graham Taylor, the former England manager has died at 72. There will be a minute's clapping in celebration of his life before the game. Taylor always came across as a very likeable man but I never warmed to his long ball football and when he became England manager his limitations were cruelly exposed. Nonetheless no one can deny that in another era, he was a hugely successful club manager with Lincoln City, Watford and Aston Villa.

At Hammersmith, weary travellers, attired in woolly hats, thick jackets and dark gloves are wheeling their buggies to the tube. In Frank Banfield Park, a lively, shaggy shepherd's dog, pisses violently on some flowers and scampers away in delight to join his mistress, a formidably, big woman with dyed blonde hair, who's twiddling a lead in her hand, like some oppressive ringmaster. Near Colwith Rd, an auburn haired youth glides down on a skateboard. By The Crabtree my backpack accidently hits a Barnsley supporter and he spills some of his beer. 'Sorry fella. Don't worry. It's only my bag.' Runners in orange bibs pass by, rigidly keeping to their fitness regimes. By the Thames, a kid enquires 'where's the Queen's Palace?' I think he must be getting his locations confused. At the passage behind the Hammersmith End, a white-haired disabled man is being wheeled towards me, asserting to his companion that 'if we can't score from penalties then we're really in trouble.' When I make my way into the Johnny Haynes Stand, at the turnstiles an animated young man in an orange bib is talking to a middle-aged colleague. 'He's not doing it for charity is he?' referring to Diego Costa's reported £30 million per year Chinese offer.

On the pitch, Billy The Badger, is waving to the crowd with outstretched arms, like a conquering hero, while selfies are taken by his adoring throng. There's four changes for Fulham from the Cardiff game One big one. Martin, the prodigal son, returns. It must be a case of kiss and make up. I'm sitting next to two Americans, who are only marginally interested in the game. The woman, fair haired with dark glasses and wearing a red woolly hat, gets upset when a

Barnsley player is fouled and bundled to the floor. 'Ooh,' she gasps. I tell her not to be too sympathetic as 'we're very partisan here.' Her companion, a man in his thirties with an obscure badge on the lapel of his jacket, joins her in hesitant laughter.

Fulham start strongly. Cairney has a shot saved, then another effort deflected. Fredericks' forward runs are causing Barnsley problems but Malone's crosses from the left are erratic. Once again Fulham can't take advantage of their ascendancy and gradually Barnsley work their way into the game with some forceful counter attacking. Adam Hammill, the Barnsley midfielder, is proving himself a handful and in the 36th minute, his surging run ends with a powerful left footed shot that hits the bar. Fulham have been warned. Thankfully such fears are allayed when Kevin McDonald is hauled down in the box and Fulham are awarded a penalty. Oh, but wait a minute we've missed five this season. Luckily Chris Martin confidently dispatches this one into the bottom right hand corner. 1-0. The crowd erupt in relief.

At half time, I talk to the young Irishman, who's back in his position today. We discuss the refusal of Costa and Dimitri Payet of West Ham to play for their clubs.

'It's a lot of money. You're not going to get another offer like that. So it must be difficult,' he responds sympathetically.

'Payet can't be about money. He won't get more dough at Marseilles,' I contend.

'Probably not.'

'Maybe its culture. It's no secret that Costa hasn't settled in London, so maybe 'Mrs Costa' and 'Mrs Payet' have something to do with it. 'In fact, the Spaniard Jozabed, who cost us £4 million, hasn't settled either. There's talk of him going on loan to Celta Vigo. He looks a good technical player (he scored nine goals in La Liga last season) but maybe not suited to the rough and tumble of The Championship.

A half time visit to that hub of opinion, Fulham FC's toilets, gives me access to the fans frustration-'we've had three fuckin' chances,' says one diehard, annoyed that such dominance hasn't put the game to bed. At the restart, Fulham again press strongly but can't take advantage. However, in the fifty fifth minute, Martin floats a cross over to the left, Malone meets it on the volley and scores in the far corner. A great goal. 2-0. We've got some daylight now. This gives Fulham confidence to create further chances. Notably Martin linking up with Johansen in an audacious move, which ends with the Norwegian midfielder's shot just going wide of the post. Fulham's control of the game continues and Adam Davies, the Barnsley keeper, makes some good saves. Fulham run down the clock and complete an emphatic win. We're now eighth, two places off the play-offs.

I make my way to The Wall and wait for the verdict.

'We played some great stuff,' says Richard, wrapped in a thick coat with a highly protective woollen hat.

'You're looking rather Russian,' I observe

'You do when you're cold, you know,' replies Richard, pulling my scarf in mock strangulation.

'I couldn't watch the penalty,' confesses Pete.' I turned my back but when I heard that roar I knew it was in. I'll watch it later on the telly.'

'Aluko and Piazon had good chances in the first half. We should have scored more. They had a good period when they hit the bar,' proclaims the author.

'The penalty changed everything,' asserts The Oracle.

'We were playing like Arsenal. Passing it around too much in the box,' says a disapproving Pete.

Alex thought that Martin certainly put in a shift.

It's cold and the intrepid Fulham contingent from East Sussex want to go to their train.

'Going to QPR?' says Richard starting to make his way down Stevenage Rd.

'No. I'm going to watch it on tv. Save a few bob.' I didn't tell him about the fraudulent scam!

'See you next home game then,' cries the departing Richard.

As Alex and I move away, Pete is moving away backwards, waving his arms in the air ecstatically but I can't hear a word he's saying.

'He's happy when Fulham win and miserable when they lose,' observes Alex.

Alex and I make our way down towards Fulham Palace Rd.

I voice my concern

'I hope we don't pay for missing chances.'

'He's looking for a striker and a centre half. Let's hope he finds them in the transfer window.'

We then discuss the similarities with the passing football of Jean Tigana's promotion side. Tigana revolutionised Fulham with his training methods and modern attention to detail, like even having the players' teeth checked. He coached ordinary players like Rufus Brevett to be good ones. No wonder other coaches used to come to Motspur Park to see his training sessions. Tigana never fully replicated his team's Championship success in the Premiership but I always felt those times were clouded by the deterioration of his relationship with Chairman Mohammed Al-Fayed, who sued him for his alleged illicit involvement in transfer dealings. Franco Baresi was suddenly made Director of Football, Tigana dismissed and Fayed lost his court cases. In true gallic style, Tigana once quoted from Proust in a team talk, only for one of the Fulham players to get culturally confused and think that the classic French writer was Prost, the racing driver! Tigana risked more than the average manager, that's why his style of football at its best was a joy to watch. Jokanović is equally audacious-both he and Tigana obviously believe that the way you play matters, not just winning.

Alex moves the conversation on to our weaknesses.

'I just hope that our hesitancy with crosses and lack of physical power won't be our undoing. You see, Brighton, with their strong players at the back, hung in there, just waited, bided their time and struck. We need to be better against canny sides with good game management.'

'At least we were better off the ball today and the togetherness of the team seems good,' counters an optimistic author.

'Yeah. We can get there. Listen. Better go,' says Alex suddenly feeling the cold.

'Ok Alex. See you.' I reply as I energetically stride up Fulham Palace Road in an effort to get warm.

More Trouble with
The Neighbours!

Donald Trump has been elected the 45th President of the United States. It's a cold but sunny London day. A third of the money hacked from my account has been recovered but so far the bank aren't budging about the rest. I'm now going through the nightmare of an elongated complaints procedure. In addition to my financial woes, I have a heavy cold so I'm glad the Rangers game is on Sky. Peter Beagrie and David Prutton are discussing the teams, prompted by presenter Kelly Cates. QPR haven't done the double over Fulham for 40 years. Let's hope this taboo isn't broken today.

Both sides are unchanged from their last match. Daniel Mann, the commentator is with summariser Don Goodman, the ex-Wolves player. Mann quotes meeting a septuagenarian fan, who told him that 'Fulham are playing the best football I've ever seen them play.' I hope that such eulogies don't become the kiss of death. In fact, Fulham start sluggishly. QPR seem quicker on the ball and are pressing intensely, high up the pitch. Fulham are struggling to get their game together. After six minutes and some brilliant twisting and turning in the penalty area, the elusive Aluko goes down. A contentious penalty is awarded. Come on Fulham, score and get more space to play our game. Martin comes up to take it. He's missed two and scored two this season. So let's hope he succeeds against our closest rival. Oh no! No such bloody luck! He scuffs his shot and Smithies dives to his right and saves easily. That's three penalties the QPR keeper has saved from Fulham this season. Quite a record. We've now missed seven. How can we expect to be in the play-offs, when we miss such golden opportunities?

QPR have been given encouragement and their French striker Sylla gets into some good positions on goal: first, he shoots tamely at Button and then miscontrols the ball, giving Kalas time to recover. After 25 minutes, McDonald looks to pass back to the keeper but loses control of the ball. Ryan Manning pounces, shoots and beats Button easily. A gift. 0-1 to Rangers. Fulham respond but Piazon's shot is blocked by a massive deflection which bounces kindly into

Smithies' arms. Then Fredericks is booked for dissent when a corner decision goes against him. This is a sign of pure frustration and Fredericks doesn't show sufficient discipline. Holloway has previously managed both our full backs, Fredericks and Malone. He knows their strengths and has successfully stopped them getting forward. The whistle blows for half time. QPR have been over physical and robust but Fulham haven't been at their best. They've kept a lot of possession but their passing has been too slow, their movement insufficiently incisive and they haven't matched Rangers' intensity.

During the second half, we control possession without conjuring up many chances. Then with a quarter of an hour to go, we have a free kick in a good position. Rangers don't clear Johansen's shot. It comes to Cairney, whose shot is cleverly redirected by the interjection of Martin's boot and the ball flies into the net. 1-1. Can we push on for the much needed three points? A fine curling shot from Aluko is tipped over the bar. Then QPR counter and Button parries a strong shot from substitute Washington. The rebound goes loose but Button falls on it before a hooped shirt can pounce.

Fulham look for a winner: substitute Sessegnon loops a header over the bar and big Matt Smith, on for Aluko, sees his left footed shot blocked. Then, in injury time, on the touchline next to the dug outs, it all starts kicking off. Marc Bircham, the QPR physio, kicks the ball away, there's a fracas and Bircham is sent off. However, that's not the end of the altercations, as on the pitch, Tom Cairney is given a yellow card for pushing Manning in the chest, after the young Irishman had kicked Johansen, which I don't think the ref saw. Thankfully, not long afterwards, the final whistle blows. We've dropped two points against a determined, but limited footballing side.

Sky make Ryan Manning Man of The Match. The twenty year old from Galway certainly gave a very committed performance, covering a lot of ground, pressing strongly and scoring their goal.

'I'm over the moon. Disappointed with the result but over the moon the way things have been happening to me. (he's just signed a new contract).' There are currently a lot of moons in Ryan's world.

Then former Sky pundit Ian Holloway, now QPR manager, has his say;

'They (Fulham) move the ball better than Reading (their last opponents). We needed to get a second goal. I'm a bit disappointed really. but we had a fighting spirit. We're still learning. We got to get tighter. We did in the second half.' Re the Fulham goal: 'We didn't step up quick enough. They're a very good team-their movement was excellent. It's a big point for us.' We then hear that Holloway's daughter, who's deaf, has given birth after several miscarriages, which puts things into perspective.

Slaviša gives an interview with his thick Serbian accent. He rues the mistakes but thinks we played well without creating as many chances as we normally do.

Prutton and Beagrie then discuss the game with Kelly :

Beagrie stresses that the first goal was due to good pressing by QPR. For Fulham's goal, he illustrates that Cairney wasn't picked up by Manning on the edge of the box, so he was free to shoot when the ball came back to him from the blocked free kick. 'No wonder the young Irish midfielder was disappointed.'

And as for Fulham's seventh penalty miss of the season?

'It becomes a mental thing,' says Prutton. 'If it goes on any longer, Jokanović should address it. Whoever takes the next penalty will have even greater pressure. It's a habit you need to break quickly.'

Beagrie didn't think it was a penalty, nor earlier (naturally!) did Holloway.

As for Fulham, David Prutton felt that their final ball let them down. Beagrie probably summed it up. 'If Fulham had put the penalty in, they would have gone on to win this game.' Ugh, that hurts. Two bloody points lost in a tight race. Still in this crazy league, we're now seventh. So still all to play for.

Reading: The Story Continues

I'm at Craven Cottage waiting to leave for Reading again. I get in the coach which has arrived from Gillingham. Barbara takes my ticket and I then approach East End Man.

'Can I sit next to you?' I ask.

'Yes'

I settle myself and await our departure. There's a pause. Apparently, we're waiting for stragglers.

A middle aged man with flowing long hair, in a thick black leather jacket, looking like a member of Status Quo, hurriedly enters and makes his way to the back of the coach. There's rumours that the fog might come down at Reading. Some passengers are concerned. Apparently Sky say an inspection is to take place at 5.30pm.'

'Tracey (in the ticket office) hasn't heard of an inspection,' says Barbara.

I ask East End Man with the dark jacket and long grey hair, what he thought of the QPR game.

'They roughed us up bit and we gave away a daft goal. One point was just about acceptable.'

He then proceeds to tell me that his daughter's partner is a Reading supporter but as he needs to get back, he's avoiding the family this evening.

Suddenly, the coach's engine starts but stalls

'Have we got a dodgy one?' an older wag cries out, 'maybe we should get out and push?'

Eventually the driver, attired in regulation white shirt and black tie, gets the coach to start.'

'You see he's not a bad driver really,' another voice pipes up.

Across the aisle, is a man with very grey hair, in dark cords, black jacket and brown shoes. He speaks in a strong middle class voice. He's discussing some paintings he bought with his companion-maybe someone who works with him?

Behind me is a man with a round cherubic face, joking about the previous postponement.

'Perhaps we should play the second half first' he cheekily declaims, laughing loudly as he does so.

Then East End Man denounces the lack of tacklers in the side, Jozabed, for instance.'

'But he's off on loan now.'

'All right. Cairney then.'

'Yes you're right,' I concur, 'we don't have many good tacklers when they have the ball and 'the turnover' starts.'

My fellow supporter then takes a nap. When he awakens. He tells me that he had to get up early and travel from the east end to Wembley to help his brother.

'Is he disabled?' I ask.

'In a sort of way he is.'

East End Man is now reading his paper

'Tunnicliffe has gone on loan. To Wigan,' he tells me.

'He'll get games there. I don't think he passes well enough for the way we play.'

'Fredericks should be back tonight.'

'I'm not so sure. He overreacts to being fouled and lacks discipline. Good going forward, he's very athletic and fast. But he can be a bit of a liability.'

'Smith isn't getting games'

'I think he no longer fits into the way we play. We're all about pass and move. He's too slow and static.'

We arrive at the ground quickly. The start was slow because of heavy London traffic but as soon as we got on the M4, it didn't take long. I now go to my seat in the stadium. Or should I say I'm climbing to it? It's like scaling Everest but I eventually get to the summit. A few rows above me is a supporter wearing a big brown cap with flapping ends. The stuffed replica of a big dog sits imperiously on the top of his head. It's a surreal sight, worthy of a character at The Mad Hatter's Tea Party. Next to me is an Asian man, who arrives just before kick off in a brown porkpie hat and a thick leather jacket, on which is embroidered that bizarre Fulham badge. Fulham have made one change: Madl in place of Piazon. Fulham are playing three at the back, Madl, Kalas and Ream, with Fredericks and Malone playing further forward as wing backs. Early on, Madl

120

plays Fredericks in over the top but it comes to nothing. My Asian friend enjoys getting up and chanting, 'YOU'RE SHIT AAAAH! at Reading's goal kicks. Buoyed by the away support, Madl comes forward and shoots. The Fulham faithful are in singing refrain. 'TAKE ME HOME AL FAYED!...'

However, Reading are attacking at the far end. Button saves a McShane header and then parries a Swift shot from a Beerens cross. 'SLAVISA'S BLACK AND WHITE ARMY!' rings round the ground. The rugged McShane is booked for a robust tackle on Cairney, who's inevitably being marked closely. 'OH WHEN THE WHITES, OH WHEN THE WHITES, GO MARCHIN' IN, GO MARCHIN' IN, OH WHEN THE WHITES GO MARCHIN' IN! I WANNA BE IN THAT NUMBER, WHEN THE WHITES GO MARCHIN' IN!' is the next tune on the song sheet. In response, Fulham conjure up some great free flowing passing football, started by Tom Cairney and ending with Stefan Johansen shooting over the bar. The fans are in great, humorous voice. 'WE WON IT ONE TIME! THE INTERTOTO, WE WON IT ONE TIME! THE INTERTOTO, WE'LL WIN IT AGAIN!' referring to our success in one of Europe's minor, now defunct competitions.

Like the first postponed match, the game's pretty even. Fredericks has another pacy run down the right, unfortunately when he pulls the ball back, he can't find a Fulham player, confirming that we really lack a natural goal poacher. The Fulham fans then launch into 'CAN'T TAKE MY EYES OFF YOU'. A young supporter dressed all in black with a surprisingly thin sweater and no jacket, pipes up. 'HAVE YOU EVER BEEN TO VENICE, HAVE YOU FUCK?' He looks a bit like a younger version of Joey Barton, but with sleeked down hair; what he's chanting is shrouded in mystery. Al Habsi, Reading's Omani goalkeeper, then makes a loose clearance and is disparaged by another vociferous fan-'ONCE A WIGAN REJECT. ALWAYS A WIGAN REJECT!' Nonetheless, Reading end the half strongly when Swift connects first time with a Beerens cross but Button pushes his shot past the post.

Fulham make a change for the second half. Midfielder Piazon comes on for Madl and the team revert to their more usual 4-2-3-1 formation. Behind me on my left, a thickset gentleman with a protruding belly, ensconced in a grey sweater and dark jacket, is berating the ref. 'That's vision, that was ref (bringing play back a yard for a throw in!). Get on with it!' Four minutes into the second half, when a cross is floated into the Fulham penalty area, Ream collides innocuously with Moore but perplexingly the referee awards Reading a penalty. A real soft one. Swift takes the spot kick but Button gets a firm punch on the shot. Unfortunately, Beerens is the quickest to react, while Fulham respond sluggishly, and the Dutchman's shot flies into the net. 1-0. Reading gain in confidence as Fulham leave more gaps, pushing forward to get an equaliser. Swift is about to score a second but is brilliantly foiled by a last ditch tackle by Kalas. McLeary shoots from distance and hits the bar with a powerful shot.

There's now less singing by the Fulham faithful, although we're still showing a determination to equalise. Fredericks continues to make inroads down the right and finds both Piazon and Aluko, who have shots blocked. Sessegnon comes on for Malone, no doubt to release new energy, but he makes a few mistakes and looks a bit raw. The game is drifting away from us but the fans rediscover their voice. 'COME ON YOU WHITES!' they passionately chant. Then, in injury time after some short passes outside the box, Piazon makes his way into the penalty area and is shoved in the back by Moore. Penalty! Oh no! Not another one! Martin comes up to take it. He shoots, but in going for power not placement, it's parried by Al Habsi and scrambled away. The keeper is then predictably mobbed by his colleagues. That's the eighth penalty Fulham have missed this season -seven in the league! Talk of throwing away points. We're now ninth. Five points off the play offs. It's still doable but we need to get on a winning run quickly.

Back in the coach, there is anger and bewilderment at another penalty miss. Martin is again public enemy number one. We've tried five different penalty takers this season and they've all missed! Perhaps that's why there's reported interest in bringing Ross McCormack back. At least, he can score from penalties. One of Barbara's friends, the white haired lady in front of me, isn't having it.' 'What about his attitude.? He can't even climb over a four foot six wall.' This is a reference to McCormack not attending training for

Aston Villa, because the electronic security gates at his home were locked. Apparently, Villa manager Steve Bruce went round to the house and discovered that the wall at the itinerant forward's home was only four foot six inches high! Long haired East End Man is similarly doom laden:

'That's why we won't go up. They made it difficult by pressurising Cairney, and pushing up on our full backs so they couldn't make runs and we lost.'

'We still managed to release Fredericks and I thought Cairney played well in the second half.'

'Wouldn't be so bad if we could score from penalties. The manager said he had faith in Martin to take them!'

My friend transfers his sorrows into looking at his messages. I bury myself in a suitably grisly Maigret novel about a man accused of murdering his wife. When I get off, I say 'safe home' to Ross's bête noir, The White Haired Lady. I wait for my mate, East End Man. He tells me that as it's not too late, he only has to get one night bus after his tube journey. I turn towards my entrance, when he suddenly stops me:

'I've got to go this side.'

'Ok. By the way, what's your name?'

'Doug.'

'I'm Roland. Safe home.'

He hobbles slowly away, as I make my way to Hammersmith bus station.

The Tigers in The Cup

The Chris Martin saga goes on. Apparently, he's signed an extended contract with Derby, extolling the club's virtues. Unsurprisingly, this hasn't gone down well with the supporters, which has led to him to being called several unflattering names. Anyway, Donny Osmond is on at the Apollo, and an idiosyncratic café down the Fulham Palace Rd somewhat righteously called Truth has a board outside saying 'coffee it's the drink if you don't get, you can't think.' The Crabtree are advertising for St Valentine's Day but also the Rugby Five Nations-maybe to keep Fulham fans away and become more obviously a middle class pub? The Thames is at very low tide and two travelling Hull supporters are discussing business- 'they're selling some units,' says one in a thick Yorkshire accent. He's wearing sunglasses, the club's orange and black striped scarf and a thick dark jacket. As I'm getting my programme, I complain to the Scottish lady that 12. 30 pm is an absurd time for a football match.

'I got up at 8.30,' she informs me.'

'The Hull supporters must have left early,' I surmise.

'5.30,' she replies.

'Crazy.'

The man clad in red doing the Bobby Moore Fund cancer collection agrees.

'Ridiculous. Should be 4pm like in Spain.'

'I agree. TV controls everything.'

I put a quid in his bucket and make my way to the stand. I'm going to the Riverside so I'm frisked. In this case, not very well. As I pass under the Putney Stand, Hull supporters are watching Federer play Nadal in the final of the Australian Open. It's the fifth set and Federer is very near winning. By the time, I get to the edge of the Riverside, I witness the final game and amazingly the Swiss master wins an Open at the age of thirty five. Legend is an overused word but it's justified in his case. Roger Federer, along with Tiger Woods and Cristiano Ronaldo are the greatest current sportsman I've seen live.

I make my way to my seat. It's a good position, three quarters of the way up, in the Upper Stand, towards the Putney End. As it's an FA Cup game, one can sit anywhere-'it's so different up here,' says a woman ensconced with her family. Her father, a corpulent grey haired man with a humorous smile, is late but finally makes it. He's missed Billy The Badger milking the crowd and preening himself, after engaging in the inevitable selfies. The Hull fans are to my right. Amazingly, there's a lot of them. When the players come out, there's the usual cursory handshakes and then we're off. Hull, now managed by Marco Silva, the Portuguese, ex-Olympiakos manager, recently beat Man Utd in the second leg of the EFL semi final. From what I saw on tv, they played well, so this won't be an easy game. Hull have made six changes, Fulham make three: Odoi and Sessegnon are the full backs and Marcus Bettinelli is back in goal.

The opening skirmishes are cautious with some good passing from both sides. The Hull supporters are singing 'WE WANT ALLAM OUT! WE WANT ALLAM OUT!' referring to their unpopular chairman, who after unsuccessful attempts to rebrand the club, wants to sell. After ten minutes Curtis Davies goes off with a hamstring injury. 'I'M CITY TILL I DIE. I'M CITY TILL I DIE!' shout the defiant Hull faithful. A few minutes later there's an exquisite move by Fulham: a free kick from Johansen is headed down by Kalas and expertly volleyed by Sone Aluko. 1-0 to the Whites. Then Hull come back into it and Fernandez hits the side netting. Meanwhile, their fans keep on the chairman's back. 'YOU SAID YOU WOULD GO! YOU SAID YOU WOULD GO!'. When Martin shoots over the bar from an Odoi pass, the Dad next to me remarks: 'some people like him but I never rated him'. This is a good open, entertaining game. Fulham then proceed to indulge in predictable defensive lunacy. Hernandez beats an onrushing Bettinelli to an over the top ball but thankfully he controls it with his hand. This is followed by an amazing piece of skill from Sone Aluko as he runs at the Hull defence, twisting and turning, feinting this way and that, beating half the Hull defence, only for his final shot to go just wide. The game continues on its lively way to half time with both sides having half chances.

During the interval, in the loo, somebody says 'it's going well.' 'Yes, but this is Fulham ain't it mate?' says his pessimistic friend. On the pitch, Brede Hangeland, our distinguished, ex-centre half, tall, fair with a thick dark coat and green scarf, is being publicly interviewed. He's been working for Norwegian tv covering The Premiership, so he hasn't seen much of Fulham, but he's been impressed by the first half. 'Bit risky at the back though,' he comments, referring to Fulham playing such high defensive line, to which there is laughter, given Brede's lack of pace, but 'he hopes to see Fulham back in the Premier League soon.'

The second half starts. The bloke next to me is lost. His daughter calls out. 'Dad!' He's at the bottom of the mountainous stairs. When he clambers over me to his seat, somewhat breathless, he complains about the queue and the awful service. 'Harrods it ain't,' he bewails. After Piazon has a poked shot cleared before it goes over the line, Hull score. Evandro is unmarked by Sessegnon at the back post and nods in Robertson's accurate cross. 1-1. However, we reply in style when Aluko sends a wonderful diagonal pass to Sessegnon charging down the left. The gifted prodigy calmly squares it for Martin, who taps the ball into the net. 2-1. Young Ryan leaps with joy into Martin's arms. Despite the jubilation, Martin is still booed by a section of the crowd for his seemingly Judas-like behaviour. Still, what a fabulous team goal, one of the best this season.

With under half an hour to go, there's another delightful Fulham move. Piazon finds Martin who plays in Sessegnon on the left and the youngster puts the ball through the advancing keeper Jakupović's legs. 3-1. Brilliant and what a game for Ryan! We could be seeing the birth of a great player here. It's as if after making a mistake for Hull's goal, he was determined to get forward and stamp his class on the game. Then with ten minutes to go, Tom Cairney, Fulham's midfield general, works a good position and squares the ball to the hard working Johansen, whose powerful shot makes it 4-1. This is the cue for Floyd Ayité, back after Togo's elimination in the African Nations Cup, to come on for the tireless Sone Aluko, who is given a thunderous ovation.

This is followed a few minutes later by the entrance of the Greek. Not Zorba but our new loan signing from Werder Bremen, Thanos

Petsos, who comes on for Martin, who departs, only quietly appreciated. It should be easy win for Fulham. but no such luck. Hull come at us and the enterprising Scottish international full back, Robertson, is on goal when taken out by the rugged Tomas Kalas. A definite penalty. Hernandez, who has looked a natural striker the whole game, takes the kick-but would you believe it, his tame shot is saved by Marcus Bettinelli, who when trying to claw the rebound, brings down Hernandez, as the striker follows up. So it's penalty number two. Hernandez looks unsure about taking it but finally decides to do so. And amazingly, he misses again! This time it's a magnificent save from Marcus. Hernandez went for power down the middle and the Fulham keeper anticipated well, stood his ground and palmed his blistering shot over the bar. After Bettinelli is effusively congratulated by his teammates, Tom Cairney makes way for Fredericks, who interestingly hands the arm band to the oft criticised Ream, who's had a really good game. The heroic Marcus makes another good save from Tynam and Ryan Fredericks ends up just missing a final half chance before the final whistle blows. We're through to the next round with a great win.

It's Wednesday and It's Burton!

I'm not going to make it to Burton. I've a horrific cold that won't go away. Going up to East Staffordshire will take five hours plus, so it's a non-starter. This is pity as it's a game we must win but I'm just going to have to rely on the usual media outlets.

Burton is a successful small club with limited resource and a ground capacity of 6,912. It wasn't so long ago that they were in the Conference. Their meteoric rise through the league has been guided by a variety of managers including Roy McFarland, Gary Rowett, Jimmy Hasselbaink and the current manager, Nigel Clough. The week before this game, Clough talked to his old club Nottingham Forest but he refused their offer, preferring to stay at Burton and help them avoid relegation. This must have given the club a lift, so Fulham have been warned.

In the current transfer window, apparently Fulham tried to sign several strikers but to no avail. Instead, we've ended up with the twenty six year old Gohi Bi Zoro Cyriac (I love the Zoro-will he be our second masked striker?). 'Zoro' has scored a reasonable amount of goals playing for the likes of Anderlecht, Standard Liege and his current club, so let's hope he can do the same for Fulham. Travelling the other way are Cauley Woodrow and Lasse Vigen Christensen, who, ironically are going to Burton on loan but can't play against their parent club in this game. Matt Smith, starved of games at Fulham, has also departed, joining QPR on a permanent deal.

After eating a nourishing omelette and watching Parliament pass Article 50 to trigger leaving the EU, I settle down to Sky's coverage of the evening's games. Julian Warren is the presenter on the Sports channel. Attired more like a banker from Canary Wharf than a football man, he's in the studio with Paul Walsh ex-Liverpool and Spurs, Alan ('Rambo') McNally ex-Celtic and Bayern Munich, Neil Mellor ex-Liverpool and Preston and Tony Cottee, ex-West Ham and Everton. Matt Murray, the former Wolves keeper, is at Burton. An urbane figure in a black coat, huddling among the crowd, he relays that the start of the game is uneventful. Plenty of possession for Fulham but no significant incidents so far. Burton were very resolute at the Cottage to earn a draw, so I hope history doesn't repeat itself. By half time Matt tells us that there's no change in the score. Time for a cup of tea.

And then there's news from Burton. When I see it on the screen I shout an ecstatic, 'yes!' 0-1 to Fulham. Mira laughs but Sky are now back with Matt. He describes the lead up to the goal, then Sky show a recording. Tom Cairney. our captain, continuing his excellent season, finds Stefan Johansen on the left and the Norwegian's shot finds the right hand corner. A good goal. Let's hope Fulham now manage the game and hit the Brewers on the break, as they press for a equaliser.

After the panel go rabbiting on about an eccentric use of headphones, we're over to Matt again for an update. And yes! Scott Malone rampaging down the left, after being put through by Lucas Piazon's defence splitting pass, scores with a powerful rising shot. 0-2. Great goal! Surely game over? And so it is, despite Burton's late spirited late response. Brilliant.

Unfortunately play-off rivals Leeds have come back from being one behind to win 2-1 but local rivals QPR have earned a draw in the last minute at Newcastle, which could help us. We're ninth, three points behind the position for the play-offs. Now where's that Lemsip, so I can get up to Birmingham on Saturday?

St Andrews Here We Come!

Mira is driving me to the Cottage to get the coach to Birmingham. There's little activity so we sail down Hammersmith Rd and Fulham Palace Rd talking about available gym and yoga classes. I have warm tea in a fantastic thermos and some well prepared chicken, so I'm not going to spend a fortune at the arid Welcome Break Cafe. 'You always like my food as long as I cook it,' says Mira with a twinkle in her eye, as she drops me off.

There's only one coach. Barbara takes my ticket and I pass our immaculately dressed driver with his familiar black waistcoat, white shirt and tie. I sit opposite an older man, possibly in his 70s, with a decorated hat. He's the aforementioned, The Man With Many Badges We talk about away trips. He tells me he's not going to Newcastle because of that absurd elevated view-'it's not worth it. Like watching from an aeroplane?' I suggest. 'Yes. Exactly.' At the front of the coach is a small, portly, middle aged Ulsterman, who with Barbara and a talkative, animated, grey haired lady, are discussing the song sung when Malone scored at Burton. Apparently, it was a version of The Logical Song recorded by Supertramp. Only instead of 'Logical, Logical', the fans sang 'MAGICAL! MAGICAL!' The Animated Lady, suitably gesticulating, then reveals that the Burton ground was so small that when our goalkeeper, David Button, collected the ball close to her, she reprimanded him in no uncertain terms. 'You're lucky to be in the first team!' 'Nothing like encouragement then,' I cynically retort.

I turn to the Man With Many Badges and ask why there's only one coach. 'I think you could get a good cheap rail deal, fifteen pounds return, if you booked in advance,' he informs me. In front of me, opposite the portly Ulsterman, there's a middle aged man wearing a dark sweater and blue trainers, who's reading The Mirror. He's with his young demanding son, who's masked by the size of the seats. 'I feel sorry for the Burton crowd.' he pronounces 'having to watch that every week. They hardly got up our end,' he tells The Ulsterman and The Animated Lady. We're about to leave but at the last minute, two bounding twenty year old lads in light grey track suits burst into the coach. Meanwhile The Man With the Kid is telling The Animated Lady that 'boys don't play offside until they're 12.' Good fun for the kids to enjoy the game but there must be a few goal hangers! Meanwhile, the two lads have settled behind me and are planning their trip.

'Before I go to the game. I'll have three pints in the pub.'

'Beep ! Beep! blares the coach's hooter.

'Was he drifting?' asks The Animated Lady.

'Yes,' says the driver, 'drifting with a mobile in one hand!'

We're on the M4. It's dark, cloudy and raining. I can't see the lads behind me. One of them goes into loquacious overdrive.

'I didn't know what the girls were like. I should have slapped her. ...I'd had enough so I kicked him.' Bravado or unpleasant reality? Who knows? He talks quickly like the staccato rhythm of a keyboard.

The Man With Many Badges is taking a nap. The kid is making demands of his Dad. Barbara's reading The Daily Mail and its extracts of a biography on Theresa May.

We brake suddenly and I spill my tea, which I've poured from my impressive king sized thermos. The lads behind blurt on:

'What you fuckin' doing?' remonstrates one of the lads

'That's disgusting!' says the other.

The mind boggles as to what they're talking about.

We're now passing a sign to Blenheim. Palace, home of the Duke of Marlborough, a relation of Winston Churchill, who was born there.

One of the lads is on his mobile:

'Hello Skip, how ya doing?...Another four hours snoring and everything.'

A huge van passes- MAERSK ENGLAND is emblazoned on its side.

We then pass a sign to Silverstone, the home of British motor racing.

The lads blather on

'Did you talk to her?'

'In Manchester, I'll take her under my wing. Not with 'how are you?' Boring. I'll try some different lines.'

We pass a sign to Warwickshire, 'Shakespeare's County'. Let's hope it augurs for The Taming Of The Brum!

Then we pass a sign to The British Motor Museum, which possesses a huge collection of British cars. We're now at the service station. We have a three quarters of an hour break.

Walking to the Welcome Break, I'm following a young boy with 'Parker' on the back of his shirt, who's accompanied by his Dad. Next to me are three elderly women stumbling towards the M40 food bastion.

'Where are we?' one of them wails.

'We could be anywhere,' I suggest.

They laugh nervously, oblivious to their whereabouts.

Inside the building I find a communal wooden seat and unpack my chicken and rice.

An older Fulham supporter with tight cropped white hair, a ruddy face and a red sweater with Fulham insignia written on it, is joined by a beefy Brummie in a dark blue jacket:

'It's fifteen years since I was in London,' says the Brummie. The wife is going to London for the first time in fifty four years. We're going to see the sights.'

After the Brummie departs, I join the Man In The Red Sweater, who then reveals his own holiday memories.

'My Mum only went abroad once. In those days, you went to the coast,'

'Like Littlehampton?'

'Yes. Littlehampton. Exactly. Now people take four or five holidays abroad a year!'

He then digresses to the football:

'The thing about Fulham is you don't know what they're going to do next. That's why we love them!'

'Do you remember 'The Great Escape' to avoid relegation in the 60s under Buckingham?'

'Buckingham destroyed Fulham. He sold Leggat. I remember we beat Man U, stayed up north and early the next week beat City!'

'Yes. That must have been the same season when we were going down and then went on an amazing run, winning something like nine of the last thirteen games. Talk about getting out of jail!'

'Yes, that's Fulham. Anyway, let's hope for good things today.'

Back on the coach, Barbara is asking the kid what books he's reading at school. The young blonde boy seems detached and hesitant and is taking ages to reply. I then get a clearer sighting of the two lads sitting behind me, as they return to the coach. One is tall and slim with a dark red jacket, blue jeans and straggly, unkempt hair. The other is brown haired, short and stocky with dark blue jeans.

The lads continue, duetting voices behind me:

'His older brother is a bit of a mess.'

'They're all a bit of a mess. The whole family.'

'He doesn't work but he has a really nice car.'

Then Straggly, the slim one, goes on about his home town.

'I hate Feltham. You can't take Feltham out of me. Shame as it's such a shithole!'

We're now in Birmingham.

The lads are back on to football:

'Martin Jol. Such a twat! With the likes of Karagounis,' proclaims Straggly.

'I liked Karagounis,' responds Stocky.

'Yeah but not at 37 years of age!'

We're near the St Andrews ground. The driver is struggling to find the exact entrance.

He's quietly berated by the 'terrible twins' behind me.

'You're fuckin' lost!'

Followed by

'You don't know what you're doing!'

And finally

'He's messed it up!'

A smart three point turn by the much abused driver gets us pointing in the right direction.

'Well done driver!' Straggly sarcastically bellows.

We pass the team bus with its dark filtered windows. There could be martians in there for all I know.

'I definitely need three pints before the game,' says Straggly with virile intent.

We advance slowly through narrow streets to the ground. A big van is front of us proclaiming 'AZKA IS GOOD FOR YOU.'

'I hate you. You're going back in a coffin!' says Straggly to his mate.

The Custard Factory is on the way to the ground. Sounds more interesting than it is. They're digital retailers involved in shopping.

'That's where your Mum is,' says Straggly pointing nebulously in the direction of the Birmingham sky. 'She was created by aliens. You can't be that ugly and get away with it!'

We pass a long line of back to back, red brick houses, several all boarded up.

We go into the car park. The team bus is there before us.

'Zola (the Birmingham manager) hasn't won in 10 games,' says Barbara, as we're about to leave the coach.

'Yes,' pipes up a fateful voice. 'That's why he'll win today!'

The young blonde kid is looking for more goodies. 'No,' says The Man With The Kid, as they leave the coach, 'not with the way you've been fleecing me off.'

The team bus has disappeared, miraculously uncontaminated by fans. We're now being searched before entering the stadium.

'Not a strip search, mate,' says a wag behind me, 'you'd like that wouldn't you?'

'Take the top off mate,' says an austere, yellow jacketed official, referring to my water bottle.

The inside of the ground, underneath the stand is a vast, impersonal concrete space, more suitable for a prison. When I go to the toilet, it's big but there's no hot water or heating. Ok, I'm only paying sixteen pounds as an OAP, which is a very reasonable price, but surely with all the money swilling around, the game can improve facilities for away fans? Amidst the bar and the food counters, a tv is attached to a pole in the middle of the concrete area. It's showing Chelsea v Arsenal. While sauntering around with a drink, I meet a young Scottish lad, Jason. He's from Ayrshire. He watches about four Fulham games a season. He's flown from Glasgow and is staying with student friends, so he's making a weekend of it. I discover that he's lost faith in Scottish football and much prefers the English game. I tell him that I remember a time when good Scottish players were in top English sides: Denis Law, Billy Bremner, Alan Gilzean, John White etc. Sadly now they're more likely to be in the Championship. I then ask him about the Scottish national team, which played well in the first half of the European Qualifiers but has since lost its way. Apparently the manager, Gordon Strachan, being ex-Celtic, isn't trusted by 'the other side'. 'Is that still going on? I enquire. 'Oh yes,' says Jason confidently. With kick off approaching, I divert our chat from tribal feuding, wish him well and toast a Fulham win.

I enter the Gill Merrick Stand. I remember Gill. He was goalkeeper for Birmingham and England. A moustachioed custodian, he was one of the best English keepers in the mid fifties. He also later managed Birmingham when they won the League Cup in 1963. It's unfortunate that he's most remembered for being the keeper who was on the losing side twice against 'The Magnificent Magyars,' the Hungarian side of Puskas and Hidegkuti, which beat England 6-3 at Wembley and then 7-1 at Nepstadion (former Fulham player and manager, Bedford Jezzard, also played in that humiliation). I'm halfway up the stand. The Birmingham mascot, Beau Brummie, no less, waves at the crowd with a young, sheepish-looking Fulham mascot in attendance. Then young boys with blue flags and yellow-sleeved green sweaters are photographed with Beau. The Fulham team are warming up. When they shoot against third choice keeper Joronen, they keep missing. As they exit to my right, the Fulham faithful give them a rousing version of 'WHEN THE WHITES GO MARCHIN' IN!' When the two teams then make their official entrance, to our left, 'CRAVEN COTTAGE BY THE RIVER,' is also vociferously bawled out by the assembled throng.

Birmingham are attacking our end. Button, our keeper. acknowledges the applause as he makes his way to the goal. The game starts and the Bluenoses are playing it long through the middle and being robust in midfield. The somewhat outdated, 'AL FAYED WHOOOAAA, AL FAYED WHOOOAAA! HE WANTS TO BE A BRIT, AND QPR ARE SHIT! AL FAYED WHOOOAA!' is then rigorously chanted. Some young fans are standing in front of me but eventually they sit down. Sessegnon as left back in place of Malone is the only change to the team that played Burton. In the early stages of the game, Fulham threaten but without any cutting edge. City's striker, Jutkiewicz is giving us problems and our central defence are not winning the aerial battle, so it's no surprise when the City striker heads Gardner's cross against the bar. Fulham's goal threat continues to be innocuous and the half ends with the oft reviled Button making a good save from that man Jutkiewicz.

At half time, I turn to the supporter next to me, impressively smart in a grey, leather jacket.

'We haven't won the headers,' I suggest.

'Not one,' he agrees anxiously.

At the far end there's a competition. Targets are displayed on a tarpaulin sheet and the various competitors are challenged to kick the ball into them to win some money. I don't think anybody is successful.

When the second half starts, Cairney is chopped by Kieta, who gets a yellow card. This prompts the fans to sing to the tune of 'Ain't Nobody' by Rufus and Chaka Khan, 'AIN'T NOBODY LIKE TOM CAIRNEY, MAKES ME HAPPY, MAKES ME FEEL THIS WAY!' Fulham must take their chance when it comes but when Aluko centres a perfectly executed cross, Martin can only glance it wide. You've got to do better with a free header! Now it's Gleeson's turn to chop Cairney. Another yellow. The officials are under threat for not protecting our playmaker. 'Fuckin' wanker, referee,' cries Mr Angry directly below me, all red face with veins bulging. I can't imagine this is how Gianfranco Zola really wants his team to play but after ten games without a win, he's had to revert to rugged 'blue collar' football, which was essentially what they were playing under their previous manager, Gary Rowett, who got sacked when they were sixth in the league. When the Bluenoses fail to clear their lines, Piazon shoots over the bar from ten yards. He's got to at least hit the target from there! Later, Kalas robs Sinclair and starts a scintillating counter attack, only to be ruthlessly fouled by Kieftenbeld. Another yellow card. This is like Sheffield Wednesday's and QPR's tactics against us. Harass Cairney, double up on the advancing full backs, stop counter attacks by fouling and look to trouble our central defenders in the air.

Now we're getting frustrated and when Fredericks has a heavy touch, he tries to recover and goes through Gardner. It's a red. Unfortunately, Fredericks is always liable to be rash. Now we're in trouble. Kalas moves across to right back and McDonald moves back to central defence. The Bluenose crowd are encouraged and get very vocal, while our support goes sotto voce. After seventy five minutes, they breach our defence when Jutkiewicz slides in Keita's cross. 1-0. We now become hesitant and a wayward Johansen back pass nearly gifts another goal but Tim Ream makes a great tackle. Maybe if we hang in there we'll get at least one chance? Cairney shoots straight at Kuszczak, who's taking an inordinate time with his goal kicks, which are denigrated with the traditional, 'OOOH. YOU'RE SHIT. AAAAAH!' Cyriac, (our Zoro) comes on for Aluko to make his debut. Then the menacing Jutkiewicz nearly seals it for City, when his overhead kick is pushed over the bar by Button. With that reprieve, is something going our way? Eventually, our moment comes. McDonald finds Ayité free in the penalty area but the Togolese international snatches at the ball and his shot goes wide of the post. Game over. In a tight contest, we lack mental strength and without a natural goalscorer, we're vulnerable.

Back in the coach, a thick set rosy-faced, cheery man is now sitting just below me to the right. He wasn't there before. Maybe he was further down the coach? Apparently, he used to have a shop in the Munster Rd. He still lives in the area and has been supporting the Whites for a long time. He even knows local Fulham legend 'Tosh' Chamberlain. He's certainly not happy about today's performance.

'That was shocking. today. They sussed us out. Like QPR. Did we have a shot on target? Not really. We got no striker. One big chance we had and we missed.'

The coach moves slowly out of the ground as Barbara tells us the police are clearing the road. She then goes down the aisle with an open envelope, collecting money for the driver. I pop in a quid. The lads behind me haven't got any dough so Barbara passes them. When she returns to the front of the coach, Stocky makes an offer, shouting out :

'Margaret, would the driver like a Mars bar?'

'No thanks, I've already eaten,' replies the waist coated navigator.

137

She's not Margaret,' whispers Straggly to his mate.

'What's your name?' shouts Stocky.

'Not Margaret,' is Barbara's measured response.

I talk to Rosy-Faced Man about young players like Roberts, Dembélé and Hyndman all leaving before they've played many games in the Fulham first team.

'Trouble is they're all looking for more money. Still, it's better than stacking shelves at Waitrose.' He then digresses:

'Fulham, they blow hot and cold. They let you down when you most need them. It's always been the same. You never know what's going on there.'

I then discuss the case of Fulham's missed penalties with the two young lads.

'We'd be in a play-off position if we'd scored from the six penalties. So who do you think should take the next one?' I air frustratedly.

'Who do you think? asks Straggly.

'Malone.'

'A full back for a penalty?'

'Straight down the middle'. Then I ask Straggly. 'Who would you have take them?'

'I don't know,' he hesitates, then decides. 'Ok. Button.'

'Really, a goalkeeper?'

'Yeah. Then, when he misses, he can say that he wasn't meant to take them, anyway!'

'If not,' I facetiously suggest,' there's always one of the kids, a supporter or a half time guest. Anybody as long as it goes in!'

We're now approaching Hammersmith. It's been a quick drive down the M40 on a Saturday night. The Man With The Kid, who is now wearing a black cap, is berating Brum's tactics-'every time they were tackled, they went down like ninepins. It was like the Wednesday game.' I gather myself, thank Barbara and the driver and make my way to Mira's in Wood Lane. We've now descended to tenth, six points off the play-offs. Still doable but we need to win our next two home games to get back on track.

Wigan in SW6

I'm at Mira's. she says she'll give me a lift to the Cottage.

Walking to the car, Mira is bracing the cold by wearing a blue woolly hat with a long extension.

'See I'm a dwarf. A blue marine dwarf.'

'Are you discriminating against dwarves?' I enquire.

I then sing 'Hey Ho! Hey Ho! It's Off To Work We Go!' from Disney's 'Snow White and The Seven Dwarves'. Mira asks me to clarify the words and then gradually joins me in an invigorating duet.

We seem to be making good progress past Westfield,

'You see, there isn't so much traffic,' exclaims Mira.

We take the short cut through the ring road to Shepherd's Bush Green. By the time we get to Fulham Palace Rd, there's more traffic and it's slower.

'I'll get out and walk.'

'No wait. Keep me company!'

'I've known this road since I was a child. It's slow.'

I wait a bit but when the traffic's not moving and it's half an hour before kick off, my departure is reluctantly accepted.

At Frank Banfield Park, mastiffs are prowling around, sniffing each other and Polish drinkers congregate around a bench, sheltered by a tall, majestic linden tree. At the River Café, steam pours out of the kitchen windows, while white clothed chefs step on to the pavement for a break. Thick jacketed figures in woollen hats make their way to the game. 'No Dog Fouling' says the notice approaching the Thames Path. On The Thames, seagulls bob on the grey water, green, red and blue-hatted rowers glide down the river. A grey coated man with a megaphone, trailing behind in a motor boat, stridently instructs them. Meanwhile, huddles of supporters spray themselves across the path. I pass the moss infested wall at the Hammersmith End and get my programme. A young man in a red hood is selling them today.

'Where's the Scottish lady?' I enquire.

'I don't know,' he replies.

'You fired her. You're ruthless, you young people!'

I get to my seat in the Johnny Haynes Stand. There are quite a few empty ones. The young Irishman, a regular in the row behind, says hello, as he makes his way behind me. Slaviša has made four changes for this game. Odoi and Madl come in for Fredericks who's suspended and Kalas who is injured. Malone and Ayité replace Sessegnon and Piazon who are on the bench. Young Ryan is wearing red boots as Fulham prepare to attack the Putney End. The two goalkeepers don't touch hands changing ends, as they did in days of yore. Fulham start well camping themselves in Wigan's half with good possession. This is a game we must win, so we need an early break through. The crowd seem up for it. 'WE ARE THE FULHAM BOYS!' rings round the ground. Aluko is booked, for what seems an innocuous foul. 'YOU DON'T KNOW WHAT YOU'RE DOING!' is the consequent retort to referee Coote's decision. Thankfully, from the free kick the ball goes straight into keeper Button's arms. Then in the twenty fifth minute, that man Aluko again, looks to make things happen. He runs past a hesitant Perkins, gets to the byline and delivers a perfect cross for Floyd Ayité, who has a simple tap in. 1-0.

Unfortunately, we then seem to show hesitancy at the back. A mix-up between Ream and Button nearly proves fatal. 'Button, you're useless,' cries the young Irishman behind me. Then a Warnock cross is missed by striker Bogle and Malone running towards goal puts the ball into his own net. 1-1. Maybe Button could have come for that? The young Irishman, smartly attired in a brown cap, now has more fuel to abuse his victim: 'Button, you're shit!' he yells. Then in the dying embers of the first half, Ream fails to clear his lines, tries to be too clever, the ball runs loose to Power, who squares to Jacobs for an easy finish. 1-2. Fulham are booed of at half time. I find that unnecessary. We have forty five minutes left to play. What's the point of demoralising the team. 'Button's awful, I never rated him,' says the relentless Irishman at half time and 'Ream, he had a terrible half.'

The second half starts and Wigan have changed their goalkeeper. Matt Gilks has come on for Jakob Haugaard, a Dane, who's on loan from Stoke City. Bogle, Wigan's striker is continuing to bully our centre backs. Big, strong with quick feet, he seems effective if a bit raw. Here he is now, getting past his man into a shooting position but

Button makes a good save. The young Irishman is silent. We were lucky there, Bogle did all the hard part and should have scored. With thirty three minutes to go, Jokanović brings on Cyriac and Kebano to replace Martin and McDonald. Taking off a defender and bringing on an extra forward is a brave tactical decision. Slaviša is going for the three points. A risk but a necessary one. At the end of this game, we can't afford to be nine points adrift from the play offs. Martin is booed as he traipses off. It seems fans think that he hasn't shown enough effort and movement. Certainly, Cyriac and Kebano are finding space and showing energy and commitment. Kebano's left footed shot clips the bar and Cyriac shoots over. Given they both aren't tall, they're never going to win many headers but they certainly seem to be giving us more thrust and pace in the final third.

Former Whites defender, lanky Dan Burn, is booked for fouling Ayité. as Wigan get behind the ball and look to play on the break. This leads to the Latics getting pushed further back towards their own goal, some desperate defending and Connolly going in the book for chopping Ayité. After some near misses, Johansen squares a free kick for Denis Odoi and wow! What a shot from thirty five yards. It powers into the bottom left hand corner. 2-2. Game on, with nineteen minutes to go. But, oh no, our defence has almost immediately been breached again. Jacobs gets through, shoots and Button brilliantly palms the ball away leaving, his Irish tormentor, speechless again. This important save is followed by the menacing Bogle getting behind our defence and shooting wide with just the keeper to beat. That was a big let off. However, Fulham are still pressing, urged on by a committed crowd. With seconds to go, Kebano beats his man down the left, cuts in and places the ball in the right hand corner. 3-2 to the Whites. The young Irishman is ecstatic. What a turnaround- would you believe it?

At The Wall, I meet Alex. We wait for Richard and Pete.

'A friend just summed that up. That's the worst victory, I've ever seen,' declares Alex.

'Yes. We didn't really play well.'

'We did our best to throw the game away.'

'Slav took a risk with those attacking changes but it worked out.'

'We got out of jail. Button made two very important saves in the second half.'

'It could be a turning point.'

'They tired and Kebano took his goal well.'

'Doesn't look like Richard and Pete are coming.'

'Were they going somewhere?'

'Yes. They had a 5.29 train to catch. They must have gone early.'

'They've got an evening do.'

'Golf?'

'Yeah. I think so.'

'Are you going on Tuesday?'

'Yes, I'll be there for the return of Ross,(after 'Wallgate,' now a Forest loanee).'

'He's not match fit so he shouldn't do much. Unless it's a free kick or a penalty.'

'Don't go there, please! The word penalty and Fulham are incompatible.'

'Who'll take our next one? It'll probably be in the last minute.'

'A lad on the coach suggested Button. I would put forward God if he's available!'

'See you Tuesday,' says a smiling Alex departing into the dark night.

'Ok mate'.

A Forest Valentine at The Cottage

It's Wednesday and it's mild and dry after the recent cold and wet weather. It's Valentine's Day, which is always a tricky match day for a football supporter. I gave Mira my card early and cleared the decks! Thankfully she's relaxed about going out for a meal over the weekend. Earlier today on the news, I heard an American couple, both over a hundred, being interviewed. Apparently, the husband has never mentioned the word 'love' once but they've been married for over seventy years.

After the usual rush hour traffic from Wood Lane, the walk from Hammersmith to the Cottage is unimpeded. There seems to be less of a crowd tonight and I comfortably reach Stevenage Road.

'You're missing your Valentine meal,' I tell the Scottish programme seller.

'I could do without that,' she dismissively replies.

I accidentally pick up an extra programme.

'You've already got one,' she reminds me.

As I walk towards the Cottage, there's a vociferous fan, in a blue woolly hat standing near The Wall shouting: 'Get your Fanzine ! Get your Fanzine!'

I give him a fiver.

'Five. That's two change. Thank you.'

Inside the Johnny Haynes Stand, the crowd is sparse, although there's a very good midweek turn out for Notts Forest. Billy The Badger is swaying to the crowd. By the time the game starts the ground is filling out substantially. Slaviša Jokanović comes out in a smart, long black coat, Gary Brazil is more conventionally dressed in a dark track suit. Brazil is Forest's caretaker manager after the sacking of Phillipe Montanier. He looks to the Forest fans and claps them ardently. Brazil is an ex-Fulham player (1990-96). I remember him as a clever but rather lightweight forward. He's been working as Forest youth team coach since 2012. Recently installed as manager until the end of the season, maybe this is his chance to step up, although a 5-1 loss against Norwich at the weekend didn't help his cause. In any case, the job might be a poisoned chalice, given the owner, Kuwaiti businessman Fawaz Al-Hasawi, is looking to sell the club and can't find buyers, after a deal with an American consortium recently fell through in acrimonious circumstances. Forest seem to be going through a precarious phase, which is certainly a far cry from the halcyon Clough days.

Fulham make three changes for the game Sigurdsson, Sessegnon an Piazon come in for Madl, Malone and Martin. Two minutes into the game, Sigurdsson miscontrols the ball badly. This leads to a cross to ex-Fulham player, Kasami, who delicately volleys the ball inside the far post, beyond keeper Button. 0-1. Would you believe it? At least Kasami's celebrations are low key and respectful. Triumphalism would be too much to take. Fulham aren't starting well, they seem nervous defensively and slow to the ball in midfield. Still when we attack with the speed of young Sessegnon, we're in business. He plays Aluko in but his shot is blocked. Then Button, indicative of Fulham's defensive hesitancy, throws the ball inadvertently straight to Forest's Osborn, who gets his shot on target, while the stranded keeper is well out of his goal. Thankfully Button recovers and gets back in time to make the save. The Young Irishman isn't here tonight, so I'm spared Button abuse.

Sensing the team needs to be lifted, 'COME ON FULHAM!' rings round the ground but we still struggle. Eventually, the team responds and it's that lad Sessegnon again with a fine shot, which Forest's Serbian international keeper, Stojković, palms away. Then just before the half hour, Slaviša makes a change. Sigurdsson is taken off. I don't think it's an injury but he certainly doesn't seem sufficiently comfortable on the ball to play our possession game. Anyway, Madl comes on and takes his place. Minutes later, there's some great passing on the left between Johansen and Sessegnon, who delivers a superb cross to Cairney, just outside the area. Cairney shoots and it's 1-1. Inevitably, our captain's song resounds around the ground. 'AIN'T NOBODY LIKE TOM CAIRNEY, MAKES ME HAPPY, MAKES ME FEEL THIS WAY!' Now, at last, Fulham are finding a rhythm to their game and when Ayité lays off a ball for Piazon just outside the penalty area, the Brazilian bursts through past three defenders and calmly places his shot beyond Stojković. 2-1. 'WHO ARE YER?' the crowd mockingly chant towards the Forest fans. The lady to my right, with black, short cropped hair and Expro inscribed on the back of her jacket, points excitedly towards the opposing supporters. Her friend, the dark haired woman next to her, with sunglasses perched on her head, is permanently on her smartphone, checking the scores in the other games. Now Aluko is accused of fouling defender Fox in Forest's penalty area. The ritual sounds of boos and clappers being banged against seats, then ring out like some rhythmic religious rite. The referee, James Linington, blows for half time and is booed off for not giving a penalty. What started dreadfully, ended well.

At half time the subs are strutting their stuff on the pitch against a background of pounding hard rock. Billy the Badger is going round the ground with two red-jacketed ladies, who are handing out flowers for Valentine's Day. It looks like they're free, which is a nice touch. As The Clash's stirring 'London Calling' rings out, the players go to the side of the pitch and run between some cones, before making their way to their positions. Fulham are kicking towards the Hammersmith End.

After two minutes, Forest make progress down the left, Fox sends in an excellent cross and the promising Brereton rises unmarked and glances a header, which goes in off the post into the top, far right corner. 2-2. Where was the marking? He seemed to glide in between Madl and Ream. We've had this aerial problem for some time.

However, the indefatigable Aluko responds by going into the Forest area, twisting and turning, but is eventually crowded out and Stojković saves. Kasami, who has been effective in spells, then finds himself free in the Fulham penalty area, but the ball falls to his weaker right foot and his shot hits the side netting. From where I'm sitting, it looked as if it was a goal. This optical illusion incites The Expro Lady to gasp: 'blimey, I thought they'd scored.'

On the hour, Jokanović makes his second change, and Kebano comes on for Ayité. Six minutes later, Kasami is brought down by Madl and the free kick is going to be taken by none other than Fulham renegade Ross McCormack. It's a good position for him, central and about twenty five yards out. Is this Fulham's death knell? As Ross comes up to shoot, I'm apprehensive as he's pretty deadly with free kicks but thankfully his shot goes over the bar. Ironic cheers ring round the ground in relief. This is followed a minute later by Kebano adroitly getting on the end of Aluko's flighted pass, and the ball, via a deflection, going out of the keeper's reach. Relief! 3-2. 'OH NEESKINS KEBANO!' chant the faithful, celebrating our new cult figure. Unfortunately, for the lively and committed Neeskens, it's later given as an own goal.

Fulham, led by substitute, club captain Parker, are resisting late Forest pressure by tackling much more strongly in the final quarter of the game. In the final minutes of injury time, on the counter, Kebano breaks free but unfortunately his shot clips the post and the ball tantalisingly goes out for a goal kick. Shortly afterwards the final whistle blows. We got there in the end but it was a precarious win. Still it's three points and we're now eighth, six points off the play-offs.

'It's never boring here!' I exclaim as Alex approaches The Wall.

'No. That's ten goals in two games!'

Richard and Pete join us

'That's two games that we've won, which we could easily have lost,' says Richard. 'Without Kalas we're vulnerable in defence.'

'It's fine margins,' says Pete 'they hit the post and the header goes in, we hit it at the end and it goes out.'

'We haven't the players to make enough forward runs with the ball. Aluko does but if he's forced sideways, the attack slows down,' explains The Oracle.

'Piazon went forward to score the goal but he should have been tackled,' I suggest.

'Once you're in the penalty area, defenders are wary of giving a penalty away,' explains Richard.

We then talk about Fulham's strong resistance in the last ten minutes.

'I thought Scotty Parker was going to 'kill 'one of them!' says Pete

Richard and Pete begin to depart for their train.

'See you Sunday,' cries Richard.

'Bettinelli will be in goal, Pete. So you'll be happy!' I shout back.

'Oh good. You know, we should never have sold Stockdale to Brighton,' declares Pete.

'That was 'Mad' Felix,' Richard reminds us as they potter down Stevenage Rd.

Alex and I say our goodbyes to the East Sussex Two and wander towards Fulham Palace Rd.

'It should be a good game versus Spurs but we wouldn't want to defend like that. Mind you, it'll be more of a football game,' says Alex.

'Yes, it will. Do you think it'll be the same eleven?' I ask.

'I think Malone and Bettinelli will come in and possibly Martin. Maybe Sessegnon will come back on Wednesday at Bristol.'

'I like the way we keep playing whatever the situation. Our style is very attractive but it's difficult playing a high line when you lose the ball.'

'That could be fatal against Spurs with their players.'

'Maybe, but we'll still keep to our game plan, squeezing the play through possession, passing and moving.'

'Anyway, the cup is a bonus, we need to beat our nearest rivals in the league. Hopefully, we'll be more solid.'

'I still think we can creep into the play-offs.'

'Let's hope so.'

'See you Sunday.'

'See you.'

Now for belatedly getting those Valentine flowers!

The Other Whites

I'm at Stevenage Rd for the Spurs cup game. Buying a programme, I tell the redoubtable Scottish lady:

'You don't need to go to Spurs, do you, as they're playing here!'

'Mmmm yes,' she replies hesitantly.

The time for the game is approaching. A facsimile of the FA Cup is on a plinth in front of the players entrance, in front of a red mat. The clappers are being rapped on the seats. Billy The Badger is conducting the clapping. The music starts. The players enter to a huge roar and congregate in front of the Riverside Stand, where there are two boards advertising The Emirates FA Cup. The game is being televised on the BBC, so the managers are followed by portable steadicam cameras. Slaviša is last out. No long black coat today but a sharp dark suit.

Fulham have made four changes to the side that beat Forest. Kalas, Malone and Bettinelli replace Piazon, Sessegnon and Button. Spurs are putting out a strong side. including England internationals, Kane and Alli, although a few players like French goalkeeper Hugo Loris, Eric Dier and Kyle Walker are missing. Fulham make a bright start from a corner, Malone shoots from thirty yards out but his shot goes wide of the post. 'COME ON FULHAM!' respond the crowd. Then after a quarter of an hour, trouble emerges. Trippier takes a quick throw, Malone is out of position, the ball goes to Eriksen, whose cross is met by Kane, getting in front of his man. 0-1 and too easy. The Spurs fans, of which there are many, celebrate. 'HE'S ONE OF OUR OWN! HARRY KANE! HE'S ONE OF OUR OWN!'

Spurs look determined to make up for losing their last two games, so that they're in good heart for the return leg of their difficult Europa League game against AA Gent. A minute later, Alli is played in over the top and plucks the ball out of the air but Marcus Bettinelli makes a good save. Playing a high defensive line against such a skilful high pressing side, does indeed seem fraught with danger. However, Fulham do have a chance when Vorm, the Spurs keeper, passes straight to Tom Cairney. Cairney hits it accurately first time but his shot isn't powerful and the Dutch keeper recovers in time. Then later Cairney inadvertently passes to Kane who plays in Eriksen, who shoots wide. 'HEY, I WANNA BE...' chant the Spurs fans. A Bettinelli pass also goes to Kane but Johansen makes a strong tackle to save Marcus's embarrassment. Spurs look in control of the game. Their ardent pressing has stopped Fulham from having much of the ball and induced errors. However, glimmers of hope emerge and after Johansen fires wide, Fulham's best chance of the half emerges. Malone gets in a good cross from the left but Ayité coming in on goal misses it and Aluko following up shoot straights into Vorm's hands. A wasted opportunity.

It's half time and the young lads from the under 8s, who are playing on the pitch, between cones, once more display a high level of natural skill and spontaneity. The subs, wearing their orange bibs, are warming up, doing their usual drills. They end up in a circle passing to each other, with one of them in the middle, trying to stop the ball. The sprinklers come on again and some of the Spurs subs nearly get drenched. Eventually, they all depart and the teams reemerge.

Spurs continue to dominate and after ten minutes Kane gets round the back of Ream and turns in Eriksen's cross. 0-2. 'WHO ARE THEY? WHO ARE THEY?' chant the Tottenham fans. Fulham are really up against it now. After fifty six minutes Jokanović makes a change and Ayité, who has been ineffective today, is replaced by Ryan Sessegnon. This seems to make us look more solid as it's been too easy getting down our left hand side. Young Ryan pushes Tottenham back, by making several positive sorties into the Spurs half, which are appreciated by the crowd, and one starts to dream of a comeback: 'COME ON FULHAM!' However, our centre backs are still struggling against Kane and co and when Tottenham's King Harry, gets beyond Ream yet again, McDonald makes a terrific sliding tackle. Later, Kane shows fallibility and lofts the ball over the bar from a free kick, when he should have scored. However, Spurs' favourite son makes amends, when he beats Fulham's offside trap, takes Alli's through ball and scores his third. 0-3. Game over.

There's still over quarter of an hour to go, so we don't want a carve up. Parker comes on to calm things down. 'SUPER SCOTT, SUPER SCOTT, SUPER SCOTTY PARKER!' is sung first by the

Spurs fans (Parker being an ex-Spurs player) and then by Fulham's. This is followed by the appearance of ex-Fulham player Mousa Dembélé, replacing the promising Harry Winks. 'OH, MOUSA DEMBELEE!' rings round the ground from both sets of fans. Spurs have been playing within themselves for the last third of the game. It's been a bit like a training session for them. The Spurs fans chant for their manager: 'THERE'S ONLY ONE POCCHETINO!' This is followed by a celebration of their absent French keeper. 'HUGO! HUGO!' The Fulham fans are mute. In stoppage time, Son Heung-min nearly scores another, heading over the bar. Ok, not a carve up but a convincing victory. Still, at least we were outplayed by a side who may well win the Premiership within the next few years.

At The Wall, Alex greets me, admitting that 'sometimes you've got to 'hold your hands up'. Later, a whole flock of friends and relations appear. I'm introduced to Alex's mother, bedecked in a thick Fulham scarf and reunite with Mikey, who's over from Norway with his partner, Benedicte. Mikey was expecting to see us play Bristol City but the fixture change meant that he was lumbered with a heavy defeat. I ask the amiable Benedicte, who's clad in a thick khaki jacket, if they're having a good trip. 'It would be better if we'd won,' she defiantly replies. Then suddenly, a jaunty Richard appears exclaiming, 'I think I'm going over to the shop to buy a ball so Fulham can play with it!' which is greeted by general hilarity. Richard is talking to a mate who's a long standing Spurs fan, who's wearing an elegant, brown felt hat and is full of praise for hat trick hero Harry Kane.

'His work rate and movement is so good. He gives his team so many options,' observes Richard.

'I'm glad we won but I was a bit disappointed you didn't come at us more in the second half,' says his Spurs mate.

'We couldn't get the ball,' says The Oracle. 'I'm surprised that Jokanović didn't bring on Martin to try and hold the ball up as we couldn't get out of our half.'

Maybe after his lack lustre performance against Wigan, he doesn't trust him, given the loan fracas and his ultimate loyalty to Derby.

'If Ayitè had converted that chance at the end of the first half, it might have given us some momentum,' I suggest, clutching at some thin straws.

I don't think the two gentleman are very convinced.

Then for some bizarre reason the discussion turns to Scottish football. I recall Gordon Strachan being asked why the '82 World Cup Scottish team didn't effusively celebrate after scoring the first goal against Brazil. 'I think we were worried we might have annoyed them,' he explained. Final result Scotland 1 Brazil 4. We then remember poor old Alan Rough clutching at fresh air as the goals accumulated. 'Not a good keeper,' insists the Spurs fan.

'Do you remember a Scottish keeper called Frank Haffey, who was in goal for the 9-1 defeat by England at Wembley.'

'9-3,' invokes Richard, The Oracle.

'Right. Thanks. Well, Haffey emigrated to Australia and twenty years or so years after the Wembley debacle, a Scotsman saw him in a bar down under. 'Are you Frank Haffey?' he enquired. 'Yes,' replies Haffey. 'Is it safe for me to go back?'

After sharing the woes of Scottish keepers, I say goodbye to one and all and make my way home on a grey west London afternoon. Oh well, that's another competition gone. We're out of the cup.

Duel at Ashton Gate

According to a tabloid, East End star and 'hardman' actor Danny Dyer is in meltdown and Sutton reserve goalkeeper Wayne Shaw, has resigned because of a betting scandal focusing around him eating a pie during the Arsenal cup game. Shaw, a large 46 year old, makes former sizeable Fulham keeper, Jim 'he's fat, he's round, he can't get off the ground' Stannard, positively svelte.

Away from such culinary matters, we're playing Bristol City tonight at Ashton Gate. When I enter the coach at the Cottage, Barbara tells me that there's been an 'incident'.

'What do you mean?' I enquire

'Alcohol. I've got to inspect your bag.'

My rucksack is overstuffed with my food in a large plastic container and a hardback novel. Barbara peers in and then let's me go to my seat.

'It's not just for you, it's for everybody,' she reassures me.

I see Doug, the man from the East End with the long, flowing grey hair. I don't want to impose myself on him again, so I go to the opposite seat next to an older, slim, elderly man in his 60s-early 70s. He's very genial and phlegmatic He tells me that he lives in Borehamwood and also goes to see the rugby league side, London Broncos. He remembers affectionately when Fulham had a rugby league team and played to a crowd of 10,000 at the Cottage.

'That was when Ernie Clay was chairman.'

'Yes, I think it was.'

Clay was a tough Yorkshire businessman whose motto was, 'don't get angry, get even'.

'He took exception to management having affairs. That's why Malcolm Macdonald went,' I remind Mr Borehamwood.

This made me remember another high profile businessman and former Fulham FC board member, Eric Miller, chairman of Peachey Property Corporation. Tommy Trinder had sold his Fulham FC shares to Miller, who later brought the controversial Ernie Clay to the club. Miller was instrumental in the sacking of Bobby Robson as Fulham manager. In 1972, the new stand on the riverside was named after him and opened with a game against Benfica and the legendary Eusebio (we won 3-2). In 1976, Miller was knighted as part of Harold Wilson's controversial resignation 'lavender' honours list. However, when he was accused of illicit financial dealings, he was forced out as both Peachey chairman and board member. After being served with four writs for restitution of funds, he committed suicide in the back garden of his west London home. A pistol was by his side. He was 50. Sometimes, Fulham doesn't half choose 'em!

I'm jolted out of my Miller reverie by Barbara telling us all that she doesn't want to give the impression that she's avoiding alcohol detection

'If anyone wants to check my bag, they can,' she insists.

The man in front of Doug, to my left is Military Man, the gentleman with the white moustache, who's wearing brown framed glasses while reading The Sun. Doug is working away at a crossword in the Mirror. The driver, an authoritative man with spiked white hair, launches into an official speech, as he did on the Reading trip. He reminds us that it's illegal not to wear a safety belt, that no alcohol must be taken on board and that if the police discover we've got some, we could go to jail.

'What's more,' he continues 'if it happens a second time I can also lose my licence.'

He then digresses

'You may also notice that there's a rubbish bag in the front of the coach. Put the rubbish there. and put the food in your mouth not on the floor. Last away game, it took me three quarters of an hour to clean the coach. You wouldn't do it at home. You wouldn't do it at work. You wouldn't do it at school. Don't do it in my coach!'After this harangue, he has a diplomatic after thought. 'Apart from that, have a good time and I hope you win!'

I then talk to Mr Borehamwood, who is philosophical about us getting in to the play-offs- 'if it happens, it happens.' Mr B W tells of how he enjoys seeing his local team in the National League, and how refreshing it is to have a club with such strong links with the community. He also has a mate who watches Preston, so he has gone up north to see them. I'm wondering just how many teams this man supports.

There's a big bottleneck out of London. Behind me I can hear The portly Ulsterman and a man with what seems a muted northern accent discussing how to adjust work to the fixture list. In front of me, a young couple have headphones stuck in their ears. The woman seems very young, in her early twenties. She's wearing an attractive mauve sweater and has purple varnish on her nails. Her companion is around the same age, fair, tall, well built and enshrouded in a smart, grey sweater. A man with brown rimmed glasses and a dark blue woolly hat is walking down the aisle, probably to go to the subterranean toilet, which is a few steps down in the middle of the coach. It's Brian, one of the stewards helping Barbara, one of 'The Committee' in reserved seats at the front of the coach.

We manage to make a lot of progress down the M4. Mr Boreham wood is now asleep and resting his head against the seat in front of him, like a travelling vagrant taking a much needed nap. Meanwhile The Ulsterman and 'The Northerner' are discussing the various merits of Fulham TV, Doug, is on his mobile arranging his domestic life and talking about a friend who's going to see giant tortoises in Brazil. When he finishes his call, he starts texting. and then returns to his crossword. Two ladies at the front, behind Barbara, are chatting away. They seem to be going to every game. One of them is The Woman Behind, from the Wolves trip, who knew The Beverley Sisters. Near the Cotswolds, we enter heavy traffic. 'We're not too far away then,' Barbara confirms to the driver.

Some fans are talking about a Sun article reporting that Slaviša Jokanović is about to sign a new contract. It's written by a journalist called Dave Kidd, who apparently has good connections with Fulham. Let's hope that The Sun, that reliable arbiter of truth, is right. Fulham need stability to move forward after too many years of chopping and changing to no great effect. At the front of the coach, a man with cropped grey hair, who's sitting with 'The Committee' is dealing with a crisis but gives the caller suitable reassurance. 'I'm on a coach but I'll let you know in ten minutes.' I think it's something to do with his child. We're now stopping for a break outside Bristol. 'Be back at ten to six,' says Barbara projecting forcefully, so everyone gets the message.

While taking his meal to a table, the Fulham fan with the grey cropped hair has an accident and glasses are smashed into tiny fragments all over the floor. Quickly a waitress in a blue dress scurries around with a dustpan and brush sweeping up the splintered fragments. Meanwhile, I'm sitting in a nearby communal seating area eating my own chicken and rice in a plastic container. A young fan, with his dark hair parted in the middle and cut shorter on one side, is at a nearby table with his taller leaner mate, who has Cairney no 10 on the back of his Fulham shirt.

'So. What you think the score will be tonight?' I challenge them.

'2-0,' replies the young fan brazenly.

'You think so?'

'Why not?' He replies brusquely. We've been playing great stuff.'

A few moments later, they notice Gentleman Jim and Jamie from Fulham TV in the W H Smith's opposite. The lads scamper over and take a selfie of them in front of the sandwich display. Nothing like being a Fulham FC celebrity.

When I get back to the coach, the driver is regally patrolling the top of the steps. I go to my seat and engage with Mr Borehamwood, now refreshed from his slumber. He, tells me how much he hates all the slagging off in football. In fact, when he discovered that he was seated next to a perpetual whinger at Craven Cottage, he decided to move. We then discuss tonight's game. I tell him that I'm concerned about our aerial ability and our centre backs being bullied by big strikers. I'm therefore relieved to hear from Mr Borehamwood that Tammy Abraham, who was at the heart of City's 4-0 victory at the Cottage, is injured and not playing.

As our conversation subsides, I hear those around 'The Committee,' at the front of the coach, talking about jobs, food banks and supplementary benefit. Behind me, The Ulsterman is asking 'The Northerner,' how a Bristolian would decide which Bristol team to support. 'The Northerner' suggests that maybe City have more obvious working class roots, as they were borne out of a gas works team, like West Ham came from an ironworks one. Meanwhile, 'The Committee' and friends are now discussing work. 'A man working?' somebody cries, 'what's happening? I must be ventilating!' Then they're on to council workers: 'they have one person to dig a hole, another to repair it and another to fill it up again!' Their next subject is fuel: 'they encourage you to buy diesel with low prices then they put 'em up and tell you it's bad for you and the environment!' As we approach Bristol, there's a sign saying 'Reduce Speed'. In response to this order, a very old fan at the front, with curly grey hair and dark rimmed glasses, chortles: 'I only have two speeds, dead slow and stop.'

Outside Bristol the traffic is piling up. It's more like being outside London. Our progress is now slow, due to some road works. Brian in the woolly hat is on his mobile-'we're still on the M32, can you pick up a programme for me? Thanks.' The driver is moving into bus lanes. I'm not sure he's allowed to do so but to quote commentator, Barry Davies, in another context, 'who cares?' While one of 'The Committee' recalls a time in the past, when the Fulham coach was stoned, the bus crawls into Bristol city centre, which is plunged in darkness. 'The Northerner' behind me surmises that the council here must have a policy of 'save energy, one light only.' He obviously missed Ted Heath's three day week in the 70s. We crawl across the dark city like snails searching for some lost haven. Eventually, we park outside the ground, only to discover, that it's the wrong area. An official I can't see, a voice in the blinding darkness, is ushering us away.

'There are no stewards here,' says Barbara defiantly.

'Doesn't your driver not know where the car park is before he sets off?' replies the official angrily

'What an unfriendly place,' comments The Woman Behind.

'I'm not looking forward to the local cider,' whispers 'The Northerner' to his Ulster companion.

'Thanks for your help,' says Barbara ironically.

We then reverse and go away from the ground to an outlying site, Avonmore Car Park. It's some way from the ground, in an awkward location.

'Come back here after the game,' orders Barbara. 'Good luck, finding the ground!'

I don't have a good sense of direction, so I write down landmark sites. The Ecobat building, part of a battery company, Marsh Road etc. Meanwhile, I follow the football herd to the stadium.

It's pouring with rain. Inside the ground, there seems to be few stewards. The facilities are limited and run down. In the stadium, the away supporters are in banked seating behind the goal, in an area named after John Atyeo. 'Big John' was an English international forward, who played for City 597 times in the 50s, and later went on to be an inspiring teacher. I remember him as a child, a large, imposing figure with a Brylcreem-style quiff, who played in the national team alongside our own Johnny Haynes. We're behind the goal. There's high tiered, red banked seating around the ground, with The Lansdown Stand, named after City's majority shareholder, to our right. The development of the stadium seems an impressive investment. Around the side of the pitch, moving adverts constantly fade in and out. By the touchline, a group of schoolchildren are waving flags and what sounds like a west country ditty is blaring out of the loudspeakers. A pack of young Fulham supporters, including several track suited women, are at the back of the stand preparing to chant. One of them, a jaunty young lad with a Fulham cap, is testing the metal wall for possible resonance.

Fulham start well and get their passing game going. The fans are in good voice with 'WHEN THE WHITES GO MARCHIN' IN!' Tom Cairney shooting just over the bar cues in 'WE ARE FULHAM, SUPER FULHAM!..' This is followed by the ritual denigration of the Chelsea captain's mother, who was arrested and cautioned for shoplifting: 'JOHN TERRY. YOUR MOTHER'S A THIEF!' The City crowd seem quiet and apprehensive. The Fulham chorus agree. 'YOUR SUPPORT IS, YOUR SUPPORT IS, YOUR SUPPORT IS FUCKIN' SHIT, YOUR SUPPORT IS. FUCKIN' SHIT!' they chant. After sixteen minutes, Fulham assert their authority on the game. Johansen finds Cairney, whose delightful defence splitting pass puts in Piazon one on one with the keeper. The Brazilian finishes coolly. 0-1 to the Whites! The Fulham choir celebrate with a rendering of 'CRAVEN COTTAGE BY THE RIVER! followed by the perennial, 'CAN'T TAKE MY EYES OFF YOU! However, City's threat hasn't gone away and after twenty two minutes, Cotterill, who is becoming influential, puts in a great cross and the tall Bosnian Durić's header flies over the bar. A let off for the Whites. Coming up to twenty six minutes, Kebano is sent away by another great pass by Tom Cairney.

He scores but is ruled to be offside. 'OH, NEESKINS KEBANO!' the Fulham fans cry, followed by their taunting of City with 'YOU'RE JUST A SHIT BRISTOL ROVERS!' Maybe we're lampooning them too soon as City force Button to tip a shot over the bar and from another dangerous cross, Taylor hits the post. However, Fulham finish the half strongly and from the left of the box, Ayité's shot goes marginally wide. 'OH, FLOYD AYITEE!' scream the faithful. The City fans are now quiet. The travelling support agree. 'IS THIS A LIBRARY?' they ask. A good end to the half but we need to complete the job.

At half time, those kids are walking around the side of the pitch waving their flags, I'm not sure what they're celebrating. A brawny Fulham fan behind me, wearing a grey scarf and blue woolly hat is wary:

'We've got to be careful.'

'Still so far so good.'

'Yes but they've hit the post and missed a sitter.'

When the second half starts, Fulham continue to dominate and when Bristol fail to clear the ball, Ayité manages to find Cairney to the left of the box. Tom then curls the ball brilliantly into the top right hand corner. 2-0 to the Whites. The fans respond with loud cheers and 'OH TOM CAIRNEY. HE MAKES ME HAPPY!..' Fulham's passing is controlling the pace of the game. It's frustrating City and Cairney seems to be the focus of their ire as he's repeatedly fouled. With about half an hour to go, he's hacked particularly viciously and just about manages to restrain himself from getting into a scuffle. Fulham retain control and 'WHO ARE YER? reverberates around the ground. However, City respond and when Taylor gets one on one with Button, thankfully the Fulham keeper, stands tall and the ball bounces safely off him.

With fifteen minutes to go, Fulham are playing deeper, protecting their lead and breaking on the counter. 'SLAVISA'S BLACK AND WHITE ARMY' triumphantly rings out from the stand. Button makes another decent save from a shot by Reid, pouncing quickly on the rebound. Fredericks is finding it hard to get away from his marker but when he does break free, he puts in a great cross for McDonald, who heads narrowly heads over the bar. 'AND

IT'S SUPER FULHAM! SUPER FULHAM FC! WE'RE BY FAR THE GREATEST TEAM, THE WORLD HAS EVER SEEN!' chant the fans euphorically. The game is drawing to a close, Fulham are slowing it down during the six minutes of injury time. 'CHEERIO! CHEERIO!' sing the fans to the beleaguered City crowd. Then, our American centre back has his name chanted for a good interception. 'R-E-A-M!' they cry in an elongated chant. The whistle blows. The fans cheer. Slowly the team comes towards to the away end. and clap us for our support. Johansen takes off his shirt, revealing his tattooed arms, and throws it to the fans. Overall a good performance. That's three wins on the bounce.

I make my way to the coach. It's pouring with rain and I can't see a thing! The Fulham contingent are mainly going to the left. I follow them, hoping I find somebody I recognise. Ah, yes, there's Military Man. The lighting is sparse, and the streets dingy as I follow Military Man over the main road. Then I get reassured by discovering the landmark Ecobat building. We make our way to the muddy car park. The driver with the white spiked hair is standing imperiously at the top of the coach's steps, back lit like a film noir gangster. I settle into my seat next to Mr Borehamwood.

The inquest starts before I sit down. 'Martin made good runs but nobody gave him the ball,' says an emotional, middle aged fair haired man, before he even sits down. I think he's a member of 'The Committee'. Doug, opposite me, is wary of being too optimistic. 'They could have had two goals,' he says forlornly. 'It'll be different when we play against Warnock's lot at Cardiff on Saturday.' I tell him that what I like is that we have clarity of purpose and keep playing to our game plan, whatever happens. He's not entirely convinced so I remind him that we've just won two nil. Doug still hopes we can up our game on Saturday against tougher, more robust opposition, who have one of the best records in the division since the new year. We'll see. In the meantime, just as we're settling down to leave, our driver makes yet another speech and forcibly reminds everybody that we're in a non-smoking vehicle. Apparently, somebody was caught having a fag in the other coach.

After Brian with the woolly hat has collected money for the driver, the journey back is quiet. Fans are tired and want to check other results. Consequently, they bury themselves in their smartphones, papers and books. In contrast, I have a fraternal discussion with Mr Borehamwood, who is concerned that his mobile battery is running out and he won't be able to contact his wife.

'If it does, you can use mine,' I volunteer.

'Oh, thanks,' he replies.

Apparently his wife is going to pick him up at 12.30 am.

'You're a lucky man.'

'Yes, most of my friends tell me their wives wouldn't dream of doing such a thing.'

'You don't train her do you?' I enquire ironically.

'Oh no. It's just a matter of give and take.'

It's slow getting out of Bristol but not the crawl that we experienced coming. When we finally make our way out of the town, the driver tries to cross a bridge that doesn't take coaches, so we reverse and go by another more circuitous route. As we gather momentum, The Ulsterman and 'The Northerner' behind me, are discussing property and the merits of housing associations. Apparently, The Ulsterman lives in a housing cooperative in the East End. 'The Northerner' seems interested in how it works.

Then suddenly the shrill tones of Mr Borehamwood's mobile ring out. It's the wife.

'Oh thank you, darling. Yes, that's fine. Yes. See you there then.'

'So you're fixed now are you?'

'Yes, she's going to meet me at Craven Cottage.'

Once we get on the M4, it's a quick drive at this time of night. It's not long before Barbara makes an announcement.

'We're coming up to Hammersmith,' she announces to the travelling throng. Please get ready if you're leaving.'

I say goodbye to Mr Borehamwood.

'Very good to meet you.'

'And you.'

'You've made me look at Borehamwood in a whole new light.'

The coach stops at Hammersmith Broadway. Several people disembark. I'm following The Woman Behind, who's draped in a union jack flag. I press the button at the traffic lights.

'No those lights don't respond. They're just for traffic. I know because I've lived here for years.'

'Ok, thanks.'

The Woman Behind crosses the road in direction of St Paul's Church and recedes into the distance.

I go towards the bus station. On the pavement, I meet long haired Doug.

'See you Doug.'

'Bye,' he replies as he struggles to get his bag over his shoulder.

I make my way to get a 220 to Mira's flat in Wood Lane. A long night but a good win. We're seventh, six points off the play offs with a game in hand.

Listening to Gentleman Jim.

There's good news, Slaviša Jokanović has signed a new two year contract. After years of turmoil, this will hopefully give the club some stability. Elsewhere, Claudio Ranieri has been sacked as Leicester manager after winning the Premiership last season and the Tories are the first government to win a by-election since 1982.

I'm not going to the Cardiff game. It's a long trip and I haven't yet recovered from going to Bristol. Championship games come so thick and fast that it's difficult keeping up with it all. However, I've now subscribed to Fulham TV and this gives me an opportunity to hear Gentleman Jim and his sidekick Jamie do the commentary.

First I devour my lunch, a tasty mackerel, before sitting down to listen to the commentary. Unfortunately, I'm having difficulty finding it. In the meantime, I look at the BBC website on my smartphone. I discover that Martin isn't in the squad. Funnily enough, at one stage in the Bristol game, Slaviša was pointing at him quite vehemently, which was followed by Martin spitting on the ground, which you could interpret one way or another. Certainly, a lot of supporters think his heart is with Derby. Let him 'hoover the dug out' was one comment. Actually, I don't think he's even available to administer such menial tasks, as he hasn't travelled.

There are three changes to the Fulham side from the last time out: Fredericks for Odoi, Malone for Sessegnon and Aluko for Kebano. It seems Cardiff are starting strongly. Hoillet is having some joy down their left hand side and Button is busy making saves from both the Cardiff winger and Harris. Then after 17 minutes, this time courtesy of Radio 5, I hear that we've scored! We've been under the cosh, then on the break, Ayité wins the ball, passes to Cairney, who plays in Johansen, who then goes on a run, shoots and scores. A brilliant breakaway goal. Now, we've got something to preserve.

I'm still cursing Fulham FC TV, for not making it clearer where Gentleman Jim and his commentary reside. Or am I just being stupid? Anyway, my frustration is tempered by us scoring. Now I read that Piazon has gone off injured after getting a yellow card. I hope it's not serious, as we need him in the run in. Anyway, Kebano is now on in his place. I give up on Gentleman Jim for a moment and make a cup of tea. Then I discover on Sky that Cardiff have equalised. It's 1-1. Apparently, Johansen lost the ball in our defensive half and their big, strapping striker, Kenneth Zohore took advantage and tucked the ball away. Oh well, still plenty to play for.

I'm walking around the flat like a restless child. Come on Fulham! It sounds as if the game is very open and that Zohore is giving our centre backs problems. He's Drogba's cousin and has a similar physique. A Danish national, he seems to have had a chequered career, undermined by ill discipline but he appears to be firing on all cylinders today. Thankfully, Button is playing well and is making some smart saves. It seems to be all action in this game. McDonald has a header stopped on the line and for Cardiff, Harris has a shot marginally wide. Then Aluko mishits the ball after Kebano plays him in-if only Sone could shoot!-and as the first half ends, Johansen fires just wide of the post.

During the interval, I finally get Gentleman Jim on air. Apparently, it's done through the Match Play Centre. Surely that could be signposted more clearly? Getting that moan out of the way, I'm now ready to hear how the two boys do. Jim is setting the scene. He's reminds us of the team changes and the problems we're having with the mighty Zohore. He's not happy with one of the assistant referees-'someone should have a word with the fella over the far side, who doesn't understand offside.' Apparently, it's teaming with rain in The Principality as Floyd Ayitè shoots over the bar, when played in by Kebano. Jamie thinks that Floyd hasn't 'hit his straps' after coming back from the Africans Nations Cup.

The rain continues. The two boys hoped that it would quicken the pitch but now it's so insistent, there's a danger that the ball will stick. After, Noone shoots over the bar, Zohore turns Ream, leaves him for dead, and shoots off the side of his boot into the net. 2-1 to the Bluebirds. The boys are impressed by this goal and Zohore is assessed as 'one of the best strikers they've seen in the Championship'. Jim's then critical of midfielder Ralls' tackling. 'He kicked Floyd'. Ayitè is taken off limping and replaced by Cyriac. According to Jim, we're struggling to find a way back. Then suddenly, Tom Cairney plays Kebano in on goal and he scores. 2-2.

'Kebano certainly knows where the goal is' states Jim, after the Congolese international strikes again for Fulham. Mind you, they're not sure if the ball came off a Cardiff player. Still, they're giving it to him. Anyway, it's in and that's all that matters. Later, Jim describes Warnock fuming about a Kalas foul- 'he should know better' says Gentleman J of the irascible, much travelled Cardiff manager. A free header is then missed by Morrison, and Aluko thinks he should have had a penalty, when felled by ex-Fulham defender, Jazz Richards, but Jim and Jamie aren't protesting excessively. In the latter stages of the game, Cardiff substitute John hits the post, Aluko brings a save from McGregor and in the final minutes, Johansen fires wide after a great run by Sone Aluko.

'A well deserved point' concludes Gentleman Jim. He ends up quoting Dickens from 'A Tale Of Two Cities'. 'It was the best of times, it was the worst of times.' Jim thinks that they were the better side in the first half and we struggled. We fought hard to get back into it and equalised, although Jim tells us that the ball 'took an eternity to go into the net'. However, 'in the last half hour we were the better side'. Despite their bias, Jim and Jamie are full of praise for Cardiff's Zohore and admired the two goals he scored-one with his left foot, the other with his right. A skilful, powerful striker. 'He's such a unit!' exclaims Jim. In the end for Fulham, it's four points out of six on the road from the last two games. The two lads think it's a good return and I agree. After today's results, we're seventh, five points behind Sheffield Wednesday, with a game in hand. So there's everything to play for. The effervescent Gentleman Jim signs off by advertising the 'kids for a quid 'next home game against Preston and a final, endearing 'God Bless!

Given that it's a commentary for Fulham fans, I found it refreshing. It was a change from some anodyne Radio 5 commentaries and the hysteria of Talksport. It informs supporters by giving a commentary that's different from those main broadcasters. Ok, there some rough edges but that's part of its charm and if you're a Fulham fan, there's some particular insights into both the game and the squad. So thumbs up to Gentleman Jim and Jamie from me.

Preston Come South

It's a mild, sunny London day. Since our last outing The Lords have defeated the Commons on a Brexit amendment and President Trump's Attorney General is being accused of lying at his confirmation hearing.

Inside the ground, I notice that behind me are a whole family of Scandinavians-Norwegians, I'd guess. The young Irishman, who sits behind me, has come to the game with his father, who's over from Ireland. He discovers that the Norwegians are in his seat. He tactfully explains the situation but the wife doesn't understand English and the husband, who's in the middle of the row, takes over. The result is that they evacuate and all five of them settle themselves in my row. Fulham can't fill the ground without relying on London visitors, so we inevitably become international. I then exchange pleasantries with the Irish contingent: 'How's Ireland?' 'Great,' comes the reply from the white bearded Dad.

Soon afterwards the game starts. Kebano, with a dramatic blonde-highlighted parting, and Martin have come in for the injured Ayité and Piazon, while Sessegnon has replaced Malone. In the opening minutes, the diminutive Neeskens looks lively. He fizzes in a great cross from the left but nobody is in the six yard box. Then the inevitable happens. After extolling the virtues of Button's form in away games to my Irish friends, he sends a throw straight out to the opposition in a dangerous position. 'Is he colour blind?' rails the Irish Dad.

Fulham are dominating with their passing game and Cairney has a good shot deflected, by an inadvertent hand, so there's no ardent appeal. Later, when Aluko is tackled too strongly just outside the box, the ref, Simon Hooper, gives nothing. The Irish Dad isn't happy. 'You're kiddin' me? You've got eyes haven't yer? And when play continues, without any foul being given, his response is a bewildered, 'Jaysus!' A few minutes later, Johansen sends Kebano down the left, he beats his man, delivers a superb ball back to Aluko, who drills the ball into the net. 1-0. Terrific! The chants ring out. 'SUPER FULHAM, SUPER FULHAM FC...' Full backs, Fredericks and Sessegnon, look to press home Fulham's advantage and their aggressive runs down the flanks inspire more chants. 'WHEN THE WHITES, OH WHEN THE WHITES GO MARCHIN' IN!...' Fulham continue attacking and Kebano and Kevin McDonald go close. 'The keeper was never going to see that,' says the Irish Dad frustrated by the Scotsman's shot not being on target. Preston fight back but following a corner, McGeady's effort is comfortably saved.

At half time, I talk to the Irish duo. The father went to see Ireland play Scotland in the rugby, the previous week. They lost.

'That was a surprise,' I suggest.

'Yes, it was. But it was still a great trip.'

'I hope it goes down to the final game against England at the Aviva.'

'The Aviva? Lansdowne Rd. You're talking to an ex-Trinity (College Dublin) man here.'

'Oh, really? My daughter is living near there.'

'She must have a few bob.' (Dublin 4 being a posh area).

'No, she's renting.'

'Then she must be getting fleeced!'

He laughs somewhat nervously and we revert to discussing the game against Leeds on Tuesday.

'It's a big one.'

'There'll be a hell of an atmosphere.'

'Still we better get this one done first.'

Indeed we must. The second half continues with Fulham attacking. Seven minutes into the half, Fredericks, who's made some searing athletic runs down the right, crosses to Martin, who peels away from his man, makes space and hits the ball firmly past keeper Maxwell. 2-0. In the Johnny Haynes, youths arise as one, pointing in the direction of the visiting Preston contingent. 'WHO ARE YER? WHO ARE YER?' they scream, intent on public humiliation. However, Preston are still showing a determination to get back into the game and eight minutes later McGeady, who's become more influential, plays in Barkhuizen, who gets behind Sessegnon (outmuscled defensively in this match) and tucks the ball in via the near post. 2-1. Game on. Preston now seem to be a yard quicker. The goal has lifted them and they think they can get something out of this game.

This is a dangerous part of the match. Surely we're not going to screw it up? With quarter of an hour to go, Preston find space for Robinson twenty yards out. Robinson shoots but thankfully miles over the bar. Was that the moment where Preston finally lost? Now we might find out as Aluko plays in Kebano and yes, Neeskens puts the ball through Maxwell's legs. 3-1. Thank God! Game over!. Neeskens (yes, he's named after the distinguished Dutch player), celebrates with an alarming double somersault. The game finishes, the crowd applaud, the players, or most of them, applaud back. The Cottage is buzzing. It's all set up for Tuesday night's match with Leeds, who are fourth. We're still seventh, five points off the play-offs, with a game in hand.

Outside the ground at The Wall, I'm greeted by a satisfied Alex, an animated baseball-capped Richard and his similarly clad mate, Pete.

'We really pressed. We were much better without the ball and with Martin there. He was a focal point, he kept their big men occupied,' says Richard'

'Pity about the goal,' says Alex

'Yes Sessegnon got caught there but he'll learn from that,' continues Richard.

'I got anxious when it was 2-1,' says a more cautious Pete.

'What do you expect? This is Fulham,' says Richard

Richard thought Martin held the ball up and found good positions.'

'He didn't win many headers,' says Pete

'I know but he put a shift in,' replies Richard

'Actually, we've also played well without him because we had more speed to shift the opposition's back line around,' I remind Richard.

'I know but Martin gives us the opportunity to play it longer,' insists The Oracle.

'We didn't play many long balls,' counters Pete

'But Martin gives us that option,' continues Richard.

167

After this lively discussion on the virtues and sins of our rebellious loanee striker, the two East Sussex residents depart for their train. Pete mentioning something about him winning something in a charity for cancer and Richard buying him a drink.

Alex and I walk sedately towards Fulham Palace Rd. As we make way for a disabled man in a wheelchair to pass us, I ask Alex what he thinks of our chances.

'Well, we're in the mix for the play-offs,' he replies. 'It's important we won today. That's Preston out of it, I think. If we could just cut out the individual errors. We've got to deal with so many games. For instance, I think he'll bring back Malone against Leeds, for his experience.'

'I hope Fredericks will keep his cool as it'll be a bit of a cauldron out there.'

'Yes, it'll be an intense atmosphere. There'll be some tackles flying in, but they're a footballing side. They're managed by Garry Monk, after all, but I don't think it'll be 0-0.'

'Is that a prediction?'

'I just don't think Jokanović is that interested in clean sheets. He believes with our football that the chances will come and we'll score more goals.'

'We'll just have to see.'

'All right mate, see you Tuesday.'

Alex has his back to a procession of vehicles on Fulham Palace Road.

'Watch the traffic!' I cry as he's about to turn into the road amidst the departing throng.

Stopping The Leeds Invasion

I'm looking forward to this one. Maybe because there's something challenging and villainous about Leeds. Walking to the ground, I see an elderly Fulham FC supporter wearing the club's cap with our crudely designed badge, which looks more like something out of Mel Brooks' 'The Producers', his hilarious spoof on Nazi Germany, than belonging to a football club. The supporter looks bereft as if waiting for a friend and peers forlornly down Lochaline Street. Unfortunately nobody seems to be appearing out of the dark night air. At Colwith Rd, the rubbish is piled on the pavements in black plastic bags. By the Thames, I can see a rowing boat with flickering blue lights parked in the middle of the river. Eventually the boat moves and glides over the water, driven by shadowy, dark figures. Nearer the Cottage, across the river, a batten of five white lights stare menacingly through the trees.

When I approach the ground I hear the animated sounds of the crowd. A group of cyclists in diverse forms of coloured gear, looking like a group that have just finished a charity ride, park their bicycles in nearby River Gardens. While I join the long queue for a programme in Stevenage Rd, I hear the voice of a Leeds supporter berating his mate with his salty Yorkshire tones: 'shut your fuckin' mouth, give us a fuckin' break.' In front of me, a hefty Fulham fan is telling his ginger haired mate. 'This Leeds fan said he was going to smash us. He said they were bringing 8,000. I told him You can bring 8,000 but we'll still play you off the park. Like we did at your place.'

He then tells me of the team changes.

'No Wood tonight.'

That's good, their leading scorer is injured. He then goes on to justify how well Fulham are playing.' We should have got something at Brighton, we should have won against QPR and Derby.'

I tell him there's a lot of 'shoulds' there.

Eventually I get my programme. The Scottish lady is off tonight and has been replaced by a young woman wearing an elegant black hijab.

On my way to the Johnny Haynes stand, I'm confronted by a cyclist weaving his way through the crowd. He's wearing a light on his head as if he's a miner searching for coal.

'Big one tonight,' I remind the laid back lad in the orange bib at the turnstile.

'Yeah,' he replies casually and smiles. For all I know, he might support Chelsea.

In the toilet, a young bloke is rapping on, 'I said you bitch, I didn't even see her!' 'He's drunk,' explains one of his mates. I concentrate on my own ablutions, only to discover that the soap machine doesn't work. One of its sides has been broken and it looks positively skeletal.

At the entrance to the stand, a young bewildered man is ushering people to their seats.

'I hope I'll be happy at the end of this,' I tell him.

'I hope so,' he says with a nervous smile on his face.

The Leeds end is packed. The young Irishman isn't here as usual, in the seat behind me. Maybe he got stuck at work. Ivan, the announcer, is doing the traditional contrasting build up of the teams. Fulham make one change, the more experienced Malone coming in for the talented Sessegnon. Meanwhile, Billy The Badger is getting the crowd going, punching the air in front of the Putney End.

After the ritual formalities the game starts. 'WE ALL LOVE LEEDS! WE ALL LOVE LEEDS!' is drowned out by Fulham fans whacking clappers on their seats. Leeds are getting off to a good start, moving the ball crisply and showing a rigorous physicality. In contrast, Fulham seem hesitant. The fans sense their nervousness and try to encourage them by chanting the plaintive, 'COME ON FULHAM! COME ON FULHAM!' After five minutes, calamity strikes. From a Bartley free kick, Ream slices the ball out of Button's reach into the net. 0-1. There was a lack of communication there. Either Button should have called or Ream should have whacked the ball out of play. The fanatical Leeds fans don't care. 'OH LEEDS AWAY!' they sing. Now Fulham are under pressure. 'CHAMPIONS! WE ARE THE CHAMPIONS!' screech the visiting supporters. The ground is nearly full, there seems to be only a few spare seats in The Riverside Stand, opposite me.

After twenty minutes, Fulham get their game together and begin to dominate the ball. Martin's header goes wide and the lively Kebano shoots against the cross bar. But wait hold on, wasn't that over the line? The game continues and despite a muted protest, Fulham continue to press. Malone's shot is comfortably saved by Green and when he's put through by Cairney, he's off target. Although we're now playing really well and imposing our game, Leeds counter quickly on the break, get past our back line and oh, help, Pedraza gets one on one with Button. He shoots and thankfully the Fulham keeper saves. He should have buried that. 'OH LEEDS AWAY!' reiterate the fanatical United faithful. Leeds remain resilient and it's still 0-1 at half time.

During the interval, I talk to the supporter next to me, who's had one eye on his mobile throughout the game. He's in his late twenties, fair haired, with a dark blue jacket and white trainers. He seems to be a friend of the two ladies in the seats opposite me, on the other side of the aisle.

'The ball was over the line,' the young man asserts.

'How do you know?'

'Sky are saying so. There should be technology in this league.'

I've a feeling that it's coming in next season but that's no good to us now.

'Leeds have got what they came for. They nicked one and then defended. Mind you, they've defended well.'

The second half begins. There's a foul on Cairney and then a more vicious one on McDonald. Fulham fans respond with an inevitable, 'YOU DIRTY NORTHERN BASTARDS!' Fulham continue to play freely but are struggling to open up Leeds. Then ten minutes after the break, Kebano switches play, finds Cairney who puts in a low cross but no Fulham player is there to meet it. Oh for that natural striker! Now, that man, Neeskens, is at it again. This time down the left, he beats his man and shoots but can't quite get the angle right and hits the side netting. The game is getting increasingly intense. The 7,000 (not 8,000!) Leeds fans try to rally their team. Once more we hear, 'WE ALL LOVE LEEDS!' With their somewhat turbulent history that isn't exactly the verb that springs to mind.

There are claims for a foul on Aluko. 'CHEAT! CHEAT!' rings around the ground.

We're into the last twenty minutes now. After a pulsating run down the right by Fredericks leads to nothing, Leeds counter on the break. A strong Barrow run plays in Pedraza. He only has the keeper to beat, he must score but no- the gods are smiling on us, he hits the post. That was close!. Let's just hope Fulham can now get something out of this game. Fredericks and Cairney play in substitute Cyriac but he seems to caught on his heels and can't get his boot to the ball from five yards out. On no! That was a genuine chance. In the eightieth minute, Barrow gets a yellow card for fouling the Fulham striker with an overzealous tackle. From the resulting Johansen free kick, Green saves at full stretch. 'It's just not going to happen,' says the young fair haired man gloomily.

Time is indeed running out. 'Come on Fulham! In the eighty ninth minute substitute Parker is taken out, not for the first time, on this occasion by Phillips That's his second yellow, so he's off. Leeds are now down to ten men. 'CHEAT! CHEAT!' the crowd scream feverishly as the midfielder trundles off towards the Cottage. Time's running out as Johansen crosses and Cyriac with a magnificent leap heads the ball goalwards, only for Green to make a great save, diving to his left. We're now in injury time. It's still all Fulham as an Aluko shot flashes wide. We're now down to the last minute. Sone Aluko is weaving down the right. He attracts two defenders, Cairney finds space and Sone passes to him. Tom wraps his left foot round the ball and his shot curls into the top left hand corner, leaving keeper Green helpless.

The Cottage erupts. The noise is deafening. Cairney charges over the barrier at the Hammersmith End, into the crowd. He's followed by the whole team, with Fredericks standing aloft raising his hand in triumph like a proud Emperor acknowledging the adoring multitude. The Leeds fans look stunned and desolate. 'WHO ARE YER? WHO ARE YER?' scream the two women opposite me, who are now standing up, aggressively pointing to the Leeds fans in the Putney End. Seemingly placid folk have now turned into vengeful harpies. This is followed by 'UP YOURS!' accompanied by an expansive 'v' sign, from an excited youth behind them. Meanwhile, the whistle has blown, Tom Cairney has been given a yellow card for the celebration, which seems irrelevant.

'We had a great view of that goal,' says the young fella next to me. He's right, as even though the drama was at the opposite side of the ground, the angle was perfect to partake in the euphoria at the Hammersmith End. The team troop out to thunderous applause. You would have thought we'd won five-nil not gained a draw. However, the fans are right. It's kept our chances of a play-off place alive. After tonight's results, we're five points behind sixth place, with a game in hand. We're still in the mix.

I congregate at The Wall.

Alex is sporting a dark green, woolly hat. I'm wearing my New York Yankees baseball cap.

'Hi Roly. That was the least we deserved.'

'Kebano's shot was in apparently.'

'No technology makes it difficult for the ref,' says Alex.

Richard in Fulham FC woolly headgear and Pete, in a dark blue beanie and jacket, join us.

'We gave them a goal,' says Alex.

'I don't know what coaching manual Ream got that from,' fulminates The Oracle.

'I've just met a guy who's saying 'if only we didn't have Ream and Martin. That spoilt it for me. Is that all he can say after that performance? denunciates Pete, who then reflects-'I wonder what they're thinking? Leeds?'

'We got a point away, we could have had three,' suggests Richard. 'They'll think, we won't meet a better footballing side in the last twelve games. After all, we battered them.'

'Although they defended very well,' I remind everybody.

Richard agrees. 'Yes. Particularly when they went deeper in the second half, it got difficult.'

'In fact, they had the best clear cut chances,' I continue.

'But we were the better side,' counters Richard.

There is then a discussion about the individual errors players have made this season.

'We play high risk football, so mistakes are going to be made but overall our attacking strategy is paying off and outweighs the occasional calamity,' I conclude.

We are then approached by two people from Fulham 1879 Fan TV, one a cameraman with a piercing white beam of light. They ask for an interview and we duly oblige.

Richard and Pete then depart for their train and disappear into the pitch black night

As Alex and I walk towards Fulham Palace Rd, we discuss the challenge of Newcastle on Saturday

'If we can start well, make no mistakes and get our game going, we've got a good chance, I optimistically proclaim.

'Yes,' says Alex, 'they've lost to several clubs at home-like Wednesday, and Brentford. They're stronger away, where they've won thirteen games. So yes, there's a chance'.

'We still can make it.'

'Let's hope so. See you at Blackburn.'

'Blackburn?'

'Tuesday night.'

'Another one. I forgot. It's never-ending. Yes, I'll be there.'

Toon on The Net

I decided to listen to Gentleman Jim again for the Newcastle game. I resisted travelling so far to have a bird's eye view. However, that hasn't dampened my enthusiasm. I really believe that Fulham can beat anyone the way they're playing at the moment. So after having a lunch of liver, carrots and spuds and while my partner Mira is on the phone sorting out some computer problems, I settle down to listen to the dulcet tones of Gentleman Jim and his cohort Jamie. It's a fine spring day and the forecast is that it's going to be cool in the north east, so it should be a good day for football.

Gentleman Jim tells us that there are two changes: Odoi for Fredericks and Sessegnon for Martin. The latter is a particularly interesting one. It probably means that young Ryan is going to play further forward, which I think is his more natural position. Maybe, he's going to develop similarly to Gareth Bale by starting in a more defensive position and moving to a more offensive one. Apparently, two thousand supporters have travelled to the north east. That's a terrific response. We're unbeaten in six games but Newcastle are twenty points ahead of us. Jim tells us that Gayle is back for Newcastle in place of Murphy and that they'll be playing 4-2-3-1. We need to quieten the crowd by imposing our passing game early on. If we can do that, we can start making their supporters feel anxious.

In fact, we're getting more of the ball in the opening stages and Ream and Button, our two most criticised players, make a good start. Jamie is telling us we need to close Shelvey down as he's playing like an American quarter back, looking to dictate the play. Apparently, there's a lot of movement up front, with Kebano and Aluko interchanging positions, which is pulling the Newcastle defence around. Then after fifteen minutes, Johansen finds Malone on the left, who passes to Cairney, Tom shoots and the ball dips in under the bar. 0-1. Brilliant! Jim goes into ecstatic orbit. 'COME ON FULHAM!' resonates across the airwaves. We continue to dominate the game. Aluko is played in by Cairney but shoots straight at the keeper and Kebano goes very close with a deflected shot that narrowly passes the post. Newcastle counter but Clark's header from Anita's cross is pushed over the bar by a commanding Button. Then Jim and Jamie are outraged by Shelvey stepping on Tom Cairney and not getting a card. 'That was a yellow,' cries Jim. It's raining heavily as the half ends, Fulham are leading and our commentators are enthusiastic about the team's performance, while remaining cautious of a Toon offensive in the second half.

Mira is now relaxing after having washed her hair. She's watching The Red Shoes on BBC 2, detached from my excitement at Fulham's progress on Tyneside. I depart to the kitchen and get a cuppa. I then pop in to the bedroom, where I'm entranced by Moira Shearer's stylish dancing in the film but tear myself away and get back to the game. Can Fulham capitalise on their impressive first half? Well according to Jim and Jamie, the answer is yes. Fulham continue to attack and when Johansen goes on a run, his cross isn't cut out and Aluko back heels the ball to Ryan Sesssegnon, who calmly shoots past keeper Darlow. Fantastic. 0-2. Brilliant. Now we've put daylight between ourselves and those Magpies!

Newcastle respond, roused by their passionate, partisan crowd. Ritchie's cross is met by Gayle's header but Button pushes it over the bar. Newcastle are now taking more risks by pushing forward to get back into the game and when, on approaching the hour mark, an attack breaks down, Aluko charges forward with pace, draws their defence, passes to Sessegnon, who calmly slots the ball into the net. 0-3. Dreamland! Young Ryan is now on a hat trick.

I rush into the bedroom shout 'yes!' and Mira laughs at my expansive enthusiasm. I tell her that a sixteen year old is on a hat trick against the league leaders away from home. She looks bemused as I go back to my study to continue listening to the broadcast. 'That's another few million on Ryan's transfer fee,' says Jim. What is extraordinary about Sessegnon is the way he's so calm for one so young. He seems to have a great temperament as well as considerable ability.

The two commentators tell us that he's been working up and down the pitch tirelessly. Of course, you can never fully predict how a young player develops but this one shows every sign of going right to the top. Jim says that 'Benitez looks as sick as a pig,' at least it's not a parrot. However, I hear that Newcastle are becoming more dangerous with two (sub Murphy and Gayle) up front. McDonald gets a yellow card for a bad foul on Murphy, and then with about quarter of an hour to go, Murphy turns the Fulham defence and scores. 1-3. Don't screw up Fulham! 'That was soft,' says Jim. A few minutes later, Shelvey takes Cairney out. Jamie is indignant. 'It should be a red. He's been booked earlier. The ref bottled it.' Jamie is also worried that Fulham are dropping too deep. He thinks there are some tired legs out there and that with seven minutes to go, it's time for some substitutions. In fact, Toon substitute Gouffran then manages to get one on one with Button but the Fulham keeper saves well. Newcastle also continue to profit from diagonal balls to Murphy, who's good at pulling off into a wide area.

Now Jim can lip read Kevin McDonald saying 'fresh legs' to the bench. In fact, soon afterwards, Fredericks comes on for Kebano, followed a few minutes later by Cyriac replacing Aluko. We seem to have ridden out the storm and Dummett, the only Geordie in the Newcastle side, gets booked for a foul on the much targeted Tom Cairney. We're now in injury time, and when Malone sends over a cross and Sessegnon is bundled over, a penalty is given. Is Ryan going to take it to get his hat trick? It looks as if he might. Then it's clear that Slaviša wants Ream to take responsibility, probably as planned. He comes up and misses, the ball going wide of the right hand post. That's ten penalties this season and we've missed eight of them! We see the game out. Pity about the penalty but still, a memorable win.

Jim sums up, praising the team for a positive performance. However, he's frustrated like us all by another penalty miss. Also, 'if we'd taken more chances and been given the 'goal' against Leeds, we'd probably already be in the top six, ahead of Sheffield Wednesday, with a game in hand. But 'football's always about ifs, buts and maybes,' says Jim philosophically. He just finds it galling that in this day and age, we can't confirm whether a ball is over the line or not. However, he think it's really good the way the team have bought into the manager's philosophy. He hopes that Reading and Wednesday can have a dip in form during the run-in. 'No one will want to play us,' adds Jamie. Jim hopes we can do the business before the last game against Wednesday away and that we can take today's form into the next game at the Cottage. 'We don't want any feeling of after the Lord Mayor's Show.' They end up talking about the remarkable Ryan Sessegnon. 'What a player he's turned out to be.' With the rain pouring down in Geordieland, Jim says goodbye. There's a spring in my step. We're two points behind Wednesday in sixth place, with a game in hand. A play-off place is on!

Rovers Return

It's the following Tuesday Nicola Sturgeon, the Scottish First Minister, has announced she wants another referendum on independence and Fulham are about to play their game in hand, which could put them in the play-off spot.

When I get to my seat in the Johnny Haynes Stand, I'm joined by the Irishman and his friend.

'I'm Patrick,' says his mate, a dark haired young man with a beard. He has a Celtic air.

'Are you of Irish stock as well?' I ask.

'Yes, indeed.'

'So how was Newcastle?' I ask the Irishman.

'Great. We played very well.'

'I just couldn't bear going up those fourteen flights.'

'There is a lift.'

'I hate lifts.'

'We took 1,200.' (So maybe Gentleman Jim exaggerated?).

'Very good. Many supporters on the train?'

'A few.'

'When did you arrive?'

'About an hour before the game.'

'And you left?'

'No. we stayed up.'

'I know. A great place to get pissed!'

They both laugh knowingly.

I continue.

'Your Dad must be scared shitless about the rugby on Saturday, after another English victory this weekend!'

'He couldn't get a ticket. His mates are going though.'

'Should be good. I wouldn't put it past Ireland to stop England's run.'

I then add

'Where were you for Leeds?'

'I'm a teacher and it was a parents evening. I just couldn't get away.'

'It was a good game.'

'I know. I was gutted.'

We settle down. The players come out. The game starts. There's only one change to the Fulham team. Fredericks comes in for Odoi at right back, which is a more offensive option. Fulham are playing towards the Putney End, where there are a substantial amount of Rovers supporters, considering it's a long trek in the middle of the week. Fulham are attacking and keeping possession but our neat passing isn't creating sufficient openings. We're overplaying and not taking enough shooting opportunities. After a foul near the box, Patrick reflects, 'we don't want a penalty, as we'll miss!' The game started with roaring support for Fulham but as it progresses it gets quieter. Eventually, Fulham's dominance pays: Cairney finds Johansen on the left, he crosses and Sone Aluko meets it first time and the ball flies into the net. 1-0. 'WE ARE, WE ARE, WE ARE THE FULHAM BOYS!' echoes around the ground. Did I also hear a song about us going to Wembley? I don't think we should count our chickens.

It's half time. The two Irish lads are discussing mortgages and house prices. Disabled fans are on the pitch taking part in a penalty shoot out. Earlier, several of them had a selfie with some players-a nice touch. When the disabled supporters leave the pitch, they're given a thunderous ovation, as they wave to the Hammersmith End. As the game is about to restart, the two Irish lads stop discussing the cost of property renovation and turn their attention to the Lilywhites.

A few minutes into the half, Fredericks is booked for scything down Conway. The ensuing free kick from Bennett goes narrowly wide. Blackburn seem to be playing with a greater intensity. Their newly appointed manager Tony Mowbray seems to have fired them up. They are well organised and our full backs are finding it hard to get up the pitch. With half an hour to go, substitute Lucas Joao, on loan from Sheffield Wednesday, seems to be causing us problems. He's big and skilful and is giving Rovers a better option in the air. Frustration is creeping into our game and McDonald is booked for fouling Conway. The referee, Andy Davies, who had the embarrassment in the first half of dropping his whistle, also books Lenihan for deliberate handball. Then the assistant referee puts up a flag so late for an obvious offside that Patrick accuses him of 'taking a nap.' The Blackburn forward surge continues and Fulham are beginning to look leggy. Maybe this game has come too quickly after their exertions at Newcastle on Saturday. The fans sense this and try to rouse them with 'WHEN THE WHITES GO MARCHIN' IN.'

With just over twenty minutes to go, Joao's free header from a Conway cross goes over the bar. The Portuguese striker should have scored there. Blackburn are certainly not looking like a side fighting relegation. Then Joao puts another header over the bar from a corner. They're getting closer. Wake up Fulham! The Whites do indeed respond, and when Sessegnon gets in to a good position, the crowd shout, 'shoot!'. Young Ryan duly obliges but his powerful effort is beaten out by keeper Steele. On seventy nine minutes, when Emnes, the Dutch striker, is put through into the area, he's fouled by Tomas Kalas. The penalty is converted by Conway, Button going the wrong way. 1-1. To be honest, it's been coming. Can Fulham find more energy and intensity to win this game? Fredericks thinks so and when he finally manages to get away from his marker, he bursts forward to the byline and puts in a low cross, which substitute Cyriac hits first time and brilliantly places inside the near post. 2-1 to Fulham. A celebratory 'WE ARE THE FULHAM BOYS!' resonates enthusiastically around the ground.

Still, Blackburn are working both sides of the pitch and putting in good crosses. These need to be cut out! When Button saves a shot from Joao, it feels like we've survived the worst. However, in the fourth minute of injury time, Blackburn come again and that man Joao is at the far post to bundle in a Williams cross. 2-2. We've blown it. The two Irish lads storm out. - 'It really pisses me off,' cries John, The Irishman. The Fulham players are spreadeagled on the pitch like defeated soldiers on a battlefield. There's an eerie silence. The crowd depart quickly. Disappointment fills the air. It's a draw that feels like a defeat. Still, we've now gone eight league games unbeaten and we're seventh, just one point behind the sixth play-off place.

Alex, fair haired and wearing a dark jacket and a grey scarf, greets me at The Wall.

'Shocking. That second half performance.'

'Yes, we lost momentum'

Richard approaches, grey haired and forlorn, with his open dark jacket displaying a club shirt. Pete, in his white baseball cap, follows.

'The first half wasn't bad but the second half was awful,' says Richard.

'They came at us in the second half. We couldn't find space.' says Pete.

'I think Blackburn deserved something,' I suggest.

'They could have won it,' declares The Oracle.

'Saturday's game was mentally draining. We were up against a team fighting for their lives and we didn't find answers to the problems they set us,' explains Alex.

'We were certainly tiring,' I suggest.

'Johansen was walking on jelly,' says Richard.

Pete then puts the matter into historical perspective:

'It's always the same with this club and I've been coming here longer than even this bloke (pointing to the grey haired Oracle). They build up expectation, only to let you down.'

'We're still on an unbeaten run and one point off the play-offs,' counters Richard.

At that moment, out of the darkness, come Fulham 1879 Fan TV, once more asking The Wall members for an interview.

'Well it gave my wife a laugh,' says Pete, commenting on the previous interview.

We agree and set forth our views for their You Tube audience. When we finish Pete asks the interviewer and the cameraman, 'what about image rights?'

They laugh, clarify their web address and we all go our separate ways.

As Alex and I make our way down Stevenage Rd we discuss the final goal.

'Could Button have come for that cross?' I ask.

'I'm not sure. I think it was in 'the corridor of uncertainty'. Perfect for that situation. Defenders not knowing whether to 'stick or twist'.'

'You know what, Alex. I think we play better on bigger pitches. It suits our game more. Like Newcastle's. That said, I think we're going to need to get more members of the squad involved. With such a turnover of games, we need some fresh legs.'

'Yes. We needed Parker's experience tonight.'

'I think he's injured. Anyway, it was good to see Cyriac step up. It was a finely taken goal.'

'Yes, it was. I felt a bit sorry for Martin though, as we couldn't give him the service.'

'Still all to play for. I fancy us away. I think it suits us, when teams come on to us.'

'Yes, it's easier for the opposition to squeeze the space at the Cottage.'

'It's going to the wire. And if we need the points against Wednesday in the final game, I fancy us. Also in the big spaces of Wembley!'

Alex laughs at my optimism.

'Let's hope so. I'll see you on Saturday, Roly.'

I go to get my bus. As I cross the road to the tube at Hammersmith Broadway, I discover that Vince and his dog have departed. There's just a solitary beggar in a grey hood, wrapped in a worn blanket.

Wolves at The Cottage

If we win today we'll go 6th into the play-off position. So it's another big one. Having witnessed the seesawing 4-4 draw at Molineux, it's best not to predict anything.

As I walk down Fulham Palace Road and come out of Frank Banfield Park, I am confronted by a notice securely fixed to a lamppost stating 'No Dog Fouling'. Given the way our players have been 'taken out' in the Championship, I don't think it's only dogs who do this. On Rainville Road, a young couple cycling side by side, hold hands as they ride. It's like a scene out of a continental film. The women is dressed in luminous white pullover. The man in an elegant brown jacket. Thankfully, there's no traffic and this attractive couple glide gracefully and carefree towards their romantic destination.

At the turnstiles I'm greeted by a cheery 'good afternoon' by an attendant in an orange bib and a navy blue woolly hat. 'I hope it is,' I reply. When I enter the stand, 80s pop is being played. Then Ivan the announcer goes through the teams, in the usual dramatic, fashion. There's only one change for the Whites. Ayité replaces Malone and Sessegnon plays in a deeper role at left back. The warm up is coming to an end. Stuart Gray, Fulham's first team coach, and Tim Flowers, the goalkeeping coach, saunter off with the players. It's good to have such experienced Englishmen on the Fulham staff. Although, Javier Pereira, our Assistant Coach, who was with Slaviša at Watford and Maccabi Tel Aviv, is probably more influential.

Six sprinklers are spurting forth to slicken up the surface. It's quite a drenching, so no wonder players sometimes lose their footing. After the saturation, track suited members of the ground staff come on to the pitch and replace divets with their pitchforks, like batsmen trying to make a cricket pitch firm. Then the clappers, which have been placed on the seats like attendant weapons of noise, are clattered against the nearest object. The substitutes come out first and Denis Odoi, our full back, waves at some of the crowd in the Riverside, who are displaying a banner saying K. S. C. Lokeren, the name of his previous club. Denis responds by giving them a friendly wave. Paul Lambert, enters in functional track suit, while Slaviša goes to the dug out in his usual smart black suit. The Serbian gets a terrific reception but doesn't acknowledge it until he arrives at the Riverside Stand, when he reciprocates with a raised handclap. He knows fans are fickle and he tends to keep a detached countenance, whether we win or lose.

Fulham start the game positively, imposing their passing game and Kebano's shot goes wide of the post. A genuine chance there. Wolves look organised. They're pressing our defence and looking to play on the counter by using long balls over our high defensive line. It's not long before Hélder Costa, the former Benfica player, gives us a warning. He gets into a good position about twenty yards out but his shot is comfortably saved by Button. Fulham aren't dominating this game as much as they usually do. They are controlling possession without making many clear cut chances and Wolves are finding attacking opportunities. A certain anxiety envelops the ground. The Fulham fans are less vocal, the clappers more sporadic. McDonald's header from a short corner goes over the bar and breaks the silence. The clappers respond accordingly. 'COME ON YOU WHITES!' is vigorously chanted.

The contest is fairly even but Fulham certainly aren't at their sharpest. Just over the hour mark, Fredericks is running back to the byline looking for the ball to go out for a goal kick at the Hammersmith End. Unfortunately, he's easily robbed by the persistent Hélder Costa, who squares the ball to Cavaleiro, who can't miss. 0-1. We've given them one there. Minutes later, stung by his error, Fredericks sprints forward on a strong run down the right but his cut back is easily gathered by Wolves keeper, Carl Ikeme, the Nigerian international.

One of the features of the opposition's tactics against Fulham is to stop Cairney, the creative inspiration behind Fulham's attacking play. Predictably, with six minutes to the break, Evans lunges dangerously at our playmaker and gets a deserved yellow card. The half ends with Sessegnon striding forward and after being tackled he ball falls kindly to Sone Aluko, who fires his shot too close to the keeper. Sone isn't having one of his best days and that missed opportunity was symptomatic of Fulham's indifferent first half performance.

At half time, I turn to John, the Irishman.

'You and your friend Patrick looked as if you were going on the piss after that late Blackburn goal.'

'Not exactly, but yes we did have a drink.'

'A missed opportunity. That game.'

'Exactly.'

'There'll be another one here if we don't watch out.'

John, looks rueful, expressing discontent with Fulham's display so far.

At half time, the young Fulham under 12s seem to be better at taking penalties than the first team. When the team's come out, it transpires that Slaviša has made a bold attacking substitution. Cyriac, a striker, is coming on for McDonald, a defensive midfielder. Wolves start the half with great intensity. They're pushing us back and three minutes after the restart, after a move down our left, the ball is played in to the unmarked Weimann, who taps it in at the near post. 0-2. That was ridiculously easy. Sometimes you get a sense that only a few players in the Fulham team can tackle. Given our rearranged set up, we're now going to have to outscore Wolves and at the moment this looks unlikely. Odoi then comes on for Fredericks and a few minutes later, he sets himself and brilliantly pinpoints his long range shot into the left hand corner. A brilliant substitution! Denis immediately runs back to his position, more interested in raising an arm to the fans from Lokeren in the Riverside, than any adulation from his team mates. 1-2. 'WE ARE THE FULHAM BOYS!' echoes around the Cottage. Game on.

Later, after Wolves break away far too easily down the right, Ryan Sessegnon is caught out of position, the impressive Costa gets to the byline, crosses and Edwards running in, taps it home. Too easy and terrible defending. 1-3. Game over? In this league, who knows? Ayitė, who has looked lively, considering he's been out for a few weeks, responds by making good contact with Odoi's cross and Ikeme makes a fortuitous save, more by instinct than judgement. As full time approaches, some Fulham fans depart early. The game fizzles out. and referee Chris Kavanagh blows his whistle. As I leave the stand, I'm given some crumb of comfort by the new Championship table displayed on the tv screen perched on the wall downstairs. We're still seventh, one point behind Sheffield Wednesday, with eight games to go.

'Schoolboy defending,' says an aggrieved Alex, approaching me at The Wall.

'Yes. We gave away the goals, rather than forcing Wolves to create them,' I suggest

'Our full backs had poor games.'

'Schoolboy defending,' reiterates a frustrated capless, grey haired Richard, joining us with his good mate Pete.

'We were just saying that,' says Alex

'Mind you, Ryan is a schoolboy! We needed Martin, somebody to hold it up,' continues The Oracle.

'They just wanted to lump it forward and we couldn't deal with it,' declares Pete.

'I'd call them long passes, purposefully trying to breach our high line, feeding their quick wingers,' says the author, attempting to retain a remnant of objectivity. 'Mind you,' I continue, 'we missed chances. Aluko scuffed that shot in the first half.'

'We tired towards the end. We looked leggy,' adds Richard.

'Mentally spent?,' suggests Alex

'Yes. Not as bad as Tuesday but I think we felt the pressure,' continues Richard.

'Maybe the international break's come at a good time for us,' suggests Alex.

'I think so. The players who go away can play their matches in a different environment. The others can recharge their batteries. Then when they all join up again, hopefully they'll be refreshed, ready to go again,' declares an ever optimistic Richard.

I then look to sum up the volatile nature of our predicament:

'Anyway. It's crazy league. Anything can happen. Look at Bristol City beating Huddersfield 4-0 last night!'

'And we beat them 5-0,' Pete reminds us.

On that note of hopeful unpredictability, we go our separate ways.

Visiting The Millers

Article 50 to leave the EU has been triggered, Spain are bringing up the subject of Gibralfor, Arsene Wenger's future at Arsenal is still being hotly debated and the international break is over. In fact, it's two weeks since the Wolves debacle so hopefully the team have been psychologically rebooted. I'm a bit knackered as I've only recently returned from a city break to Berlin and last night I was at the Theatre Royal Stratford East seeing my cousin's teenage daughter in a powerful play about the current 'Prevent' strategy.

Still, I'm up for going to Rotherham, and have an extra sweater, in case we encounter the Yorkshire cold. When I get in the coach and Barbara has taken my ticket, I notice that cardboard signs with 'Reserved' are again lying on several of the front seats. Probably for 'The Committee'. I notice Jim, the Tipperary Irishman and Doug, the long haired regular from the East End, are there. The coach is nearly full, so I'm lumbered with going to the back, always the noisiest part, although others would say it's merely the most lively. I end up in front of two students. One, slim, dark and tall in a grey sweater, the other with short fair hair in a dark blue one. Oh my god, it's the return of Straggly and Stocky! Opposite me is a young, heavy, bald bloke in a pink shirt, a blue track suit top, jeans and trainers. He's immersed in his smartphone and has heavy headphones around his ears. I don't think I'll be having any conversation with him. He's sitting next to a slightly gaunt, older gentleman, who's snuggled against the window and is reading a book entitled '1913'. The digital clock at the front of the coach is an hour behind. The clocks going forward on March 26th seems to have been blithely ignored.

As we make our way out of Hammersmith on to the M25, I can hear the students behind me indulging in a lot of macho chat. Our friend in the grey sweater, Straggly, seems to pepper all his sentences with 'street' talk, like a middle class boy trying to be 'hard':

'It was so good, the atmosphere was popping off. It was like I didn't give a shit and just drank. I wasn't there for the fight. I wish I'd been in the scrap. How the hell did none of you get chucked out?

...Will just felt like beating the shit out of anyone. The guy did nothing. It was only a little brush but it kicked off.'

Suddenly a coach full of Chinese tourists runs parallel to ours. A benign gentleman gives a dignified wave.

'That's my Dad!,' says Straggly.

Straggly is on a monologue jag, his flow only briefly interrupted by his mate Stocky's short, quiet, staccato replies. This time it's about his proposed Barcelona trip.

'I've got no money but I don't care about the price. Jamie got robbed out there. I better not get robbed-I'll sink my phone up. All I need is a table to drink on.'

Then he moves on to traduce one of his other mates.

'He's bought a Harley Davidson but he can't fuckin' drive!'

Ahead of me, further towards the front, there's an Asian guy reading The Guardian. Is he the deranged screamer at the Reading game? Jim, the Tipperary Irishman, is in the seat in front of me, ensconced in The Daily Telegraph and lower to my left, a genial looking man in an old Adidas Fulham shirt, is reading the Mirror. As we make our way up the M 1, Straggly is off again, interspersed with chants of 'RYAN SESSEGNON,' eulogising Fulham's teenager. He's now going on about his own football team.

'We scored in the ninety second minute to stay in the league.' Apparently, a bloke called Laurie is still pestering him to pay for the pitch-'listen, you still have a debt of four pounds ninety eight pence.'

'Oh fuck off, Laurie!' was Straggly's riposte.

Then he deviates to his court appearance, accused of drinking on the pitch.

'A four hundred and fifty pound fine. Fuck me, my mate was caught possessing drugs and got nothing! Still I was determined not to get banned. I got dressed for the part. Chinos, brown shoes, jacket. So I didn't look like a scumbag. Some guys go into the dock in track suits. I called the judge 'your honour' and talked respectfully. There was one magistrate, a fat geezer. I thought he wasn't going to let me off easily. Thankfully, I had all my good character references ready. It seemed to swing it and I didn't get banned. My mate got a fine as well. I think his parents helped him pay it but he's behind with the instalments.'

'Why's that? asks Stocky.

'I don't know but I think he does dodgy dealings, selling on the streets.'

We're now approaching Welcome Break, somewhere outside Derby. I the challenge the benign supporter behind me, who's wearing that Adidas Fulham shirt.

'Time for Fulham trivia. How many Fulham players have been inside?'

'Tony Finnigan? Ronnie Mauge?' volunteers Adidas Man.

'And Peter Storey. He lives in Spain now.'

'Oh does he?'

'Well there is a British criminal tradition there!'

We could have also added Elliot Omozusi, Ahmad Elrich, Nathan Ashton, John Pantsil and George Best to the list of Fulham jailbirds but Barbara now makes an announcement. We're going to have an hour's break at a nearby service station. Apparently we're somewhere near Derby. I go to a patio area at the rear of this complex. There, I eat my prepared meal like a miscreant child evicted for a misdemeanour. It's fairly chilly outside and amidst the pebbles, at the wooden table across from me, there's a buxom blonde lady in a thick, dark blue jacket. She's smoking heavily and is joined by a man in black, who immediately proceeds to read his newspaper. Eventually, they give each other a smile and the man departs, followed later by the lady herself, after she's finished her fag. On completing my rice and chicken, I return to the coach, where I engage in a conversation with one of the students. Not Straggly, the macho 'fuck' one but Stocky, his more taciturn friend. Apparently, his first game was Fulham v Hertha Berlin in 2002. He was three. Blimey that ages me. He's soon joined by Straggly, who asserts that there are 15,000 hard core Fulham fans. I tell him that I think that's a bit high.

'Do you thinks so?' says Straggly.

'West London has four different clubs: Fulham, Chelsea, QPR and Brentford. Apart from Chelsea, which is a big club, the rest have a relatively small hard core pool of supporters.'

'How many do we have then?'

'I'd say 10,000 at the most, probably less.'

We then get in to how we've missed chances and so many penalties. Eight out of ten, at the last count. The two lads think we could have been easily in a play-off position, if it hadn't been for such profligacy

'This could be a season of missed opportunities,' asserts Straggly. We're just preparing to leave, when Straggly, observing an old man with a walking stick moving towards one of the coaches, turns to his mate and asks:

'What would you prefer in later life-a wheelchair or a walking stick?'

'A walking stick,' replies Stocky placidly

'I can't imagine having a walking stick later in my life,' replies the eternally youthful Straggly.

As we continue our journey, Straggly continues yapping about one of their friends who keeps saying, 'oh no, I don't believe it!'. So when he loses his drink, he cries, 'I must have lost the vodka in the kitchen. Oh no, I don't believe it!' Or when he loses his mobile. 'Where's my phone? Oh no, I don't believe it!' Straggly then challenges his mate. 'If you could get in to prison for free would you come?' 'No,' says a quietly defiant Stocky.

We're now moving towards Rotherham, past an outlying McDonalds and several semi detached houses, perched on a surrounding hill. In the town centre, we slow down, as the traffic gets heavier. We pass the Get Sorted Academy of Music, Sabirs Grill Bar and signs to the Minister Quarter, which houses the elegant fourteenth century All Saints Church. We move down Westgate, an area of modest terraced houses, cross a bridge at Main St., go past the council offices at Riverside House and the derelict Guest and Grimes factory, former Brass Founders and Manufacturers. Finally we arrive two hours before kick off at the New York Stadium, which is named after its original New York Island site. While walking around the ground, you can see Millmoor, Rotherham's previous stadium, in the distance. Apparently, the club moved to the current site, when relations soured with the previous owner, the late Ken Booth, whose scrap metal and recycling business is located next to the old ground.

Attached to the walls of the new stadium are various plaques in memoriam to fans who've died and a turnstile, number 9, named John's Gate after one loyal supporter. Surrounding the Rotherham FC shop is a quote by commentator Brian Chapple in celebration of The Millers' automatic promotion to the Championship in 2014. 'There's ninety seconds left on the watch. Everybody's gone mad. I've gone mad!' I then proceed to get into a brief conversation with a Fulham fan about Rotherham's travails and inevitable relegation from the Championship. However, this bespectacled, poker-faced man is showing no sympathy for their plight. 'As I said to the wife, you can't feel too sorry for them. It's like The Premier League, nobody gives anybody anything.'

Leaving this man of harsh but realistic judgement, I go to collect my duplicate ticket, as despite getting my booking confirmed, my original one didn't arrive in the post. Dead on one thirty, the grey metal shutters of the away ticket office are lifted and a dark haired woman in a red shirt, with a security pass entwined around her neck, is fully revealed. 'Are ya alright,' says the woman in a broad Yorkshire accent, and it's not long before I'm sorted. So far the team hasn't arrived. 'We might be needed,' I joke to another elderly fan, 'I hope they'll pay the same money!' he replies. Then suddenly, dead on cue, our heroes arrive. Manager Slaviša signs a few autographs, Ryan Fredericks accepts a selfie and the rest trundle into the stadium, headphones glued to their ears. Around this area is a dark haired man in sunglasses, keeping an eye on his kids, who have been getting autographs. While he agrees that things at the club are a lot better than in recent times, he has some doubts.

'I just question the owner. Is Shahid Khan really interested in investing in Fulham or is he more concerned in getting a foothold over here for his American Football team?'

'Probably both,' I reply

'Anyway we'll see,' he concludes as he sweeps up his kids and goes for a walk around the ground.

The stadium is surrounded by a an attractive panoramic view of church spires, municipal offices, outlying streets and houses. Nearby is a river, which flows beside one side of the ground, creating a vivid, picturesque setting. Moving further away from ticket office, I venture on to a grass verge where there are benches close to the water. Two Fulham fans, a middle aged man and woman, are eating sandwiches viewing the nearby weeping willows at the water's edge.

'Do you know the name of this river?' I ask the man in a short striped t shirt.

'Do you know? 'he asks a lady in a light, flowery spring dress.

'River Don,' she replies flatly.

'It goes to Sheffield, I think.'

'I don't know,' says the man. 'Oh yes, it does. Look there,' he declares, pointing to a nearby sign.

It's getting closer to kick off so after a bit of reflection by the river, I make my way towards the away entrance. Inside the stand, the decor is much smarter than that at Bristol City. Maybe Rotherham have spent all their money on the new stadium, rather than players. There's a plasma on the wall showing the Liverpool v Everton game. While sauntering about, I hear a voice behind me; 'can I see your ticket, sir? Somewhat alarmed, I immediately extract it from my wallet, only to turn round and see a smiling Richard declaring 'I always knew it was a forgery!' Apparently, this comic Inspector had made a late decision to come to the game, leaving Tunbridge Wells at nine thirty, so The Oracle has indeed landed!

Luckily we're able to go anywhere, so we can sit together. On first sight, the stadium is impressive. It may only hold 12,000 but it seems more than that, with its high-banked red and blue seats, mushroom-like designed floodlights and imposing screen. Just before the start, we hear that down the road, Barnsley have got an injury time equaliser against local rivals Leeds. That means if we win this game, we go sixth. This is an opportunity Fulham have to take. 'COME ON YOU WHITES!' After the teams come out and pass through a sentry guard of flags, there's a minute's silence to acknowledge the recent passing of former Millers manager, Jim McAnearney. This is respected by everybody in the stadium but unfortunately some loud Fulham fans can be heard in the bar below. This racket is countered by insistent 'sshes' from Whites supporters in the stadium but I don't think the inveterate revellers below can hear them.

Once the minute is completed, we're off. 'WE ARE FULHAM SUPER FULHAM!' rings round the stand. Fulham have made a few changes for this game, probably influenced by the exertions of those players who were away during the international break. Out go Ream, Sessegnon and Ayité. In come Madl, Malone and Martin. Fulham are starting sluggishly and after two minutes Rotherham should have scored, an unmarked Danny Ward putting Newell's excellent cross past the post. It's Rotherham who look the more dangerous and Lee Frecklington's curling shot seems goal bound, only to be magnificently saved by David Button, acrobatically diving high to his right to push it away.

During this passage of play, there has been an incident to my left. Various Fulham fans have sat in a few seats uncovered by a tarpaulin, which lies over most of that particular area. A couple of guards have told the fans to leave there for security reasons. However, one of them, a sturdy man of medium height in a brown shirt, refuses to budge, and stays rooted to the spot like a rebellious protestor facing off policeman in a Trafalgar Square sit down. One of the guards is pleading with him and getting to be more insistent. When the Fulham protestor criticises the club, the guard tells him that he's not from the club but a freelance security firm. 'Well what's the problem?' says the protestor, 'it's not as if we're Chelsea or Millwall.' Negotiations continue but prove fruitless. Another fan, a gentleman, with flowing grey haired locks, who looks like an ageing 60s rocker, tells him it's not worth it and proceeds to sing drunkenly about fighting down the Fulham Road and Fulham FC times of yore, his hands spreadeagled in open supplication to some higher power. Eventually, the security people wisely leave 'The Fulham 1' alone. As these authorities disappear, some of the crowd cynically sing 'CHEERIO! CHEERIO! CHEERIO!' A fairly dismal half then comes to an end, with Rotherham marginally the better side. We need to up our game.

After some good five a side football by local youngsters during half time, the second forty five minutes gets underway. After eight minutes, Kebano's pace makes inroads into the Millers' defence down the left. He slips the ball to Cairney, who crosses it to Martin, unmarked six yards out. Our international striker then proceeds to stumble over the ball and miss a sitter. The fans are fuming. Below me, a bald headed sixty year old wearing dark rimmed glasses and a long brown coat, goes beserk. 'Fuck off Martin! He did that on purpose! Diabolical!' says Brown Coat, ejecting out of his seat in protest, as if he was insisting that our deviant striker should face criminal prosecution.

Shortly afterwards, for some unknown reason, a bloated Rotherham supporter in a red shirt and jeans, runs on to the pitch. He's middle aged and, to put it politely, not quick. He also looks a bit the worse for wear and his attempts at a body swerve to avoid the marauding security staff is comically slow and clumsy. Eventually he's whisked away by the rather excessive presence of six security men. Meanwhile, Rotherham may not be having that much of the ball but they still are finding ways of threatening Fulham's defence and Button and co are fortunate to scramble away a Newell shot. Fulham respond but Martin heads over a Kebano cross.

The game continues uneventfully but in the sixty sixth minute, Martin finds Johansen, who plays in Cairney. Cairney shoots but his shot is blocked, Ayité hits the rebound, which comes out to Aluko, who finally scrambles the ball home. 0-1. Relief! After the initial cheers, 'CRAVEN COTTAGE BY THE RIVER' resounds rapturously in the away stand. Meanwhile, the game proceeds but somewhat nervously for Fulham.

We are trying to slow the game down but seem to be defending too deeply, as Rotherham continue to come at us. Fulham appear vulnerable to the Millers' long throws and, in injury time, when one of them isn't cleared, the ball runs loose to Belaïd, who thankfully balloons the ball over the bar. In relief, the fans give our manager a somewhat dubious chant-'SLAVISA, WOAH, SLAVISA, WOAH! HE COMES FROM SERBIA! HE'LL FUCKIN' MURDER YER!' When Ream comes on for Malone to eek up time and break up the game, an extended chant of 'R-E-A-M' is heard but the American doesn't even touch the ball. The referee blows. It's the end of the game and an energetic chant of 'FULHAM AWAY' greets the satisfactory result.

At the final whistle, Richard, looking at me as if to say 'thank goodness we came out of that alive', gives me his thoughts: 'I said to the Rotherham fan I met on the train, I'll take 1-0, off somebody's bum in the last minute!' I'm keen to get to the coach, so we can get away quickly. Consequently, I say goodbye to Richard and immediately leave the stand.

Back at the coach, when a fair haired young lady in a grey sweater and wearing a silver medallion around her neck, brings an envelope asking for contributions for the driver, Straggly is not amused.

'I'm not paying twenty quid for the coach and then a collection-unless the driver's dead!' he fumes and then goes on to tell his mate that 'he likes jumpers on girls. I think it's sexy.'

Further stunning revelations emerge when he talks of his mother choreographing both him and other children in a version of Queen's 'We Are The Champions' at his school's concert. Maybe he imitated Freddie Mercury, who knows? I think he and his mate Stocky went to the same seat of learning. Straggly recalls a fellow pupil with such a temper that 'he used to throw chairs at people, he got so angry. A real sicko!' After informing us that Beckham could do two hundred keepy uppies at four years old, the two lads recoil into their smartphones, like most other travellers.

The journey back is smooth and I get off at Hammersmith, where I encounter Doug.

'It took four shots to get it in the net,' says Doug as we walk towards the tube.

'Yes, we were a bit lucky.'

'Still, we're now sixth and in with a chance of the play-offs.'

'Absolutely. See you, Doug,' and I saunter off to get a bus to Wood Lane.

The Rams Away

It's the following Tuesday at 1pm and I'm making my lunch. I'm just surveying the vegetables when I think blimey what am I doing, I'm meant to be at the Cottage at 2pm to get the coach to Derby? I'd been hypnotised by my usual routine. I abandon my repast, shove everything in the fridge, switch the computer off, do a final security check, hoist my backpack over my shoulder and leg it to the tube. Then after all that rush, I discover that the coach hasn't even arrived.

I eventually meet up with Mikey, who's come over from Norway for the game. He left his Scandinavian home at 5 am. There's devotion for you. We clamber into the first coach, which is being managed by Barbara. Unfortunately, it's very full and we can't sit together, so we recover our tickets and go into the second coach, where we're met by the comely young lady in the grey sweater, from the Rotherham trip, who's wearing that dangling silver medallion. She's obviously the steward for this coach.

I sit next to Jim, the Tipperary Irishman, who's doing the Metro crossword. Mikey takes the seat across the aisle. He tells me how he lives fifty miles outside Oslo, on the coast near fjords. He explains how he migrated to living there. Apparently, he was originally working in Lanzarote teaching English when he met a Norwegian woman and proceeded to live with her in Norway for nine years. After they split up, he's been living with his partner Benedicte, who was at the Spurs cup game. Mikey says he came over to see the team sixteen times last season and we only won two games! I hope he's not a bad omen.

'Tiredness Can Kill Take A Break' says a road sign ominously, as we bomb down the M1. Tipperary Jim is now on the Mail crossword. Mikey is speaking to his girl friend on his mobile in Norwegian. When he finishes, I ask him how long it took to learn the language. 'Two years. However, I've an English friend who's lived in Norway for twenty odd years but only speaks English. He gave up on it as most Norwegians speak English. I didn't want to do that and when I'm with Norwegian friends I sometimes insist that we talk in their language. In fact, I work for a German firm and some of the info on the computer is in German, so I 'm taking in a bit of Deutsch as well.' He tells me that in Norway, the air is so clean. 'You get used to the cold. It can be pleasant as the air's so dry unlike the wet in England.' Our chat has made the time pass quickly and we're now pulling up at the Welcome Break, outside Leicester.

Inside the restaurant, Mikey persuades me not to go out on the patio with my own meal-'I don't think they'll chuck you out'. He gets a Kentucky fried chicken, while I surreptitiously open my rucksack and dig into my rice and chicken. After finishing our food, we leave the motorway café monolith, return to the coach and make our way to Pride Park Stadium. On the way, we pass various wind turbines and the River Derwent. The ground isn't far from the motorway so we don't enter the town but travel down Brian Clough Way, named after the former Derby manager, who led the club to winning the old First Division.

It transpires that the football ground is part of a complex which offers facilities for other business services. We see the team arrive Their entrance to the stadium is camouflaged by both the coach and silver metal barriers but Mikey still attempts to get Johansen's attention by shouting in Norwegian. Given the gargantuan headphones around the midfielder's ears, I'm not surprised by the lack of response. When Mikey and I enter the stadium, we have a beer. The cold lager is refreshing and good preparation for the battle ahead. While we're imbibing, we're interrupted by a plump security officer wearing a large yellow bib. He overhears us talking about David Moyes being reprimanded for unacceptably but jestfully threatening a BBC female journalist with 'a slap,' and can't resist making his own contribution.

'I do that to my missus. What's the problem?'

'Maybe the incident has been overblown,' I placatingly suggest.

'Just a bit,' responds the affronted official.

When Mikey tells him that he's come from Norway, the security man tells us that he went there when he was in the navy.

'I can't remember the place. Where do you live?'

'Sandefjord, fifty miles outside Oslo'

'I think that's it. I used to have photos of these places but my previous missus sodded off with a toy boy and took the photos.'

We leave our loquacious security man and go into the stand. It's big and impressive, with its floodlights beaming down from roofs like dramatic searchlights. Unfortunately, Mikey's seat is far away from mine and I make my way much higher up in the steeply raked stand. In fact, I'm not far from the back and witness young Fulham fans testing the corrugated at the back of the stand, in preparation for their chanting accompaniment. A young blonde girl has a union jack draped around her neck, while her smartly jeaned male companions are indulging in some loud but indecipherable banter. There's a big Fulham turn out. On the pitch, the Derby mascot, Rammie, with his yellow ears, white shirt and green socks, is prancing about. The teams come out, the formalities are completed and we're off. Our elevated stand is to one side of the pitch and Fulham are playing toward us.

Slaviša has made three changes: Ayité for Martin, who can't play against his parent club, Ream for Madl and Piazon for Kebano. 'SLAVISA'S BLACK AND WHITE ARMY' rings out from our friends above me. We start well. We're moving the ball much more quickly than against Rotherham and pushing Derby back. Then after eight minutes, Derby score against the run of play. There's a big gap down our right side, Olsson, their left back, plays a long ball forward and Nugent lobs it over the advancing Button. 1-0. Despite this initial setback, we continue to control possession and Cairney finds space to shoot but his effort is too close to the keeper. The fans remain positive. Chants of 'FULHAM AWAY! FULHAM AWAY!' roar on the team, interspersed with a comic refrain about our former defender Chris Baird (known as Bairdinho because of his free kick ability), who's now with Derby and on today's bench. 'BAIRD IS TOO FAT FOR US!' is their current assessment of our former defender.

The game continues evenly but then after thirty five minutes, Fredericks goes on one of his devastating runs, the Derby defence only clear the ball to Ayité, whose low left footed shot goes into the net. 1-1. 'OH, FLOYD AYITEE!' is sung in celebration, followed by the predictable 'WHO ARE YER?' After a melee in the Derby box which comes to nothing, it's the tale of two Czechs, when Tomas Kalas upends compatriot Vydra in the penalty area, following a misdirected Aluko pass, and-ugh!-it's a penalty. Nugent takes the kick but Button makes a fantastic save, diving full stretch to his left. The resulting corner comes over, and I don't believe it, we're slow to react, don't clear it and Nugent turns the loose ball into the net. 2-1.

I've now moved down to an empty seat a few rows down, to avoid the intense reverberation of the chants-maybe I'm showing my age! In the final moments of the half, Aluko strikes a ferocious shot against the bar. We could have done with that going in before the break. Instead, we'll have to settle for being a goal behind. We've been overplaying in the last third and when our full backs have put good, low crosses into the box, nobody's anticipated them. However, if we can erase silly individual mistakes, we can win this game.

Mikey clambers up the steep steps and sits next to me for the second half. Soon after the restart, Piazon is booked for diving in the penalty area. A bit unfairly, I think. Carson, the Derby goalkeeper, seems to be wasting time already. 'You useless tosser!' is the verdict of one irate, scowling Fulham fan. Still, confidence in the team remains high and, that celebrated Fulham ditty from the 70s, is being sung, somewhat incongruously-'OH THIS YEAR WE'RE GONNA WIN THE CUP, OH VIVA EL FULHAM!' Meanwhile, the game remains evenly contested as the Fulham fans move into current political territory with a mocking chant of 'WE PAY YOUR BENEFITS!' Now Derby are on the attack, a loose ball is being chased by Nugent advancing on goal. Button rushes out but only clears it against the Derby striker, who recovers and places it easily into the empty net. 3-1. Another gift. Button wasn't sufficiently quick or positive. Otherwise the ball would have gone into the nearby stand.

After this calamity, we seem a bit shell shocked but try to reassert our game. Then, in the sixty seventh minute, Button misplaces a ball out from the back, Russell willingly accepts the gift. 4-1. An outpouring of criticism of Button ensues. 'Fuckin' useless' is probably the kindest one I heard. This is now becoming a bit of a disaster, not because we've been outplayed but because of careless, individual errors. Derby have just waited for this to happen and taken their opportunities. Nugent goes off with twenty minutes to go, having scored a hat trick. 'YOUR KEEPER IS ONE OF OUR

OWN!' shouts the Derby crowd, acknowledging the hapless Button's contribution to the scoreline. The home supporters then continue with chants about their loaned striker: 'MARTIN'S TOO GOOD FOR YOU!'. Our fans counter humorously with 'MARTIN'S TOO FAT FOR US!' Fulham are still trying to rescue a point. Then in the seventy ninth minute, Sone Aluko, attacks down the left, draws their defence, passes to the unmarked Ayitė, who calmly slots the ball into the net. 4-2.

'Now if we could get another in the next few minutes, who knows?' says the ever optimistic Mikey. Certainly, substitute Sessegnon is using his pace down the left and in the closing minutes he crosses to Ayitė, who's free but can't make proper contact. 'That was the moment,' says Mikey. Now there's no chance of a grandstand finish and the game peters out to an inevitable Derby victory. Meanwhile, we hear that Sheffield Wednesday won 2-0 at Rotherham, so that means that we're now seventh, two points behind The Owls, who are sixth.

Back in the coach Tipperary Jim is fuming, 'Rowett's a proper manager (referring to the ex-Birmingham City man, who's recently replaced the ill-fated Steve McLaren, who has now been sacked twice by Derby). And Cairney is a waste of space, trundling around on one peg,' alluding to Tom's inability to use his right foot, 'all this passing around aimlessly.'

We leave the ground fairly quickly but then get into a traffic jam near the motorway. The police redirect us to proceed by another route. I think this is because Leicester are also playing at home and they don't want all the traffic congregating in the same place. The coach is dark and quiet, everybody retreating into their own private online world.

Unsurprisingly, Mikey is tired and tries to get some kip. He's got his flight back to Norway at 5am. I discover that we're taking a route that I don't recognise but when we come out at Northolt, I decide to get off at Shepherd's Bush Green. I give Mikey a warm handshake and make my way to Mira's. It's around 1.30 am, which isn't bad timing, considering the detour. I trudge wearily up Wood Lane, a solitary figure in a dark landscape. I feel knackered and disappointed. Why do you do this to me, Fulham?

The Tractor Boys Challenge

It's a hot spring Saturday. President Trump has just attacked Syria over its use of chemical weapons. Meanwhile Fulham must beat Ipswich to get back on track for the play-offs. I'm travelling from Mira's at Wood Lane.

Once in the ground, I reunite with John, the Irishman. , I don't recognise the approaching figure in shades and a yellow Fulham away shirt, but when he removes the glasses, all is revealed. 'I didn't recognise you but I'm glad to see with the gear you've become a man of the people. About time, too!' He laughs and we discuss the Derby game, in which his bête noire, Mr Button, had a nightmare. 'He makes too many mistakes,' says the Irishman.

In fact, for this game, the popular Bettinelli replaces Button, Madl comes in for Ream and Martin returns after being ineligible for the Derby game, in place of Piazon. Slaviša comes out in an immaculate, light black suit. Mick McCarthy, the Ipswich manager, is in a dark blue track suit and acknowledges the away fans with a raised clap, as he walks to the dugout with the purposeful strides of a former rugged defender. Slaviša and Mick then engage in a formal handshake and take their seats. From the early play, it seems we're mixing it up more in this game, sometimes kicking it long at goal kicks to get us further up the pitch more quickly. We start with confidence and energy, which is good after Tuesday evening's debacle and, in the early stages, Ayité and Johansen have shots saved.

However, after ten minutes, Bettinelli's clearance is charged down by McGoldrick and he's lucky that the ball fortuitously runs his way, unlike the cursed Button in the previous game. Seven minutes later, there's some fine interplay between Aluko and Fredericks. Fredericks runs freely to the right byline and his cross is met by Martin's shot, which the Ipswich keeper, Bialkowski, can only palm away to the approaching Floyd Ayité, who steers the ball into the net. 1-0. The crowd explode into song-'OH WHEN THE WHITES, OH WHEN THE WHITES GO MARCHIN' IN, GO MARCHIN' IN!' In response, Ipswich do come more into the game but Fulham are still in control and on the half hour, Ayité and Johansen create a series of passes down the left, which releases Malone to slot the ball into the far corner. Great move. 2-0. 'SLAVISA'S BLACK AND WHITE ARMY!' chant the Haynes Stand. Later, Polish keeper Bialkowski makes a fine save to stop a shot by McDonald going into the top corner. However, approaching half time, Fulham go to sleep at the back and an unmarked McGoldrick gets straight through on goal. Thankfully, he only hits the post but the warning signs are there. Shortly afterwards, the whistle is blown for half time.

During the interval, I talk to John. Apparently, he's Deputy Head Teacher of a primary school in Paddington. His friend Patrick, who came to the Blackburn game, works for the British Transport Police and has just bought a house. Hence their previous property discussion. I naively thought that was a well paid job but John tells me that it's only on a monetary level with the lower end of the teaching profession. Our conversation ensures that the usual half time entertainment passes me by and it's not long before the teams are back on the field.

Fulham are playing towards the Hammersmith End. McGoldrick and Sears. the Ipswich strikers, are making dangerous inroads down the middle of Fulham's defence and the Tractor Boys are still very much in this game. Slaviša responds around the half hour mark by replacing Madl with Ream, a like for like central defender. I'm not sure if Madl has an injury or whether Slaviša thinks that Ream can deal better with their front two. Then, just after the sixty minute mark, that man McGoldrick is through again but thankfully the newly reinstated Marcus Bettinelli stands tall and stops the shot. A counter attack ensues and we move quickly down the right flank. While Ipswich are struggling to get back, the ball finds its way to Johansen, who cuts in on his left foot and puts the ball into the right hand corner. 3-0. The crowd chant an emphatic and pronounced 'FULHAM,' followed by the rhythmic banging of clappers. Despite this setback, Ipswich are still looking to score and in injury time, they get a free kick. It's well floated, Marcus Bettinelli comes out to collect, doesn't make it and Berra scores. 3-1. Numerically a meaningless goal but can we ever keep a clean sheet?

At The Wall, I'm approached by Alex, who's holding a colourful bag with a small balloon inscribed with 50 on it. Yes, he's just reached the big 5-0 and he, Richard and friends have celebrated at a pizzeria in Putney.

'That's where Mikey told me he saw Barry Hayles,' I inform Alex.

'That's right. He had a photo taken there with Barry,' replies the birthday boy.

Mikey must stop coming. He's a bad omen.'

'Yes, I know.'

'His record seeing Fulham win is terrible.'

'Isn't it just?'

Richard joins us with burly Shane, wearing dark sunglasses and strikingly garbed in black apparel. He's making one of his occasional appearances.

'We played off Martin and got up the pitch quicker,' asserts The Oracle.

'I know but I don't like that way of playing so much. We played better football against Derby but individual errors gave them two goals there,' insists the author.

'But we watched the game together at Rotherham, we didn't create enough chances,' explains Richard.

'You're right,' I admit. 'It was probably necessary. Particularly with the accidents at the back at Pride Park.'

'We had more chances in this game,' continues Richard.'

'I suppose we countered their high pressing strategy by being a bit more direct,' I concede.

We are then interrupted by Fulham 1879 Fan TV for another interview. This time there's a dowdy, middle aged cameraman rather than the previous Asian female operator.

'With respect, your last camera operator was much prettier,' says Richard referring to the beguiling woman at the Wolves game.

We then do our stuff, Richard with his hands over nearby shoulders, grouping us together, Alex, radiant in a Visit Florida Fulham t shirt, clinging on to his bag, as his 5O balloon sways gently from side to side, Shane looking like a menacing dark-shaded member of the Marbella set and the author, lean and haggard in a New York Yankees cap.

When the interview finishes, I discover that the absent Pete, who must have gone to the Fulham shop for a few goodies, bet on the score being 3-1 and has won three hundred and fifty pounds. Apparently, when it was three nil, he was urging Ipswich to score! Nothing like switching loyalties for a few bob. After this idiosyncratic revelation, Richard and Shane depart and I walk along with Alex, and, of course, his balloon.

'We still can look very vulnerable defensively,' I contend.

'Slaviša has said that we need to be better without the ball.'

'They could have scored two or three.'

'I know. Let's hope we can tighten it up.'

'Must go. Got money on the Grand National!'

'Right. Happy birthday, Alex!' I cry as he makes his way across Fulham Palace Rd amidst the departing crowd, with his bouncing balloon decorating the early evening air.

I then discover that we're still seventh, two points behind Sheffield Wednesday, but at least we're keeping in touch with that play-off position, after the Derby debacle.

I decide to walk to Hammersmith for some much needed exercise. On my way, I encounter the following placard outside the Distillers pub: 'Take plenty of water in this heat. Beer is 97% water!'

Carrow Road Drama

It's Good Friday but rather than issuing seasonal goodwill, the press is full of dire warnings of imminent nuclear war as America pursue a more aggressive policy against North Korea. Meanwhile, I take refuge in more parochial matters. Mira drops me off at Craven Cottage to get the coach for the Norwich game. Now that we're in with a chance of making the play-offs, there's more away support, aided by the club reducing the price of a coach ticket to five pounds. I choose to go in the last of three coaches.

Before we can take our seats, a disabled boy in shorts and sunglasses is entering on his wheelchair. The side of the vehicle is opened, the boy is then placed into position and ascends into the coach like an ancient king rising to his throne. This is a most impressive piece of hydraulic engineering and marks great progress in extending access. A slim, grey haired man wearing glasses is taking the tickets. With his elegant red shirt, smartly pressed brown trousers and polished matching shoes, he appears like a benevolent schoolmaster. Once seated, I notice that the three seats in front of me aren't in use to accommodate the disabled boy.

At the top of the coach, East End Doug is talking to the driver and a bald middle aged man in a pink shirt. They're discussing the absurd discrepancies in away ticket prices, when Barbara enters the coach and informs The Schoolmaster that there will be no break on the way, as three coaches can't enter the Welcome Break car park at the same time and that we're due to leave at 10.10.

After Barbara departs, a breathless fan, clambers up the coach steps. He's wearing a red t shirt with the dates of some rock band's tour on the back. Fair, with lightly spiked hair and softly spoken, he tells the assembled throng that it wasn't a good idea for him to go out last night as he's very much the worse for wear. As he makes his way to the rear end of the coach, where most of the younger fans congregate, I notice a middle aged black guy on his mobile. He's a few rows up to my right, and explaining to a friend, that he'll chat later because 'phone conversations aren't encouraged on the coach'. This made me wonder why Fulham don't have more black fans. We certainly have some but you'd have thought that we'd have more. Eventually, the battalion of three yellow Fulham coaches leave the Cottage.

It's now just gone 10.15 and the traffic gets heavier as we make our way to Hammersmith. The driver has Radio 2 playing and interspersed with the music, there's a pop quiz. Questions are being asked about Cream and David Bowie. Once we get on the M11, the journey is smooth but there's a lot of traffic because of the Easter holiday. It's not long before a sign proclaiming Welcome To Essex greets us as we then proceed into the county of Norfolk. You can't see that much of its landscape from the motorway, apart from some pastoral corn fields. However, noticing the distinct lack of undulation, I recall playwright Nöel Coward's observation: 'very flat, Norfolk'.

When we get nearer our destination, the final entry into the town is tortuously slow and time is now ticking away. Eventually, we are within sight of Carrow Road about forty minutes before kick off. I'm a little apprehensive as although I have a ticket booked, it didn't arrive in the post. Consequently, I need to get a duplicate from the ticket office. We finally make a circuitous journey around the ground. I don't know if this is due to traffic redirection or error but it's taking an inordinately long time. When we finally get to the Lower Clarence Road car park, there's less than half an hour before the game starts. I walk briskly down Carrow Rd, over the railway bridge, overtaking supporters as I go.

After being directed to the wrong place three times by various darkly suited Norwich officials, the duplicate tickets eventually arrive ten minutes before kick off and I breathe a sigh of relief. Apparently they came via one of our coaches. 'Very Fulhamish,' observes a jovial Fulham fan, in the queue. I now rush round to the Jarrold South Stand and go through the turnstiles. In the bar, a group of young supporters in Fulham shirts are jumping up and down as beer spurts from their cans like a streaming fountain. They're singing our anthem 'CAN'T TAKE MY EYES OFF YOU'. It's raucous, loud, lively and funny. After a quick visit to the expansive grey toilet, I make my way to the stand.

The Norwich ground like Ipswich's is near the railway station. It's an impressive modern stadium. We're in a good position to the side of the pitch, adjacent to the goal in front of The Barclay Stand, named after Capt Evelyn Barclay, City's former Vice President. My seat is a particularly good one in a short row of only three, close to the exit. I'm next to two young blonde twenty year olds in white Fulham shirts. 'I actually live in Norwich,' one of the boys tells me. Behind me is a young family with two young kids and immediately in the row below is a stout, grey haired man in a white Visit Florida Fulham shirt and his younger, smaller, thinner, dark haired mate. A sort of Laurel and Hardy combination.

The Canaries beat Reading 7-1 in their last home game so they won't be lacking confidence. Fulham are unchanged and early on, Floyd Ayité, in particular, makes a lively start. After five minutes he runs at the Norwich defence, passes to Martin, whose blocked effort falls to Stefan Johansen. The Norwegian international then hits a powerful shot into the right hand corner from twenty yards out. 0-1. Fantastic! 'SLAVISA'S BLACK AND WHITE ARMY!' reverberates around the stand. Just the start we needed. 'WE'RE WINNNIN' AWAY! WE'RE WINNIN' AWAY!' chant the fans.

When Norwich respond, Ream stops a counter attack by Pritchard with a crucial tackle. 'R-E-A-M!' is then chanted as a suitably elongated response. Fulham are playing their passing game with confidence. Even though we have Martin in the side, we're not playing so many long balls as we did against Ipswich but more out from the back. Ayité is again figuring prominently: first he puts Tom Cairney through on goal but our skipper's shot is comfortably saved and later he sends in a great cross that is nearly met by Sone Aluko. The crowd chant his name in unison. 'FLOYD AYITEE!'

Nonetheless, Norwich are still mounting dangerous attacks. Wes Hoolahan's cross is put behind for a corner by Tim Ream and Swiss centre back, Timm Klose, heads over the bar. 'WE'RE ONLY HERE FOR THE FULHAM' sing the Cottage choir. It's now towards the end of the half and Norwich are pressing to get back into the game. Come on Fulham, hold on until half time! The promising Murphy then fires a powerful shot but Bettinelli tips the ball round the post. From the following corner, Klose powers in a fine header but

Bettinelli again makes an agile block and Pritchard puts the rebound over the bar. 'MARCUS BETTINELLI!' is belted out rigorously. Followed by the ruder, 'YOU'RE JUST A SHIT TEAM IN IPSWICH!' which is geographically a bit muddled, to put it mildly.

Never mind, we're now in added time but when Martin goes up for a header, he seems to elbow his marker. Several Norwich players instinctively appeal to the referee. Martin could be in trouble here. Oh no, my worst fears are confirmed. It's a red and we're down to ten men. Just when things are going well, we go and create self inflicted bloody problems. 'CHRIS MARTIN YOU'RE ONE OF OUR OWN!' sing the Norwich fans, reminding us of Martin's previous appearances for Norwich. Supporters like nothing better than a bit of humorous, ritual humiliation. 'He's fuckin' slow anyway, like a tub of lard,' asserts a voice behind me, trying to remain optimistic, while continuing our volatile relationship with our on loan striker.

During half time, I turn to the family behind, whose kids are vigorously exercising themselves on the nearby steps, telling them that I've discovered that one Fulham fan is accusing Martin of being 'a subversive agent'.

For the second half, Fulham have kept to the same remaining ten players. We're continuing to play 4-4-1, with Ayité as the lone striker, which is how we've set ourselves up since Martin's departure. A few minutes after the restart, Kalas makes a surging run into the penalty area and is brought down by substitute Bennett. And yes! The ref has given a penalty. But wait a moment, this isn't a time for assumption as we've missed eight out of ten penalties this season. Who's going to take it? Immediately, Tom Cairney steps up. A good choice, even though he's one of the culprits who's previously missed. I feel nervous about this. Come on Tom, bury it! Cairney looks concentrated, waits for the whistle and yes, he calmly puts the ball into the right hand corner as keeper Ruddy goes the wrong way. Tom does the traditional slide on the grass towards the supporters, who give him ecstatic acclaim. 0-2. We've got breathing space. 'WE'VE SCORED FROM THE SPOT! HOW SHIT ARE YOU? WE'VE SCORED FROM THE SPOT!' sing the faithful.

However, the game is certainly not over and the Canaries are looking to test our aerial vulnerability with crosses. Marcus Bettinelli meets the challenge by collecting them with agile confidence and authority. However, he's also being very slow taking his kicks so he gets booked for time wasting. The supporters then offer some comic relief singing. 'WE'LL WIN IT AGAIN! THE INTERTOTO. WE'LL WIN IT AGAIN!' once more recalling our 2002 appropriation of minor silverware. In the latter stages, Cameron Jerome comes on to create an even greater aerial threat. Jerome looked ponderous in The Premiership but has a good record in this league. The pressure is increasing on the Whites. The ball goes to Pritchard on the right, he floats in a cross in that 'corridor of uncertainty' and no Fulham player is marking the big man Jerome, so he heads it in. 1-2. 'WHO ARE YER?' scream the Norwich supporters vengefully. Game on with fourteen minutes to go.

Norwich are now making Fulham face a constant barrage of high balls and Sigurdsson comes on to help combat the intense aerial threat. However, we seem to be coping well. The team are really digging in and looking more durable than in earlier games. Norwich are forcing the issue and throwing men forwards but, on the counter, with three minutes to go, Ayité, who's been holding up the ball brilliantly, plays in Tom Cairney. Tom sends his marker the wrong way, he only has the keeper to beat. But, oh no, he's missed! I don't believe it. This team certainly don't do things the easy way. I just hope we don't pay the price for that.

Thankfully, Fulham are still keeping hold of the ball well, breaking purposefully on the counter and when, with one minute left, Lucas Piazon plays a great ball to Ayité, Floyd cleverly goes past keeper Ruddy and walks the ball into the net. 1-3. Brilliant! Game over. Surely? The team descend upon Floyd in an orgy of celebration. During the prolonged, seven minutes of injury time, Neeskens Kebano, who's now replaced Ayité, nearly scores another, when he has a shot blocked on the line. Soon afterwards, the final whistle blows. What a great win. At the end of the game, the whole Fulham squad come over to the supporters in appreciation. Bettinelli arms akimbo in delight, then points to friends in the crowd and chucks his jersey in their direction. Meanwhile, Slaviša Jokanović, in his black suit, white shirt and dark tie, joins the team, and slaps hands with substitute Scott Parker. 'HE COMES FROM SERBIA!..'

chant the crowd. Slaviša acknowledges the adulation and claps the supporters. The manager and squad depart with the cheers ringing in their ears. It's been a momentous Fulham away victory.

When I arrive at the coach. The Schoolmaster is there with the driver.

'That was a special one,' I declare.

'Yes, it was.'

'I fancy us if it goes to the last game. Ever the optimist.'

'Indeed.'

I clamber into the coach and talk to the black bloke, who's been sitting in front of me. He tells me that he lives near Kingswood Rd, so he's a Fulham lad. Although he works a lot on Saturdays, he finds it hard to get to lot of games. I think he's taken time off for this one. He tells me that he went to a lot of away games in our promotion year in 2001. He asks me for a look at the programme, which I happily lend him. Meanwhile, at the top of the coach, Doug, Mr Pink Shirt and The Schoolmaster are all discussing the game. I suppose supporters are never fully happy and they're talking about how Kalas left Jerome free for the goal, the pace of the Norwich left back going stride for stride with the speedy Fredericks and how video assistant referees should aid decision making, like sending offs. Still overall they seem to be content and so they should be.

It's slow getting to the motorway but once we're there, it's a straightforward drive back. While travelling, I discover that Sheffield Wednesday have beaten Cardiff. So unfortunately, despite the exhilaration, we're still seventh.

On getting off at Hammersmith, I talk to the departing Doug, walking gingerly, throwing a blue bag over his shoulder. We make our way across the Broadway to the tube.

'A memorable one, Doug,' I suggest.

'Yes it was. It helped that we scored first.'

'Certainly.'

'When Martin was sent off. I thought that was it. Mind you, I've seen Fulham struggle against ten men.'

'The defence certainly dug in.'

'I think it helped that Bettinelli came positively for crosses. Particularly in the last ten minutes. It gave the defence confidence.'

'Actually, Button was getting better with crosses as well. It was his footwork that got him dropped but you're right Marcus was good today.'

'Thought the Martin foul was a yellow.'

'Couldn't be certain from where I was but it didn't look good and several Norwich players appealed straightaway.'

'Where's Denis Odoi?'

'Injured.'

'We needed him today in the last ten minutes when they were going for it as Piazon can't tackle.'

'The team will be tired so it may need freshening up on Easter Monday.'

'Will they appeal over Martin?'

'I don't know but I think it's unlikely to succeed.'

'Derby lost, so it's now between Leeds, Reading, Sheffield Wednesday and us.'

'It could go to the last game.'

'Are you going up there to Sheffield Wednesday?'

'No. I'm in New Orleans, so I'll have to find the best way of getting communication.'

'Still. We've got Villa first.'

'And they play tomorrow. Mind you, Bruce will find a way of rejigging his squad.'

'Probably. Still all to play for.'

'Absolutely. Yes. Must go,' says Doug departing briskly to the Fulham Palace Rd entrance, as I make my way in the opposite direction to get a bus to Wood Lane. Yes, a memorable one, indeed.

Villa on Easter Monday

It's coming up to 1.45 pm I'm at home and about to have my lunch when I suddenly discover that the Villa game starts at 2.45 not the traditional 3 pm, because it's on tv. Bloody Sky! Immediately I unload my meal into the fridge, forego my usual domestic ritual, hurriedly put on my jacket and rush to the tube. Out of breath, I hurtle down the stairs and find out that luckily my train to is due immediately.

I arrive at Hammersmith at 2.15. That gives me the necessary half an hour to get to the Cottage. I pass Vince, who's there with his labrador. 'See you in The Premiership!' he cries, clutching his Big Issues. I explain that I'm in a rush because I forgot the kick off time. 'TV?' he asks. 'Exactly mate,' I wail as I accelerate towards Fulham Palace Rd. Down by the river, The Crabtree pub is in festive mood, with its garden full of vociferous drinkers, while other imbibers spill on to the pavement. The Thames is at very low tide. There are no rowers. A stationary white yacht is marooned in solace in the middle of the river with a union jack fluttering in the breeze. A bearded Villa fan and his thickset mate are walking behind me. 'When did you first go to Villa?' the brawny one asks. '66. It was cold enough to skin you. I took you,' the bearded one replies, pointing to a smiling, fair, middle aged woman accompanying them.

This conversation reminds me of the Villa of my own youth, when Ron Saunders was the manager and a mate of mine referred to him as 'Il Duce,' because of his shaven head and Mussolini-style, thick leather jackets. With his demanding fitness regimes ('if you want to enjoy your football go and play in the park'), his disciplined team won the League Cup (1976) beating Liverpool 5-1, the Division I Championship (1980-1) and the European Cup (1982). Ironically, the volatile Saunders had left over a contractual issue before Villa reached and won the European Cup Final and his assistant Tony Barton, a former Fulham winger (1954-59), took over. I remember Barton as a solid reserve player, who made occasional first team appearances and later sadly died from a heart attack, when only fifty six. Saunders, now eighty four, has lived in relative anonymity since leaving football in 1987. Regrettably, he's currently suffering from dementia. Quite possibly, a result of heading heavy balls when he was a bustling forward in the 50s and 60s for several clubs, including Portsmouth and Charlton. Then suddenly my memories of 'Il Duce' are jolted by some kids attempting hazardous cycling manoeuvres on the Thames Path. I extricate myself from their imaginative swerves and go to get a programme. I greet the Scottish woman with a courteous 'Happy Easter'. 'Did you have a good one?' she enquires. 'Yes,' I reply. 'Of course it was good, Fulham won away!'

Once inside the Johnny Haynes Stand, I'm greeted by John, the Irishman, who's accompanied by a white haired man in his seventies, who has a mild northern accent and a twinkle in his eye. The Irishman returns to his school tomorrow, so let's hope Fulham send him back on a high.

After the usual formalities, the game starts. Slaviša has only made one change: Sessegnon for the banned Martin, Fulham's appeal having been turned down. Villa played on Saturday as a local church objected to there being a game on Good Friday, so Fulham have had a day's extra rest over their opponents. Both Fulham full backs make forceful opening runs: Scott Malone fizzes across a couple of great crosses but, not for the first time, nobody gets on the end of them and Fredericks finds the right byline but his cut back is kicked away for a corner. A good start by The Whites, they're taking control of the game and Villa seem to be still on the coach.

Just after quarter an hour, Ryan Fredericks crosses, Sessegnon volleys the ball against the bar and, yes, he bundles the rebound into the net. 1-0. Just the early goal we need! The Haynes Stand rocks with a rendering of 'WHEN THE WHITES GO MARCHIN' IN!' Later, after twenty minutes, there's a clash between Fredericks and, Ivory Coast striker Kodjia. It's difficult to see what actually happened from my position but the ref is now consulting the assistant referee, who's running the line on the Riverside side. After these deliberations, Kodjia is sent off and trudges off the pitch to howls of derision, accompanied by mocking chants of 'CHEERIO! CHEERIO! CHEERIO!' and dismissive waves. As he passes the Haynes Stand, his eyes are wisely focused on the ground. His departure is then followed by a rendition of 'WE ARE THE

FULHAM BOYS!' Shortly after this incident, another Frenchman Amavi, the left full back, hacks down Fredericks. In revenge? Maybe, especially as there's a possibility that Ryan might have had a 'nibble' before Kodjia reacted. After half an hour, and with ten men, Villa finally get their game going. A Gardner volley is deflected behind and from the ensuing corner, Elphick's header goes wide. When Aluko is then hacked down, there are howling cries of 'OFF! OFF!' We're in injury time now and after Tom Cairney mishits a volley, the ball comes back to centre back Tim Ream but his shot hurtles past the post. A real chance there. Pity it went to the wrong player. Shortly afterwards, the ref blows for half time. So far so good but let's hope we can complete the job. I then turn to the old'un and ask him what he thinks.

'You're playing well but you need the second goal.'

He's right we need to get some daylight between us and the Villains.

'You've put in some great crosses,' he adds.

I agree but it's a pity that we haven't capitalised on them. Our forwards are quick and skilful but just don't react like natural goalscorers.

During the interval, the biggest attraction is our former black striker Leroy Rosenior (1982-85,87-88 and 1990-91), who's being interviewed during the break. Leroy also holds the record for the shortest reign as a manager, ten minutes for Torquay United in 2007! Apparently, he's been in the club shop signing his book, 'It's Only Banter'. Ancient cries of 'LEROY! LEROY!' are chanted in appreciation, as he speaks warmly of his Cottage years, which is good considering the racism that was still around the game at that time. After Leroy departs, the players come out to renew battle.

It's not long after the restart that the talented but mercurial Jack Grealish gets the ball on the left, close to the Haynes Stand. He goes inside of Fredericks, who's lacking support, and unleashes a fantastic shot, which nestles perfectly in the far corner, leaving Bettinelli diving in despair. 1-1. Game on. One has to admit that was an excellent goal. The match now grows in intensity and Gardner is booked for fouling the tireless Johansen. Coming up to the hour mark, Floyd Ayité uses his pace, finds Aluko, whose volley diverts off Baker into the net. Brilliant. 2-1. 'WHO ARE YER? WHO ARE YER?' scream the Fulham faithful, followed by an improvised accompaniment of cardboard clappers. Then, with eleven minutes to go Johansen finds Kebano on the right. There's plenty of space as Villa's attacking substitutions mean that there's now no meaningful left back. The Congolese international fires a low shot across goal, and finds the far corner. 3-1. Game over!

'SUPER FULHAM, SUPER FULHAM FC, BY FAR THE GREATEST TEAM THE WORLD HAS EVER SEEN!' chant the fans in hyperbolic refrain. This is followed by a celebratory battle cry of 'SLAVISA'S BLACK AND WHITE ARMY!' Now Fulham are playing 'keep ball,' running down the clock. The happy crowd continue the party mood singing another anthem, 'CRAVEN COTTAGE BY THE RIVER.' Finally the whistle blows. A deserved and necessary win. The team clap the fans at the Hammersmith End home. As they come off, Bettinelli and McDonald make signals to their nearest and dearest in the Cottage. Cairney and Kebano share a joke. Tim Ream follows them, and when he acknowledges the Haynes Stand with a clap, the fans respond with an expansive chant of 'R-E-A-M!'. The ground is buzzing as I say goodbye to the Irishman and the moustachioed old 'un, who make a hurried exit to beat the traffic.

As I pass the tv monitor downstairs, I discover that Wednesday are still leading QPR 2-1 at Loftus Rd, so no change there. Our earlier kick off means they have a further fifteen minutes to play. However, there's good news elsewhere. Leeds are losing 2-1 against Wolves.

At The Wall, I meet Alex, who tells me his thoughts

'A good result, we played well. Helped by the sending off, of course.'

'Yes. Great,' I reply, 'especially following the good Norwich result.'

'Leeds are losing but we could do with a goal for QPR.'

Richard and Pete now join us.

'We were good apart from a period at 1-0 where we were passing the ball about a bit aimlessly,' says Richard.

I then notice the inscription on Pete's black t shirt. It reads:

'Grumpy Old Fulham Fan
Lifelong Supporter
Only Happy When Winning.'

'I like your t shirt, Pete,' I venture admiringly.

'Got it on the internet. Put the words on myself.'

The Oracle is now scrolling down his smartphone.

'Leeds have lost. We're sixth on goal difference as Wednesday beat QPR 2-1,' declares Richard.

I then bring up Pete's winnings.

'Oh no, that's another Pete.' says Richard.

'Not our Pete?' I enquire.

'No, not me,' insists our Pete

'This Pete bets 3-1 on each Fulham game,' explains Richard.

'On Fulham 1879 Fan TV, he said it paid for his forthcoming season ticket,' I reply.

'What he didn't say was that it would also pay for all the money he lost on other bets!' says Richard, with a twinkle in his eye.

We then discuss going to the final game at Sheffield Wednesday.

'It's best we book quickly. We need to leave early. It's a 12 o'clock kick off,' says Richard.

'Oh, right,' I respond. 'Are all the games kicking off then?'

'Yes. We'll look to share a car from Sussex. Your coach will probably be leaving the Cottage at 6 am!'

'Bloody Sky!' I remonstrate yet again.

And on that philosophical thought, Richard and Pete depart towards Putney and Alex and I go towards Fulham Palace Rd.

'You know Wednesday are asking twenty nine quid for the game? I'm only paying fifteen for the Huddersfield game. It's outrageous,' I moan.

'Yes. It's certainly too much.'

'You'd think there was some fair price regulation so there's not such a wild disparity.'

We then talk about the team's chances.

'We're getting better without the ball,' I assert.

'Yes let's hope we can keep at it.'

'We were very strong against Norwich with ten men. And there seems to be good body language in the group.'

'Yes today it was good to see Button supporting Bettinelli and passing on his observations.'

'At Norwich, it seemed Scott Parker had more of a coaching role as he didn't warm up with the other subs at half time and at the end he and Slaviša grasped each other's hand like they were part of the same management team. I imagine, as an experienced club captain, he has a big influence. I also think Kevin McDonald is a bit of an unsung hero. He's very consistent.'

'Yes, he's holding it all together at the back.'

Suddenly Alex's phone rings.

'It's Mikey from Norway. I'd better talk to him'

'Ok. But tell him not to come to any more games as we don't want to lose!'

And with that ultimatum, I make my way to the tube and a quiet evening in Ealing.

A Triumph in Yorkshire

Prime Minister Theresa May has called an election, Brenda of Bristol has cried 'not another one!' and sadly, Ugo Ehigou, the former Villa and Middlesborough centre back and recently the Spurs Under 23 coach, has collapsed and died from a heart attack at Tottenham's training ground. Meanwhile, apparently Wolves are interested in Chris Martin, leading one Fulham wag to comment-'with his size he should produce a big meal for the whole pack!' John Terry is finally leaving Chelsea at 36. When it was suggested that Fulham might buy him, a fan commented 'John Terry Vodka. Made in London. Bottled in Moscow,' (referring to his missed penalty in the 2008 Champions League Final).

Mira has just returned from a brief visit to Poland but she generously drives me to the Cottage to catch the coach to Huddersfield. The radio isn't working, so I'm purposefully loquacious to keep her alert. After a bizarre conversation about the mechanics of acceleration, she unceremoniously ejects me at Stevenage Rd and drives off, back to bed. It's now 6.25 am, the coaches haven't arrived but I engage with Dukey, the middle aged gent with the balding dark hair. He has a Fulham scarf wrapped around his neck and tells me that 'we haven't won four on the bounce since 2001' and that 'Huddersfield was the ground where promotion was confirmed in that year.'

I decide to go in the first coach. Stewarding the journey is that elderly man with a highly decorative Fulham cap, The Man With Many Badges. Some familiar older supporters are on the coach: apart from Dukey, there's a squat man in a red shirt, a sturdy, bald headed bloke and Tipperary Jim from the Norwich trip. I'm in the middle of the coach as five, strong, muscular twenty year olds make their way past me. I recognise two of them from the Rotherham game., including our friend the incessantly swaggering Straggly. The Man With Many Badges, informs us that we'll be stopping for a break in three hours time at 10 am. The driver, who is the man who gave the previous 'rules' speeches, is dressed in stern grey today. He's had a haircut, his beard is now trimmed, less shaggy and he's smartly dressed in his usual attire. This time, his speech is mercifully brief but he warns us that 'if you're not wearing a seat belt and the police stop us, you'll be fined fifty quid. Also remember, no alcohol and use the white sacks attached to the seat for rubbish. The toilet is in the middle of the coach, the door is on the right, not the emergency door in front of you. So don't get run over! Oh yes, if you've food to eat, put it in your mouth, not on the floor!'

I'm sitting next to a Malaysian middle aged man with dark, slightly greying hair. He asks me politely if I can move to accommodate his daughter, who's sitting further up the coach, next to Tipperary Jim. I'm reluctant to do so as the leg room in her seat is negligible and I'll be squashed like a sardine in a tin there. He understands as this is a five hour journey. He then asks the tall, dark, thirtyish looking man to our right but he responds similarly.

We're now on our way. The Malaysian is wearing an exotic, multi-coloured sweater and scarf. We have an amiable conversation about the merits of the management of Mark Hughes, and the way the German league strikes a better balance between having a strong competition and supporting the national team. I suggest that the German national team is almost a club in itself these days. I discover that although he's lived in England for forty years, he's hardly been outside London. He tells me about his uncle, who was imprisoned by the Japanese in World War Two, where he met an American who encouraged him to go to the States. His uncle then became a GI to get residency and when this legislation was reversed, he joined the marines, became an American citizen and via university and a period in Bologna, established himself as a doctor in New Jersey. After this unusual story, it's not long before we arrive at Woodall Service Station, off the M1. I go to the forecourt with the smokers, where I eat my specially cooked rice and fish, while a group of young supporters linger and banter away

Back in the coach, I discuss with The Malaysian, former Fulham keeper, David Stockdale's misfortune, in scoring two own goals for Brighton against Norwich, which surely must be a first. We then pass Chesterfield on our left. 'Oh, that's where it is,' says The Malaysian, as if discovering a new found land. We're an hour or so away from Huddersfield. When we finally make it off the M1, we gradually wind our way to the town. I'm entranced by the beauty of the Yorkshire countryside on a sunny spring day. A plethora of yellow oilseeds glisten in the sun. Old country houses, farms, barns, overarching hills and an early season cricket match, all contribute to an idyllic rural landscape. As we get nearer the town, there are some Barratt style homes but also more traditional sites like the local Methodist Church and the Heritage Museum. We pass over the River Colne, which flows through the Pennines, past various. textile and turbo technology firms and the university. Finally, we make our way up St Andrews Rd to the stadium. We arrive in the car park at 12.18. The gates won't open until 1.30 at the earliest, so there's time to kill. As I disembark, I'm next to the tall, dark man, the one who refused to move, who was watching a film about surfing.

'Was the film any good? It seemed to have some exhilarating shots.'

'Actually, it got quite scary when they encountered sharks.'

'Oh I must have missed that bit. I only saw a slim blonde woman in a bathing suit, effortlessly gliding over waves.'

'Later, I had to stifle my screams. It was so scary. Oh sorry, I've forgotten something' and he suddenly returns to the coach.

I then walk down St Andrews Rd and after a bit of sauntering, I go to the Premium Inn for a drink. It seems to house both sets of fans and appears relaxed but I take no chances and remove my colours before entering. After getting a Guinness and plonking myself at one of the bar's oak tables, I go to the toilet, which is flooding because of some drainage problem. I share my toilet adventure with two Fulham fans and discover that one went to school with John Chamberlain, son of the legendary 'Tosh'. We have a laugh about the eccentricities of past Fulham teams and, after sinking a pint, I make my way back to the ground

Inside, the stadium is impressive. We're behind one of the goals in The Chadwick Lawrence Stand, named after the law firm sponsors. To the right of the stand are the Town fans. Compact high banked seats surround the stadium. Huddersfield are fourth in the table and are already in the play-offs, which is an amazing achievement given their resources. As the teams warm up, a member of David Wagner's staff, wearing a blue and white track suit, is staring intensely at the Fulham players. Is he trying to psych them out? Or is he looking to discover who doesn't look sharp? He's certainly a menacing presence but I'm doubtful as to whether his hypnotic glares will have any effect.

I then watch the Fulham team practice shots against that ever available keeper, Joronen. One of them flies way over the bar, prompting the man next to me, a grey haired bloke with brown rimmed spectacles to recall a time, many years ago, when he was hit smack in the face by shot by diminutive Fulham striker Paul Peschisolido's, misfiring effort.

To our left, children now create a formal gangway for the players. They wave their blue and white Huddersfield flags earnestly in the air. The teams come out. The sound of 'SLAVISA'S BLACK AND WHITE ARMY' crescendos in the away stand. The home fans to our right respond, fluttering a Huddersfield flag, with a picture of Wagner. The Fulham supporters apparently number about 1,700. They realise the importance of the game and make their presence strongly felt. 'SUPER FULHAM, SUPER FULHAM FC...' chant the fans as the game gets underway.

The home team start with intensity. Fulham seem a bit slow out of the blocks. After three minutes, Löwe, Town's German left back runs into the box and is clipped by a covering Floyd Ayité. A penalty is awarded. Löwe takes it himself and his left footed shot goes into the right hand corner. 1-0. Not the start we want. However, Fulham immediately respond and Johansen plays in Sessegnon but his shot goes over the bar. 'RYAN SESSEGNON' chant the faithful. With just over quarter of an hour gone, a misplaced pass by a Town defender, twenty five yards out from goal, sees the ball cleverly played out to the left, where Scott Malone finds space and yes, scores with a great shot into the far corner, beyond keeper Ward. 1-1.

Later, Schindler narrowly glances a header just wide of the post, exposing our aerial weakness. Shortly after this narrow escape, we're back up Town's end. Floyd Ayité gets into the box, draws in players, looks to fully control the ball but is brought down. Yes, it's a penalty. Tom Cairney steps up. Now let's get this penalty jinx fully behind us, Tom, please! And yes, the captain delivers, drilling it deceptively into the right hand corner, giving the keeper no chance. 1-2. 'WHO

ARE YER? WHO ARE YER?' scream the black and white army. Town supporters now go very quiet-'SHALL WE SING FOR YER?' suggest the away fans.

Fulham then initiate a period of possession, which leads to Town frustration and Billing gets a yellow card for a nasty foul on the industrious McDonald. The fans respond with an inevitable chant of 'YOU DIRTY NORTHERN BASTARDS!' Fulham are now playing with confidence. The lively Ayité has a shot comfortably saved and Tom Cairney goes inches wide. Then the tireless Sone Aluko shows considerable trickery down the left avoiding Town's efforts at fouling him. He finds Sessegnon, whose shot is deflected. The ball then runs to Stefan Johansen, whose shot rifles into the net. 1-3. Brilliant Stefan! 'WE ARE GOING UP! WE ARE GOING UP! echoes around the stand. Followed by 'SUPER FULHAM! SUPER FULHAM FC!'

However, the Terriers still pose a threat and from a corner, Billings' header goes marginally wide. We're coming to the end of the half when Hogg is caught lingering on the ball outside the box. The tireless Johansen closes the defender down, keeps his feet, avoiding crude attempts to foul him and we're now in dreamland, as he places the ball beyond keeper Ward. 1-4. 'QUE SERA, SERA, WHATEVER WILL BE WILL BE, WE'RE GOIN' TO WEMBERLEE, QUE SERA SERA!' Nothing like our own version of a Doris Day hit.

At half time, we hear that about how our rivals are doing. It's 0-0 in the Leeds game, Reading are losing and Sheffield Wednesday are drawing. So everything to play for. For the second half Denis Odoi replaces Ryan Fredericks at right back. Ryan is on a yellow card so it's a good call, given his volcanic nature. The supporters are happy. 'FOLLOWIN' FULHAM AWAY!' they chant. I just hope we can now play a solid game, see it out and not make too many errors. Ironically, Odoi gets a yellow card within five minutes of the restart. As the half proceeds, one gets a sense that Fulham are playing within themselves, managing the game. It's becoming a bit of a damp squib but then suddenly Odoi, who's been solid, chests a ball down in the final third but fatally, it's to no one. Colin Quaner, the tall German striker, intercepts but his footwork is laboured and Marcus Bettinelli comes out to make a great save.

We then hear that Leeds are losing at Burton 'LEEDS, LEEDS ARE FALLING APART, AGAIN!' is the celebratory response. This is followed by Malone trying a shot with his 'wrong' right foot that goes past the post. 'WE ARE GOING UP! WE ARE GOING UP!' cry the Fulham support. Ryan Sessegon miscontrols a pass for a chance on goal but the faithful are too busy getting into party mood with 'WE LOVE YOU FULHAM, WE DO! WE LOVE YOU FULHAM WE DO! OH FULHAM, WE LOVE YOU!' and when, with four minutes to go, a limping Stefan Johansen is substituted he's given an appreciative send off with 'OH, STEFAN YOHANSEN!' In contrast, the Town fans are subdued. 'IS THERE A FIRE DRILL?' is the mocking Fulham riposte to the home fans leaving early. Sessegnon again fails to control the ball in front of goal-on another day he could have had a hat trick! But who cares? We hear Leeds have lost and we're in sixth place. So if we beat Brentford next week at the Cottage, we'll be in the play-offs. The Fulham team come over to the fans and applaud them. Bettinelli is the last to leave. As he punches the air in celebration, the fans joyfully sing his name-'MARCUS BETTINELLI!'

As I approach the coach in the car park, an elated, inebriated middle aged Fulham supporter, with hands flying anarchically, is chanting 'LEEDS, LEEDS ARE FALLING APART AGAIN!' which a policeman finds very amusing. Given local rivalries, that's not surprising. The supporter continues ecstatically 'WE'RE THE OLDEST TEAM IN LONDON AND WE'RE GOIN' TO WEMBERLEE! WEMBERLEE!' The Man With Many Badges is outside the coach. 'That was a good one,' I enthuse.' Yes, it was,' he replies with a satisfied smile. When I settle back in my seat, he looks to collect the tip for the driver. 'The driver will probably do well now there's a lot of happy supporters,' says The Malaysian. Our steward does the rounds and yes, The Malaysian is right, the big white envelope looks distinctly bulky. After putting in my quidsworth, an elegantly dressed supporter in a brown hat and jacket, cream trousers and a yellow shirt is making his way to the toilet.

'How do I get down here?' says Brown Hat, staring at the steep steps.

'Turn right,' says the diplomatic lady in front of me.

'Thanks darling.'

'Don't go left. You'll be outside the coach!' she warns.

Brown Hat is about to make his way gingerly down the steps to the toilet door. I think he's had a few but he's not drunk, just a bit worse for wear. Before fully descending, he talks to a nearby group of supporters including Dukey, The Man In The Red Shirt etc.

'I'm Fulham through and through,' he tells them. 'My Dad went to Fulham. He was an Irishman. He could have taken me to Loftus Rd. Thank God he didn't otherwise I'd be supporting that lot! And as for our next game-Brentford? We mustn't let those insects take over!'

We make our way out of the town with little difficulty. The Malaysian falls asleep. Others are looking at the Chelsea-Spurs game on their smartphones. A short man with a shaven head and 'HAYNES MAESTRO' displayed on the back of his Fulham shirt, is talking earnestly to the men in the middle of the coach, Dukey and Co. I think they're discussing the problems of family home care. It grows darker, time passes, and it's not long before we're approaching Hammersmith.

'I hope Johansen is fit,' says The Malaysian.'

'Slaviša in his post match interview, has said he should be ok.'

'Good. See you at Wembley!' replies The Malaysian, clasping my hand.

I take my bag, thank our steward and then the driver. I walk towards the tube with Tipperary Jim, who this time is in a more optimistic mood. We agree that it was a good day and that we have a real chance now. I say good night and make my way back to Ealing, where I arrive home just before ten o'clock. Come on Fulham, win next Saturday and we're in the play-offs!

The Bees Swarm to The Cottage

My bus from Wood Lane got stuck in a traffic jam, so I got off and went to Goldhawk Rd tube station. While waiting for a train, I bemoan the bad service with a black guy, who's wearing a dark blue uniform and has probably just finished work. When I tell him I'm going to the Brentford game, he engages in football chat. 'You're having a good season, man.' He then declares his loyalties. 'I'm a Spurs fan. The nearly team'. 'Still, they're a young squad,' I reply, 'they've still got a few seasons yet to win the title.' 'Yeah. You're right. We'll see,' he cautiously responds, as we leave Hammersmith station. 'Have a good one,' he cries as he disappears into the embrace of the Saturday shoppers.

Now I start my canter to the Cottage. I've got twenty five minutes. I should just make it but it won't be easy. I pass Frank Banfield Park, where in the adventure playground, kids are clambering up and down various equipment like playful animals and reluctant corgis are being rigorously exercised. It's low tide on the Thames. There are few rowers and only a sprinkling of moored yachts. Maybe they're all away for the Bank Holiday. I wriggle past a phalanx of elderly supporters who are taking over the width of the Thames Path. As I pass, a smartly jacketed young couple are discussing properties, while clutching pieces of swaying paper, full of flat specs. At Stevenage Rd, I'm reunited with the white haired Scottish Lady, who sells the programmes.

'I hope it's not the last time I see you this season.'

'Oh, no.'

'Fingers crossed'

As I go to my seat, a frail, pale looking man is in front of my seat. He moves tactfully to one side, where he 's seated with the rest of his family. Behind me as usual is John, The Irishman. His Dad's over from Ireland.

'You're back!'

They laugh.

'Let's hope we have a good one.'

'With the luck of the Irish,' I suggest.

'Of course!'

This isn't going to be a push over. Brentford are also a form team, unbeaten in seven games, winning the last four. There's a thunderous din as the teams come out. It isn't just the clappers, everybody is getting very vocal. Brentford supporters are taking up most of the Putney End but they're being drowned out. Fulham start well. They look confident and their passing game is pushing Brentford right back. After eight minutes, the pressure tells and when Sone Aluko puts Ryan Sessegnon through on the left, the teenager squares a perfect pass for Tom Cairney, who guides the ball into the net from close range. 1-0. 'WHO ARE YER? WHO ARE YER?' scream the fans as they indignantly point towards the Bees supporters at the Putney End. 'WHEN THE WHITES, OH WHEN THE WHITES GO MARCHIN' IN! I WANNA BE IN THAT NUMBER WHEN THE WHITES GO MARCHIN' IN!' sing the passionate crowd.

Cairney, our pivotal playmaker, who really makes the team tick, has another shot at goal but this time it's comfortable for Bees keeper Dan Bentley. Fulham are on top but we need that second goal. as Brentford are gradually playing their way into the game. Then, with a third of the match gone, Floyd Ayité beats Brentford's high line and only has the keeper to beat, this is it surely? Ugh! Unbelievably, he blasts the ball sky high, with a shot more akin to that game they play at Twickenham. I think the ball might have taken a bobble. Or am I being too kind? I just hope, we don't regret missing such a gilt-edged chance.

The crowd console themselves singing 'WE ARE, WE ARE, WE ARE THE FULHAM BOYS!' Fulham still seem to be controlling the game. Then after thirty four minutes, Brentford go on a counter attack. There's some good passing between our lines and gawd, the spaces open up and when the ball comes to Yennaris, just outside the area, he scores with a blistering shot beyond Marcus. 1-1. Game on. Now it's role reversal. 'WHO ARE YER? WHO ARE YER?' scream the Brentford fans, gesticulating wildly at their closest rivals.

Still, I'm confident that this Fulham team believe that they can score at any time and will respond. The athletic Fredericks agrees as he careers down the right like a man possessed, leaving defenders trailing in his wake, and puts in a great cross, Ayité pulls away from his man, rises and. oh no, his header's gone over the bar. What a golden chance! If only we had a cutting edge to our game.

We're now coming up to the end of the first half. Johansen finds that man Ayité again. He twists and turns in the area, a tackle comes in, Floyd goes down and surely ref? Yes, it's a penalty. Cairney gets ready to take it. There's a protracted delay. Tom comes up, again goes for the right hand corner and I don't believe it, we've missed another as Bentley saves diving to his left. The ball rebounds off him, Cairney sticks a leg out but doesn't get there and the keeper grabs it. We've now missed nine penalties this season! Their keeper had done his homework and our penalty problems have come back to haunt us. The whistle goes for half time. There's no doubt we're making life hard for ourselves and the game is in the balance.

At half time, the academy players compete in a penalty competition and a stout Barry Hayles, the former Fulham striker, is interviewed by our announcer. I can't hear the interview clearly but I think Barry is saying is that we're playing well and should be two or three goals up. When he walks off the pitch towards the Cottage. 'BARRY! BARRY!' is chanted and he raises his hand in acknowledgement. Apparently, Barry's still playing non league football for Chesham United at forty four years of age! The Irishman and his Dad have gone for some refreshment but on their return they tell me that Leeds, who have to win to stay in play-off contention, given their inferior goal difference, are losing 3-0 to Norwich. That means if it stays like that, we're in the play-offs!

The game restarts. Cairney has a shot going to the top corner, well saved by Bentley. Johansen fires inches wide. Fulham are spending a lot of time in Brentford's final third and keeping possession well but the Bees are still proving effective on the counter attack. Just after the hour mark, Vibe runs at Ream and his shot brings a good save from Bettinelli, warning us of that Bees threat. Then the persistent Aluko wriggles through their defence but loses control and ends up poking the ball to the keeper. As we come into the last third of the game, some Fulham players seem to be tiring. We then hear that Leeds have now managed to dramatically claw their way back to 3-3! The tension in the ground is palpable. We've got to at least hold out and hope. The crowd cry out desperately 'COME ON FULHAM! COME ON FULHAM!' The wan man next to me, looks apprehensive. 'They never make it easy, supporting this club do they?' I suggest. 'They certainly don't,' he replies mournfully.

Brentford are still coming at us and would love to spoil our party but substitute Kebano forces a corner and from Johansen's kick, Piazon just misses getting a header on goal. We're now in the final ten minutes and Fulham are passing nervously. 'Stop messin', bellows the Irishman's Dad. When they start taking risks at the back, John, the Irishman, gets splenetic-'what the fuck are you doing?' It's all getting to be a bit fraught. Eventually, after what seems an eternity, the whistle blows. There's then a tense pause, while we await the Leeds result.

Suddenly, the Fulham players embrace each other and Slaviša comes on to the pitch. Apparently, Leeds have drawn. They can't catch us. We've made it to the play-offs. Brilliant. The crowd celebrate. 'OH NOW, YOU GOTTA BELIEVE US, OH NOW YOU GOTTA BELIEVE US, OH NOW YOU GOTTA BELIEVE US, WE'RE GOIN' TO WEMBERLEE!, WE'RE GOIN' TO WEMBERLEE!' The players move to the Hammersmith End and acknowledge the Fulham faithful. Tim Ream's left hand punches the air, the team clap the fans. As they trundle off to the Cottage, many supporters in the Haynes Stand stay behind to give them a standing ovation.

By The Wall, a haggard man is neurotically puffing at an electronic cigarette, as an army of departing fans from the Hammersmith End march out of the ground chanting: 'WE ARE ! WE ARE! WE ARE GOING UP!'.

'Mad, wasn't it?' says the approaching Alex 'but we finally got there.'

'Yes,' I reply.' Just about.'

'Phew!' says Richard 'we started misplacing passes and playing too deep. Still all that matters is the result.'

Richard's mate Pete has gone to the shop with his grandson. He's with Shane who's elegantly dressed in a light blue jacket and a multi-coloured scarf, sartorially tied around his neck.

'Ayité changed his boots at half time but it didn't seem to make a difference!' says Richard.

'No. Floyd didn't have one of his best games. Ream and McDonald played well,' propounds the author.

'I thought Ream was crap but he was good today.' chimes in Shane.

'I agree about McDonald,' says Richard, 'he's the glue that sticks the team together.'

There's then a discussion about the play-off dates. Richard discovers that he's got a competitive golf match on one of those days.

'I think I might be going to be ill on that day!'

As they leave, I call to Richard:

'Fulham should be in the drama business.'

'You mean more twists and turns than Agatha Christie!' he yells back.

'Exactly!'

Alex and I then wander up towards Fulham Palace Rd.

'I think he's got to give some of the other squad members a run out at Hillsborough.'

'Maybe he will.'

'Many of them have had little game time recently. What happens if there are injuries or we need them as vital substitutes?'

'Piazon was certainly off the pace and he hasn't played much recently.'

'Still the defence has become more resilient.'

'Resilient. that's the right word.'

'Previous Fulham teams would have lost today. But bloody penalties is still a problem.'

Alex then tells me that he took penalties himself and moves his feet with agile dexterity to show me how Cairney could have been less predictable and gone for the other side of the goal.

After this illuminating insight, I say goodbye to Alex and walk to the Hammersmith Bus Station, to get some exercise. Outside Bristas, next to the Chicago Grill, is a sign saying 'Arrogant, Superb Coffee.' Not sure where that comes from. I'd prefer 'Brilliant. Superb Fulham Make Play-Offs!'

Seeing It Out

I'm getting up at 3.30 am to watch a football match that is a non event. Apparently, 3,000 Fulham obsessives are going up to Sheffield for the 12 pm game with Sheffield Wednesday. They booked believing the game would decide our play-off place. As we settled that at 5 pm last Saturday, this game could be a bit of a damp squib.

At the Cottage, I have to undergo an alcohol inspection. 'It's got to be done otherwise the coach firm will lose its licence,' says our steward, The Man With Many Badges. A white haired man with square, grey framed glasses asks me to open the bag. He peers in. Then, as I put the bag on the pavement, he says, 'I heard something heavy.' 'That's my thermos,' I reply, alleviating his worst fears.

I then take my seat and recognise the grey bearded portly Ulsterman, who lives in the coop in East London and who's wearing a grey sweater and a blue collared shirt. We talk about the likely make up of today's team. 'Maybe, he'll play both Cyriac and Martin?' Suddenly, a group of hyperactive young women make their way down the narrow aisle. One has a Marathon Bet Fulham t shirt, another, who is wearing large sunglasses and a light brown coat, desperately clasps a foam coffee cup, while stumbling in the aisle. 'She's been on the vodka,' jokes Miss Marathon Bet. As it nears 5.30 am, when we're meant to leave, breathless stragglers come rushing in. A pale, young dark haired woman in jeans bundles herself into a seat and The Man With Many Badges inspects her bag. Then in comes The Ulsterman's mate and a weary voiced 'The Northerner' stumbles down the aisle. 'The train didn't come as usual,' he explains, 'there was a problem as police emerged out of the tunnel.' He then adds drowsily, 'I don't feel I've had a good night's sleep.'

'Don't worry about that,' I reassure him. 'Can you take penalties?'

'Oh yes, I take good penalties,' he replies with a glint in his eye.

After discovering that our support is going to supplant that of the 2,700 fans who went to the Brighton away game, The Man With Many Badges makes a short speech stating that 'we're going to stop at Toddington for breakfast in two hours time.' I've had mine but I suppose I'd better compensate for a lack of lunch. I ask our steward if everybody's arrived. Apparently, only twenty haven't turned up. 'Given that now we've made the play-offs, you'd expect that,' I suggest. 'I guess so,' replies The Man with Many Badges. Eventually, the cohort of coaches leave the Cottage.

Behind me a bearded young man in his twenties and presumably his middle-aged father are chatting away. 'I love Phil Collins. Mum gave me a ticket for him,' he gushes. Meanwhile, our Asian driver's Indian music is percolating pleasantly through the coach's speakers. 'I've received a tweet from a friend of mine in Detroit,' continues The Bearded Youngster, 'he asks if he should buy tickets for Wembley?' In fact, dead on cue, we pass that very town. Is this a portent of things to come? We then proceed into Hertfordshire, followed by Bedfordshire, not far from Woburn Abbey and eventually enter Toddington. We then pass a dreadful car crash. A yellow ambulance's red light is throbbing menacingly. 'I think there was a three car pile-up. One of them was upside down,' says The Bearded Youngster. After passing a sign to Silverstone, we finally arrive at the familiar service station. It's 7.45 am.

Inside this mecca of consumerism there are a huge variety of services ranging from WH Smith to Costa Coffee. Outside the food counter is a flashing red neon sign, enticing us to 'Order Here! Order Here!' Surreptitiously, I sit at one of the oak tables and unpack my own rice and chicken. At the table opposite me, there are a couple of middle aged Fulham supporters, one in his forties with a shaven head, tattoos on his arm and a Visit Florida Fulham shirt. His younger mate is more conventionally dressed in a blue jacket, shirt and jeans.

'Bloody awful kick off time,' I tell them.

'Absolutely,' says The Shaven Headed Man.

'Bloody Sky!' I predictably exclaim.

'Mind you, I was just saying I prefer the Championship, 'cause you play Saturday. In the Premiership, they'll play anytime.'

'You don't know where you are,' suggests his mate.

Suddenly I'm thinking that maybe breakfast football will be the next launch!

'And we haven't got to the play-offs yet,' I remind them.

'Yeah,' says The Shaven Headed Man, 'why can't the northern teams play-off against each other and then the southern teams?'
'The building of the new Wembley went so over budget, they'd take anything,' I proclaim.
'That's right. They'd take blow football or tiddlywinks competitions, if you paid them!' says The Shaven Headed Man.
Back in the coach, the girls are last in-'What? What are you talkin' about?' says Miss Marathon Bet to The Girl In Shades. 'Shut up, that's totally ridiculous,' she insists, as they meander to the back seats. When we resume our journey, it's not long before we're greeted by a sign stating, 'Nottinghamshire, The Robin Hood County'. The Bearded Youngster and his Dad, who's casually dressed in blue denim jacket and jeans, are talking about the election. 'She's done nothing,' says the older man, referring to Prime Minister May, who is supposedly on course for a landslide victory, in the forthcoming general election, if we believe the polls. Finally we arrive in Sheffield. We make the inevitable circle around the stadium confines to get in the correct parking position. It's now two hours before the game, so I decide to go for a local Yorkshire walk.

The ground is near Hillsborough Park and the River Don, which is bisected by a small bridge. Hillsborough Primary School, a children's care centre, light industrial complexes and many residential back to back houses complete the local area. This is a club in the heart of the community with arterial Supertram lines criss-crossing the neighbourhood.

Although I'm strolling about in Fulham colours, people say hello or 'hey up' and are very friendly. Outside the ground's West Stand there is a memorial to those who died in the Hillsborough tragedy. 'Never Forget The 96. 15 April 1989' is inscribed into a simple abstract monument, behind which are the draped scarves of various clubs. Further down, a fair haired middle aged man in a yellow bib is selling programmes. I hear him talking to two young women about the miner's strike of 1989. 'I wasn't going on the picket line....Thatcher's police had a licence to do what they wanted.' The area seems to be still haunted by that period.

Further down, there's an idiosyncratic shop for old programmes run by a large, imposing gentleman in a black sweater and grey trousers. The programmes are carefully placed in different sections. Many are displayed on the walls. For a lover of football, it brings back treasured memories of forgotten names -Terry Curran, David Hirst and Peter Eustace, let alone Fulham's 1975 FA Cup Semi Final game against Birmingham City. Outside The Spion Kop South Stand, there's also a huge painting of the club's badge with its central picture of an Owl and its motto underneath, Consilio Et Animis. While there, a man in a green felt hat smoking a cigar asks me:

'What do you think about today then?'

'I think we'll put out quite a few reserves.'

'Wednesday will probably do the same,'

His strong cigar fumes are beginning to invade my throat.

'What was it like coming up?'

'Smooth. There was very little traffic. But getting up at 3.45 was difficult.'

'I got up early 'cause I came from Doncaster.'

We're then interrupted. A young lad asks The Cigar Man to take a selfie of him with a very, big, tall, athletic blonde man in his late thirties, early forties. When it's done, The Cigar Man asks him:

'So are you summarising today?'

'Yes, that's right.'

'So what do you think the result will be?'

He agrees it depended on the team selection.

'If there are changes, it makes sense. You don't want silly red cards or injuries to key players,' says The Athletic Blonde.

He's obviously an ex-Wednesday player. After he departs to join the local radio team, I ask The Cigar Man for his name?

'I've forgotten. I think he also played for Norwich.'

We then go down memory lane and when I mention Derek Dooley, Jackie Sewell and Albert Quixall ('he didn't do good when he went to United. He should have stayed here'), he's genuinely shocked.

'How old are you then? '

'Seventy one.'

'You don't look it.'

'I'm seventy three myself.'

'You're looking good on it!'

After such mutual flattery, we digress to discuss how physical and dirty the game was in the past. The Cigar Man sums up that violent sporting culture.

'Yes if you had made such challenges on the street, you'd have been arrested. On the pitch here, you got away with it in front of 30,000 witnesses!'

After agreeing this match is really a warm up before the important stuff, we depart, wishing each other well but those cigar fumes are really getting to me.

As I start to wander around the ground, at the bottom of Leppings Lane, I bump into Tipperary Jim, who's wearing a baseball cap and a light, casual jacket, while his luggage lies on the pavement. He's looking a bit frustrated but still greets me with a cheery grin.

'I'm waiting for our coach to take our bags. There's no sign of it yet.'

'When did you come up?'

'Last night. I stayed at a hotel.'

After wishing him good luck, I leave Tipperary Jim and make my way back to the ground. I pass a supporter with 'Sheff Wednesday FC' imprinted on a blue shirt with white sleeves. 'This is a relaxed weekend compared to next week,' says the fan, foreseeing the tension of the forthcoming play-offs.

When I enter the West Stand, I climb up the steep steps to the biggest football lavatories I've ever witnessed. Good to accommodate a large crowd, although the blue and white decor could do with sprucing up. In the bar, the fans are bouncing up and down. 'DON'T KNOW HOW I GOT HERE, I DON'T CARE. FULHAM AWAY! FULHAM AWAY!'

We're behind the goal in the Upper Stand. Below us are some home supporters. To our right is the entrance to the pitch. To our left, the perimeter of the high raked stand's roof is full of a plethora of adverts. Suddenly, as if by some magical osmosis, a yellow plastic banana floats innocently above our head. This surreal object is pursued by black and white balloons. These are trailed by a yellow and pink beach ball and a bunch of white balloons, which fly upwards like released pigeons from a coop. A chant of 'SUPPORT FULHAM AWAY! SUPPORT FULHAM AWAY!' is followed by a rendition of 'SUPER FULHAM!, SUPER FULHAM FC! BY FAR THE GREATEST TEAM, THE WORLD HAS EVER SEEN!' It's carnival time as the Fulham faithful decide to poke fun at their nearest competitors. 'WE'RE ALL HAVING A PARTY! WE'RE ALL HAVING A PARTY! WE'RE ALL HAVING A PARTY! BECAUSE LEEDS HAVE FUCKED IT UP! OH LEEDS HAVE FUCKED IT UP! OH LEEDS HAVE FUCKED IT UP!'

The teams enter through an aisle created by flag waving youngsters. The procession is followed by rudimentary handshakes and the introduction of young mascots. Fulham are playing in red, defending our goal. Slaviša has made four changes: Odoi for Fredericks, Piazon for Johansen, Kebano for Sessegnon and Martin for Ayité. We start lethargically as if we haven't yet arrived in Yorkshire. After nine minutes, the referee, Graham Scott gets in the way of a Kalas pass, the ball moves out to Sam Winnall on the left of the penalty area and the striker calmly guides the ball across Bettinelli into the net. 1-0. 'WEDNESDAY!' scream the home fans. Not a good start.

Fulham are nearly undone again when there appears to be a mix up between Kalas and Ream. Neither goes to clear a ball over the top. but fortunately Jordan Rhodes' control is poor. When the game settles down, Fulham control possession and start to dominate the game. Meanwhile, the substitutes warm up in front of us. Chants of 'RYAN! RYAN SESSEGNON!' and 'SUPER, SUPER SCOTT, SUPER SCOTTY PARKER!' greet the men on the bench. Then Odoi, whose crossing up to this point has been erratic, is played in down the right; he centres and yes, Neeskens Kebano meets it first time and scores. 1-1. The fans celebrate with an effusive denigration of their powerful neighbours: 'WE ARE FULHAM, WE ARE FULHAM, WE ARE FULHAM FFC. WE ARE FULHAM, SUPER FULHAM, WE ARE FULHAM, FUCK CHELSEA!'

Unsurprisingly, this doesn't appear to be the most intense of games. Wednesday have made many changes and most of their regulars are missing. Fulham continue to play good passing football but again lack a cutting edge in the final third. Still there's still time to teasingly taunt the locals with a chant of 'OH, SHEFFIELD UNITED!' in support of their bitter rivals. The Wednesday crowd are quiet. 'SSSSHHHHH!' hiss the Fulham fraternity. Then, suddenly there's a huge, unnecessarily vicious lunge at Aluko and Matthias is sent off. Wednesday are now down to ten men. 'YOU DIRTY NORTHERN BASTARDS!' echoes spontaneously around the stand. Silly really, Aluko wasn't in a dangerous area and this is in one of the least important games of the season.

A few minutes later, I'm interrupted by a young, auburn haired bloke in a black track suit top and his dark haired female companion, who's wearing big oval, black rimmed glasses. They're going early to the bar. 'It's not that bad is it?' I enquire. He grins and continues on his way to beat the queue. Fulham look to capitalise on having the extra man but at the break the score remains 1-1.

During half time, Kieran Westwood the Wednesday keeper (not playing in this game) is given his Player of the Year Award and a dance troupe in black track suits expertly perform a modern dance, to throbbing music. Meanwhile, some young Owls are having a team photo taken.

When the second half starts, Fulham continue to dominate possession but still aren't clinical with their finishing. The bloke next to me and his lady now reappear. 'You're missing the good bits!' I temptingly suggest, 'surely Fulham can't drive you to drink? 'No mate, it's not that bad,' he replies cheerily as he and his bespectacled lady friend, take their seats.

With eleven minutes to go, Fulham get a free kick in a wide position, Piazon floats in a good, quick delivery and yes, Kebano flicks it in. 1-2. The Wednesday players are protesting that there was a handball but their pleas are rejected. Fulham celebrate by chanting exultantly: 'THE WHITES ARE GOIN' UP! OH NOW, YOU'VE GOT TO BELIEVE US! THE WHITES ARE GOIN' UP!' This elation is followed by Kebano nearly getting a hat trick but keeper Joe Wildsmith makes a great save, tipping the Fulham forward's shot on to the crossbar and behind for a corner.

The game then peters out, three minutes of injury time are played and Fulham see them out comfortably. The players come over to the fans, Ream claps them and gets an energetic 'R-E-A-M!' chant in response. McDonald displays a victory sign. Bettinelli pumps his fist in the air and gives McDonald a mock kiss! A playful end to a good win in a less intense game.

The Lad In the Black Track Suit makes his way out with the Lady With The Oval Glasses. 'Ok, don't go on the piss now,' I advise. 'See you mate,' he replies buoyantly. After my last visit to the expansive toilet, I leave the ground and have trouble finding the coach. It's moved from its original position but a policeman puts me right. I'm greeted by the smiling Asian driver in a dark blue sweater.

When The Man With Many Badges has done his collection for the driver and counts the heads, I note that The Bearded Youngster and his Dad are no longer present. They must be staying in Yorkshire, or have gone on the piss! Making our way out of central Sheffield is slow. As we drive through the suburbs amidst semi detached houses, we pass three funeral homes in quick succession, which is a bit ghoulish.

Approaching the motorway, nature becomes remote as we are propelled into the concrete world of the M1. Still we now move quickly as the traffic is light. We stop at Newport Pagnell for a quarter of an hour's break. The Ulsterman and 'The Northerner' go to sleep. We get into London in good time.

I get off at Shepherd's Bush Green and go to see Mira. I arrive in Wood Lane just before 9 pm. I'm a bit knackered but it was a good day. Well, of course it was as Fulham won! Now for next week and the real stuff. The first leg of the play-off against Reading. I do believe we can go all the way.

Battle with The Royals

It's Saturday May 13th and it's the first leg of the play-off semi-final. Chelsea have won the Premiership by beating West Brom away, and a rather docile general election campaign goes on apace. In contrast, there's feverish excitement in west London about Fulham's play-off chances. Although, we beat Reading easily at the Cottage earlier in the season, this is a completely different situation.

At Hammersmith Broadway, Phil Collins is advertised as coming to the Apollo in June. At the top of Fulham Palace Rd, The Duke of Cornwall pub is lively with punters displaying an array of various Fulham t shirts, while enjoying the sunshine and sipping their beers on the nearby pavement. It's high tide on the Thames. A crew of female rowers have dropped oars as their demanding cox barks instructions. Sporadic yachts float elegantly on the cusp of waves. Kids run amok down the pathway and a robust Fulham fan in dark sunglasses stops an overactive infant in his tracks. 'Mine do that as well,' he says sympathetically to an advancing young mum, who has breathlessly chased after the young miscreant. In Stevenage Rd, I say goodbye to the Scottish lady who sells the programmes.

'Have a good summer?'

'Well, I could see you at Wembley.'

'Oh. You do Wembley as well?'

'Maybe, we'll see you there?'

'Of course, we'll see you there,' says the nearby ruddy faced, white haired man doing The Bobby Moore Fund cancer collection, while his small, soporific, brown-coated dog lies asleep on the road, oblivious to the world

I'm going to meet Alan, a mate of mine, by the Johnny Haynes statue. Alan is an avid supporter of Notts County, who are currently languishing in sixteenth place in League One. Alan's father, Jack Dunnett, who's approaching his ninety fifth birthday, was a Labour MP in Nottingham, Chairman of Notts County (1967-87) and President of The Football League (1981-86,1988-89). At 5 pm, Alan arrives. With long greying hair and a rucksack over his back he greets me with 'you're looking thin,' which makes me feel as if I've been on hunger strike, when I've only been keeping to a diet. As we pass the turnstiles, Alan says he's surprised that his rucksack hasn't been checked-'why was it they looked into my bag when I went to the Putney End and not here?' 'Away supporters go into the Putney End and you're with trustworthy Fulham supporters in The Johnny Haynes Stand!' He doesn't look convinced at my spurious attempts at an explanation.

When the teams come out, there's a huge wall of sound. This is the most important game at the Cottage for years and the fans are up for it, violently banging their clappers on accompanying seats. Such intense noise drowns out a significant Reading following. Slaviša gets a thunderous reception. The atmosphere is electric. The Irishman gets to his seat just in time but there are a lot of latecomers, who aren't regulars. They're blocking the view and taking a long time to get to their seats. I'm controlling my irritation while these 'intruders' settle down. When the game starts, we're playing towards the Putney End. There seems to be a lot of nervousness. Unsurprising, considering what's at stake. Not just a place in The Premiership but £90 million.

There's a frenetic start and when our centre backs, Ream and Kalas, collide, they nearly let in Grabban but the ball is nervously scrambled away. Eventually, Fulham compose themselves and a terrific curling shot from Cairney, goes just wide of the post. Then comes the clamorous roar of 'WE ARE, WE ARE, WE ARE THE FULHAM BOYS!' We're nearly twenty minutes into the game, when Scott Malone and Floyd Ayité combine down the left, Floyd is away, it's a great pull back but on no, Aluko's shot goes wide of the far post. That was a great chance. He should have buried that. Sone Aluko has been terrific for us this season but his finishing is erratic, to put it mildly. We just don't have a natural finisher and we can't afford to miss such chances in a 'cup' game. There's less margin for error.

Reading are doing job on us in this half, rather like Sheffield Wednesday did here. They're pressing strongly, not allowing us to pass from the back, they're marking Cairney very tightly to counter the hub of our creativity and they're preventing Fredericks from using his pace on the right, although Malone, our other full back, seems to be more successfully escaping their clutches on the left. In addition, they're fouling a lot and breaking up the play. Towards the end of the half, Ayitè sprints away towards goal but unwisely shoots from an acute angle when others were unmarked in the box. The referee blows his whistle for half time. It's exciting but more for the game's intensity rather than its quality.

During the interval, the Irishman rushes to the bar to 'settle the nerves'. Meanwhile, Alan reminisces about muddy pitches when there were no substitutes. He remembers Bobby Moore once having to go in goal for West Ham.

'Didn't he save a penalty,' I enquire.

'Yes, he saved it but they scored on the rebound.'

I also get the thoughts of a young, rugged bloke behind me, who's proudly displaying his Fulham Visit Florida shirt.

'If we get a goal, they'll have to come out and that'll make it easier.'

'True but it's been hard to break through so far. We'll see,' I cautiously respond.

Seven minutes into the second half, Fulham give possession away, in the final third. There's an appeal for handball, several Fulham players hesitate, the ball makes its way out to the left, where Obita is unmarked. He shoots and oh no, here we go, the ball goes in off the far post, past the despairing dive of Marcus Bettinelli. 0-1. That was a harder chance than the one Aluko missed! Ugh! Come on Fulham, fight back! Now, Malone gets a yellow card. I think it must be for verbals about the handball incident. In any case, the referee, Stuart Atwell, seems to be overawed by the occasion and has been inconsistent with his decisions. Now we're totting them up, as Kevin McDonald also gets a yellow. He took one for the team there, to stop a dangerous counter attack as Reading pressed forward.

However, as The Royals tire, the game opens up and after sixty five minutes, Cairney finds Floyd Ayitè, who flicks the ball on the volley to Scott Malone, who's free on the left. He crosses, Al Habsi fumbles, the ball goes in the air and Tom Cairney heads it in. Yes! 1-1. 'WE ARE THE FULHAM BOYS!' implodes around the ground.

With ten minutes to go, the Reading captain Paul McShane, lunges dangerously at McDonald, and receives a red card. Initially, he walks off in the wrong direction but is unceremoniously directed towards the Cottage. The ginger haired Irish international departs slowly, his eyes looking straight ahead, relishing breaking up the play and wasting time. The crowd shout 'CHEERIO! CHEERIO!' and wave as he departs. There is a crescendo of booing and the woman to my right is getting particularly animated, screaming abuse as if she was at a public hanging of yesteryear.

Now Fulham, come on, get a winner! The crowd are ferociously roaring the team on. The support in this game has been the most boisterous for many years. Fulham are pressing, looking for a way through, almost trying too hard. Unfortunately, they're forced to resort to long distance efforts. The whistle finally blows. Not what we ideally wanted but still all to play for.

Alan has to skedaddle home and I meet up with Alex at The Wall, where I give him money for my Reading away ticket

Richard arrives.

'Ok mate. We're doing a bit of wheeler-dealing here,' I warn him.

'Oh right a bit of 'Minder' stuff.'

'A bit straighter than that!'

Then Richard gets on to the football:

'We were nervous. We were trying to force it.'

'When we put crosses in, nobody was on the end of them,' says Alex.

'We didn't play to the whistle for their goal,' I pronounce.

'Still away from home, I fancy us as they've got to come out more,' says Pete, now joining us.

'We were bad in the first half. Better in the second, when Fredericks found more space down the right. The ball was coming too slowly to Martin. Slaviša was going crazy at Bettinelli, wanting him to be quicker with his kicking,' concludes The Oracle.

I then accompany Richard and Pete who are going to Hammersmith tube. I leave the lads at the station and make my way to Wood Lane, pondering on what might happen in Berkshire in a few days time. I just hope we can go all the way.

The Final Reckoning

I'm at the Cottage waiting for the coach to go to Reading for the second leg of the play-off semi-final. As I wait for Alex, I talk to The Ulsterman. I discover that he's from Co Armagh, 'bandit country' during 'the troubles'. He's lingering near the wall to the Johnny Haynes Stand as we discuss the possible team for tonight and whether to start with Chris Martin or not? There are four coaches and when Alex appears we clamber into one of them. Barbara, our steward, hears Alex call me Roly and thinks that he said Julie! On the way to finding seats, I pass East End Doug, who's been in New Orleans.

'Listen to some good jazz then?' 'I ask

'Yes and blues. Also managed to book a ticket for this match online from Detroit airport!'

Alex and I settle in the middle of the coach. It's a humid evening so we turn on the much needed ventilation. Alex has got a new Fulham t shirt, inscribed with 'Slaviša Jokanović. Making Fulham Great Again!' He also has a flag, which combines the Serbian national flag with Fulham's. Like Slaviša, Alex's partner, Dragana, is Serbian and works as an Education Manager for The Royal College of General Practitioners.

Unfortunately, our mates, Richard and Pete, are indeed tied up with that golf competition. As they're known to be committed Fulham fans, it wouldn't take a Hercule Poirot to discover their whereabouts, if they threw a 'sickie'. During the journey, Alex and I have a wide ranging discussion regarding the club's football structure, which seems to be in a better place now Director Tony Khan, Shahid's son, is basing himself more in London and Brian Talbot, the former Ipswich and Arsenal player, is assisting him with 'football operations' .

By the time we arrive at the ground, we have a short wait before going into the South Stand. I have a lager poured for me by a young blonde girl, whose name Tilly is displayed diplomatically on her Fulham FC shirt. On the screen, they're showing reruns of previous Fulham games. We seem to be losing most of them. 'It just winds me up,' says a Fulham fan in a brown flannelled shirt. 'Oh that's one's a draw. Thanks a lot!' says the man, pointing at the screen, as his protruding paunch emerges more fully into view. In the steep stand, we're next to a bloke with shaven greying hair. He's wearing a dark track suit top and blue jeans. He peers at us through round brown rimmed glasses. Apparently, his nephews are in seats far away from him, so he's asking us to move. When Alex is reluctant, the bloke tells him that one of the nephews is suffering from cancer, which is a bit sudden and dramatic. Alex tells him that he's a bit superstitious about moving, so he prefers to stay, which The Man In Brown Glasses seems to accept.

The Royals announcer is now trying to rouse the crowd. 'Reading We Love You' appears dramatically across the stadium screen. 'Confident?' I ask the Man In Brown Glasses. 'Yes,' he replies, 'because even when we go behind, we continue to play our football, the best since the Tigana days.' The fans chant, 'COME ON YOU WHITES!' and 'SLAVISA'S BLACK AND WHITE ARMY!' cranking up the support. The mascots wait at the centre circle. A St George's flag drapes over the edge of the stand to our left, proclaiming 'Ipsden Royals.' The Fulham faithful now sing 'TAKE ME HOME, AL FAYED...CRAVEN COTTAGE BY THE RIVER' and 'AL-FAYED WHOOAAA! HE WANTS TO BE A BRIT AND QPR ARE SHIT!' The tension is increasing. Some young Royals in yellow shirts and red shorts form a guard of honour. Then orchestral music reaches a crescendo, four fire flames explode into the air and the teams enter the arena like gladiators ready to wrestle over their fate. After the obligatory handshakes and the toss, overseen by international referee Martin Atkinson, we're off.

Reading in their usual blue and white hoops are playing towards us. Fulham are in their red away strip. The Royals start with intensity. Mutual taunting is going back and forth between the fans. 'CHELSEA REJECT! 'they scream when loanee centre back Kalas touches the ball. 'WHO THE FUCKIN,' WHO THE FUCKIN,' WHO THE FUCKIN' HELL ARE YOU?' respond the Fulham loyalists. Yann Kermorgant, the Reading striker, is looking sharp and fit for a thirty five year old and when he swivels, and shoots, Marcus Bettinelli makes a great save, diving to his right to push the ball round the post. It seems we haven't yet got the pace of the game. Then after eighteen minutes, Ryan Fredericks, goes haring down the right, evades three tackles, goes inside and shoots with his weaker left foot and Al Habsi dives to his left to make a comfortable save.

'COME ON FULHAM!' shout the crowd, sensing that the Whites are beginning to assert themselves. Tom Cairney then bends a free kick and Al Habsi claws the shot away and smothers the follow up by Sone Aluko. That's more like it. The travelling fans respond with their traditional cry against their neighbours, 'WE ARE FULHAM.... FUCK CHELSEA!' which is followed by the equally disparaging, 'YOU'RE JUST A SHIT QUEEN'S PARK RANGERS!' yelled tauntingly at their Reading counterparts. We're a few minutes over the half hour mark now but when Kebano plays in Aluko, he spoons his shot wildly into the air. On no, Sone, not again! This is followed by Kevin McDonald, who has been his usual purposeful self sweeping up and recycling the ball, getting booked for a challenge on Williams. The whistle blows for half time. A cagey half, no one fully in the ascendancy. Let's hope our passing game will emerge triumphant as legs tire.

Alex and I remain in our seats in the precipitous stand. It's too much like descending from the London Eye to make the effort to go and congregate with inveterate mortals in the bar. We might as well stay in the sky.

When the game restarts, the home team, now playing towards the far end, reassert themselves with intensity but thankfully Grabban's flick from a Kermorgant cross is easily saved by Bettinelli. Then, after forty eight minutes, the ball bounces to Kalas in the box and, oh no, it looks as if he's handled the ball. Was that accidental and just a natural part of his stride? The stern Mr Atkinson doesn't think so. He points confidently to the spot. In fact, there aren't many protests from the Fulham players. After a short wait, Kermorgant comes up and fatally plants the ball inside the left post, beyond Bettinelli's despairing dive. 1-0. Marcus guessed correctly but such was the accuracy and power of the shot that it comfortably found the net. Fulham have got it all to do now. The home crowd go wild. 'WE'RE GOING TO WEMBERLEE!' chant the Royals fans.

Reading's play now seems much quicker. So much is at stake and bookings begin to abound: Kermorgant for a challenge on Johansen and Moore for a lunge on Aluko. Reading continue to press and

Gunter on the right gets in a great cross. It reaches John Swift unmarked, five yards out-help! Are they going to get a second? No, I don't believe it, he shoots tamely at Marcus, when he had the whole goal at his mercy. What a let off! Maybe it's a good omen. Let's hope so. Fulham certainly respond and Aluko plays in Ayité but the Togolese international is crowded out.

Soon after his arrival on the hour mark, substitute and ex-Reading loanee, Lucas Piazon, is found in the box by Fredericks. He shoots first time but the ball bounces off a hooped shirt for a corner, which unfortunately comes to nothing. Still Reading are now tiring and they're unable to press us so quickly. Fulham are now finding more space and dominating possession. 'COME ON YOU WHITES!'

The tension rises and Malone gets a yellow card for arguing. The persistent Aluko releases Sessegnon but on no, Ryan's shot is weak and Al Habsi saves comfortably. Then Piazon is wrestled to the ground in the box by Van De Berg. A penalty? Surely? Yes, please! The authoritative Mr Atkinson doesn't agree. Was he right? Possibly. Fulham still continue to attack determinedly. Sone Aluko cuts back on to his left foot, is this it? No, predictably, he shoots over the bloody bar!

With fifteen minutes to go, Aluko has possession in the right corner. He leaves his man for dead with a fantastic twirl and pulls the ball back for Kevin McDonald, who meets it perfectly, it's going into the far upper corner but oh no, it can't happen-Al Habsi has managed to tip it over the bar. What a brilliant save! Could it be a match winning one? Reading are now time wasting, doing anything to manage the game. Mind you, we did the same thing at Norwich.

Then Sone Aluko is at it again, this time teeing up substitute Martin in the box, the striker turns and is going to shoot, when that man Al Habsi dives bravely at his feet and takes a knock, which is the cue for treatment and another delay. Time's running out now and in a final throw of the dice, keeper Marcus Bettinelli, comes up for a corner. Come on Fulham, let's go for it! Eventually, Johansen crosses, Martin gets on the end of it but his header goes agonisingly wide of the post. Shortly afterwards, Martin Atkinson's harsh, shrill whistle brings both the game and our season to an end.

The Reading fans swarm on to the pitch like an invading army. So much for the earlier notices warning them of arrests if there's an invasion. In fact, the screen is now proclaiming 'KEEP OFF THE PITCH!' A bit late now, methinks. It only needs the musical accompaniment of the Sex Pistols to complete the anarchic scene. The Reading players get embraced by the manic throng while some Royals supporters jeer at the Fulham faithful, to which there is an inevitable combative visual and aural response. Most of the Fulham players have scampered to the tunnel, probably fearing for their safety. A few: Ream, Sessegnon, Tom Cairney, Marcus Bettinelli and Kevin McDonald, emerge from the scrummage to applaud the fans. Ex-academy team player Marcus comes close to the supporters. 'MARCUS BETTINELLI!' chant the defiant faithful. Eventually, they all wearily trudge off the pitch, weaving their way through the Royals fans, who have now completed their land grab.

'They shouldn't have let 'em on in the first place,' says one hefty departing fan. Because of the steep incline, exiting the stand is a slow process. The brawny fan's brown rimmed glasses are misting up and he's now getting irate, 'let's get out of this shit hole!' he cries despairingly. You can understand the disappointment but to coin a well worn phrase, the Fulham players definitely 'left everything on the pitch.'

The journey back is short but quiet. Alex and I try to console ourselves. I tell him that I think play-offs are a marketing construction to make more money and attract more tv viewers That said, all the teams know the rules before the season starts, so I suppose in that sense it's fair. Fulham should look to avoid the lottery of the play-offs next season and be promoted automatically.

Alex and I consider where to strengthen. We agree that our priority should be a goal scoring striker as we miss too many chances. Not easy to find but hopefully we'll strike gold. It seems churlish to be over critical of the current squad as they seem to be a good group. However, we need to be ruthless to succeed. Therefore an upgrade on our current goalkeepers, a sweeper-keeper, better with his feet and a taller, more powerful centre back, who regularly wins the ball in the air, would complete a better spine for the team, to seriously compete for automatic promotion.

As we reach Hammersmith, we finish our efforts at being Fulham manager, or should I say, Head Coach. On reaching The Broadway, I take Alex's address, wish him well during the close season and depart. I trundle down the dark aisle, thank Barbara, as well as the white-shirted driver, who's submerged in his seat below me. On evacuating the coach, I share commiserations with East End Doug and make my way back to Wood Lane. It's been a great adventure. Thank you Fulham and here's to promotion next time around.

Our Fulham

So in the end, it was a case of so near but so far away. At the start of the season, most supporters would have regarded achieving a play-off place as a sign of a good season. Slaviša has met that target, which is no mean achievement, considering that fourteen new players had to be integrated into the squad.

After a difficult introduction to the club in 2015-16, this season Slaviša started to forge his own team and way of playing. A passing style of possession football with high line pressing began to emerge. You feel that the players enjoy playing this way and it's certainly been very entertaining to watch.

When we won the Championship in 2001, Jean Tigana's team outplayed other teams with their own brand of brilliant, passing football. These days the league is more competitive and it's not possible to do that so easily. Given the punishing schedule of 46 games, often with two a week, you need to know how to win 'ugly' on occasions, by establishing a physical presence and adapting your game. Slaviša has shown some flexibility and has played it long in parts of games but too often we've have lacked players with a combative cutting edge without the ball, who earn the right to play against hard, resolute and more physical opposition. We've also missed too many chances, given away too many unnecessary goals and failed to convert nine out of the thirteen penalties we've been awarded. Hopefully, next season, we'll add a more clinical approach to our existing attractive, creative play. We'll need to do so, especially as our rivals will be much more familiar with our tactics.

In an individualistic, materialistic world, football still provides a focus for the community. Its long traditions, emanating from such institutions as boys clubs and, in Fulham's case, a church, have been handed down from one generation to another. Fulham is one of the oldest clubs in our leagues and has a unique history, spanning over generations. It's picturesque ground, next to the Thames, makes it one of Britain's most attractive sports venues. However, since being relegated from The Premiership in 2014, the club has struggled to develop a team of which supporters can be really proud. This season we found that again. Galvanised by our appealing play and its accompanying success, fans got behind the team in a way not witnessed for several seasons. Watching the team both home and away, I've seen that commitment grow from myriads of supporters, whether male or female, or from whatever ethnicity or background. The Fulham family has been rehabilitated. Long may that continue as owners, managers, coaches and players come and go but supporters are here forever!

25693763R00142

Printed in Great Britain
by Amazon